"The precarious situation found within professional work raises questions about how society will organize expert knowledge. This book provides valuable insights about the reasons for and implications of the decline of these elite occupations."
**—Arne L. Kalleberg, Kenan Professor of Sociology,
University of North Carolina at Chapel Hill**

"This well-written and engaging book demonstrates how economic, social and political changes have undermined professional work and career opportunities in the United States. Long considered among the very best jobs in the economy – secure, well-paid, autonomous and fulfilling – professional work has become more precarious and hence less appealing. Leicht and Fennell document these changes, masterfully linking economic, social, and political trends to the changing labor market for professional workers, demonstrating how social change has implications for current and future professional workers. In so doing, they provide rich insights of interest to a broad audience."
—Tracey L. Adams, Professor, Western University

"Leicht and Fennell marshal evidence from many sources to document the declining prospects for the traditional professions – and the glimmers of hope for students who are hoping to become scientists, academicians, attorneys, or physicians."
**—Teresa A. Sullivan, President Emerita and University
Professor, the University of Virginia**

Crisis in the Professions

Crisis in the Professions: The New Dark Age presents a wide, panoramic view into the state of modern professional work in the United States. Struggling labor markets, growing inequalities, and increasing amounts of cultural and political mistrust are but a few major changes undermining the people seen as essential in society and needed to compete in a globalized, highly skilled world.

The authors explore this profound dilemma through a variety of methods, each one allowing them to identify significant areas of change and concern. They address macro-level social, political, and economic forces at the root of these changes and pair these explanations with illustrative vignettes of young, would-be professionals to paint a comprehensive, albeit complicated picture of professional work in the 21st century. Amid a backdrop of increasing globalization, technological advance, and cultural devaluation of expertise, the authors point attention to the mounting implications these shifts have for new generations of professionals and consider alternative models to address signs of precarity and instability within the professions.

With piercing insight and compelling evidence, *Crisis in the Professions* probes deeply enough to stimulate scholars and researchers invested in the sociological study of work and provides a valuable, versatile read for advanced students in these areas as well.

Kevin T. Leicht is Professor of Sociology at the University of Illinois Urbana-Champaign, Former Program Officer for the Sociology and Data Intensive Research Program in the Social Sciences at the U.S. National Science Foundation, and Founding Director of the Iowa Social Science Research Center at The University of Iowa, United States. He is the former editor of *Research in Social Stratification and Mobility* (the official journal of the Social Stratification Section of the International Sociological Association) and *The Sociological Quarterly* (the official journal of the Midwest Sociological Society).

Leicht has written extensively on issues relating to organizational and workplace change, economic development, globalization, and political sociology. His work has been funded by the U.S. National Science Foundation, Spencer Foundation, the Ford Foundation, and the U.S. National Institutes of Health, and his published articles have appeared in the American Sociological Review, American Journal of Sociology, the Academy of Management Journal, Law and Society Review, and other outlets. His published books include *Professional Work* (with Mary Fennell, Blackwell, 2001), *Post-Industrial Peasants: The Illusion of Middle Class Prosperity* (with Scott Fitzgerald, Worth, 2008) winner of the Midwest Sociological Society Best Book Award for 2009, and *Middle Class Meltdown* (with Scott Fitzgerald, Routledge, 2014).

Mary L. Fennell is Emerita Professor of Sociology at Brown University and Emerita C.V. Starr Professor of Commerce, Organizations, and Entrepreneurship. She is the co-author of three other books (including *Professional Work: A Sociological Approach*, with Kevin T. Leicht) and dozens of peer-reviewed articles. She has served as Editor of the *Journal of Health and Social Behavior* and Associate Editor of *Health Services Research* and is Former Chair of the ASA Section on Medical Sociology. She was Director of the Brown program in Business, Entrepreneurship, and Organizations, Former Chair of the Department of Sociology, and Former Dean of the Faculty.

Fennell has written extensively on change in professional organizations, managing change in healthcare organizations, and recognizing and managing the connections between changing technologies, changing populations of care, and conflict between providers, insurers, and healthcare organizations. She has consulted extensively for the National Cancer Institute and taught courses on healthcare organizations, research methods, and theories of organizational change. Her research work has been funded by the National Science Foundation, the National Institutes of Health, the National Cancer Institute, and the National Institute on Aging. She has served as Editor or Co-Editor of five special issues on topics related to healthcare policy and change in healthcare organizations, for multiple leading peer-reviewed journals. Her collaborative work on community-based cancer care and research has been recognized by the National Institutes of Health with Director's Awards in 2009 and 2012.

Crisis in the Professions

The New Dark Age

Kevin T. Leicht and Mary L. Fennell

Routledge
Taylor & Francis Group

NEW YORK AND LONDON

Designed cover image: © Shutterstock

First published 2023
by Routledge
605 Third Avenue, New York, NY 10158

and by Routledge
4 Park Square, Milton Park, Abingdon, Oxon, OX14 4RN

Routledge is an imprint of the Taylor & Francis Group, an informa business

© 2023 Taylor & Francis

Library of Congress Cataloging-in-Publication Data
Names: Leicht, Kevin T., author. | Fennell, Mary L., author.
Title: Crisis in the professions: the new dark age/Kevin T. Leicht,
     Mary L. Fennell.
Description: New York, NY: Routledge, 2023. | Includes
     bibliographical references and index.
Identifiers: LCCN 2022044029 (print) | LCCN 2022044030 (ebook) |
     ISBN 9781032126296 (hardback) | ISBN 9781032126258
     (paperback) | ISBN 9781003225485 (ebook)
Subjects: LCSH: Professions – Social aspects. | Economics—
     Sociological aspects.
Classification: LCC HT687. L38 2023 (print) | LCC HT687 (ebook) |
     DDC 306.3—dc23/eng/20220919
LC record available at https://lccn.loc.gov/2022044029
LC ebook record available at https://lccn.loc.gov/2022044030

ISBN: 978-1-032-12629-6 (hbk)
ISBN: 978-1-032-12625-8 (pbk)
ISBN: 978-1-003-22548-5 (ebk)

DOI: 10.4324/9781003225485

Typeset in Bembo
by Apex CoVantage, LLC

Contents

Figures

Tables and Boxes

Tables

Boxes

Part I
Systemic Changes

1 Crisis in the Professions

The New Dark Age

There is something happening to skilled jobs in America. Nowhere are these changes more dramatic, less studied, and at the same time more subtle, than among the holders of the elite jobs we call professionals. These are the kinds of jobs – as doctors, lawyers, scientists, managers, and college and university professors – we would love to see our children achieve. These are the job holders that we want our students to emulate. These *were* the jobs that were the bedrock of the skilled, post-industrial economy representing the career aspirations of generations of young people. Land one of these jobs and (historically) you've "made it" and achieved the American Dream. But now these jobs are becoming less stable, less fulfilling, less desired, and more precarious. How could the jobs we thought were central to our international competitiveness end up like this?

Professional jobs are best exemplified by the list of positions earlier: these are classic examples of jobs that require a lengthy period of university training, culminating in an advanced degree such as the PhD, MD, or JD. Professionals do work that is of value to society: healing the sick; educating young people; and providing legal advice and representation in a court of law. Professionals typically claim control and power over their own area of expertise and often over other occupations within the field that are expected to work with the professional. Because their work is based upon expertise and lengthy training, professionals expect the quality of their work to be assessed *only* by other professionals, and they expect the work they do to be autonomously performed. They may perform their work within bureaucratic settings of various sorts, but ultimately, their loyalty is focused on their profession or their professional association. Professional associations often wield peer review and/or practitioner control over the profession. This and other central concepts of this work are briefly defined for easy reference in Box 1.1.

Researchers and commentators have sensed the development of problems with the professional paradigm for many years. In our prior work (*Professional Work: A Sociological Approach*, Blackwell 2001), we cataloged the many ways that the work done by professionals and high-level managers had changed dramatically since the 1970s. In that book, we argued that

DOI: 10.4324/9781003225485-2

Box 1.1   Concepts and Definitions

Profession/Professional (based on Leicht and Fennell 2001): (1) used as a folk concept to signify (a) prestige, respect; (b) full-time work for pay; (c) to perform some task with great skill or proficiency; (2) used as a sociological concept to study: (a) elite classes of occupations with a focus on the characteristics or attributes of such occupations as a taxonomy (the attribute model of professions; see Carr–Saunders and Wilson 1933); or more recently, as (b) a process model, to study the processes through which certain occupations come to acquire power, develop monopolies, and/or lay claim to the status of a profession (see J. Roth 1974).

Professional Work: typically used to think about the conditions under which work performed by professionals is done. A particularly useful framework was provided by Hafferty and Light (1995) and Friedson (1986): there are three ways to think about how the nature of professional work can change: through (1) change in the content of the work (referring to the standards of work procedures, or expectations of the use of technology to accomplish the work); (2) the terms of professional work (i.e., work contract); and (3) changes in the conditions of work (the setting in which work is performed).

Precariat (based on Standing 2011): an emerging class of workers, including unemployed and underemployed workers, who lack access to stable jobs, and who often need to combine work from several part-time jobs in order to "get by," none of which lead to a meaningful career with predictability or security.

Seven Forms of Labor Security (based on Standing 2011): labor market security; employment security; job security; work security; skill reproduction security; income security; and representation security.

Post-Truth (from the Oxford Dictionary 2016): "relating to or denoting circumstances in which objective facts are less influential in shaping public opinion than appeals to emotion and personal belief."

Expertise as the Basis of Authority (based on Weber 1947 and Friedson 1986): within modern bureaucratic structures, authority rests on two bases: the *legal* order or formal structure of positions, in which certain positions are clearly defined in terms of their authority rights over other positions. The *rational* basis of authority is grounded, however, in expertise, acquired through training, experience, and ability.

Globalization (based in the Global Workforce Project, Levin Institute of SUNY (n.d.)): "the process of interaction and integration among the people, companies, and governments of different nations, a process driven by international trade and investment and aided by information technology." In our work, the globalization of professional work and professional markets applies this basic definition to the broadening labor markets of various professional sectors that are no longer confined by political boundaries or information systems.

Entrepreneurship (from The Free Dictionary): "the state, quality, or condition of being an entrepreneur, an organizer or promoter of business ventures." An entrepreneur is someone who creates, funds, or originates a business venture and assumes the risk for it. From the old French (entreprendre) meaning "to undertake."

managers and professionals were changing places in an increasingly unified elite division of labor and that the workplaces where such elite work was done were characterized by flatter hierarchies, greater reliance on temporary and subcontracted workers, downsized permanent staffs, and a greater reliance on virtual organizations and work settings rather than recognizable brick-and-mortar workspaces. The work settings themselves became more diverse, professional interests became more diverse (through specialization), and professionals themselves became more demographically diverse (in terms of gender, race, and ethnicity).

Now, barely two decades later, we find that professional work and careers have changed again and, in many ways, not for the better. In fact, we would argue that these elite jobs of the 20th century are not nearly as desirable now in the 21st century – these jobs have continued to lose work-setting control and have also lost status, financial rewards, and stability on multiple dimensions. Professional work is still dependent on a lengthy period of university-based training and the achievement of an advanced degree, and it is still work that is inherently valuable to society – or at least relevant to key social values (such as medical care, legal rights, scientific inquiry). However, that value is no longer commonly shared across all sectors of society and it does not translate into generally assumed status, power, or financial rewards. And as an additional marker of uncertainty, it is not clear what has happened to those trends toward greater demographic diversity within and across professions.

Theories of Professions and 21st-Century Professional Work (See Box 1.2)

The history of the study of professions is a long one and extends back to the founders of sociology, especially Emile Durkheim and Max Weber. Some of this prior work has aged well, while some has been modified considerably or abandoned as the world of professional work (and analysis of it) has changed.

Trait theories of the professions focused on defining professional work (some of which are reflected in our definition of profession/professional in Box 1.1). Much of this work settled on a set of traits analysts believed professions had that average occupations did not have.

These traits varied from author to author but generally focused on the following:

1)   Knowledge based on theory and complex intellectual techniques;
2)   Mastery of a knowledge base that requires a long period of training, usually university-based, technically specialized, and that socializes the trainee into the culture and symbols of the profession;
3)   Tasks that are inherently valuable to society and relevant to key social values (health, technological progress, legal rights, etc.);
4)   Practitioners who are motivated by service to the client's welfare and to the profession;
5)   A high degree of autonomy in the performance of tasks;
6)   Practitioners exhibit a long-term commitment to the profession;
7)   Practitioners enjoy a well-developed sense of community within the profession;
8)   The profession has a well-developed code of ethics that guides professional behavior and defines the profession's values.

Box 1.2   Theories of Professional Work

Scholars have expended a lot of energy attempting to explain why professional work exists as it is and how it is organized. Generally, these explanations come in one of five groups;

Trait theories focus on the characteristics that professions have that other types of occupations do not.

Liberal/technocratic theories focus on the technological changes created by global capitalism and the distinctive world views and outlooks among educated professional elites.

Power theories focus on ways that professions themselves manipulate supply and demand for their services and (often) gravitate toward specialties and practice locations that benefit the rich and powerful. Some variants question whether professional workers are increasingly used to generate profits for private shareholders at the expense of a service ideal that focuses on client welfare. In some versions, the value of professional knowledge itself is viewed as questionable.

Hybridization and institutional theories focus on ways that different ways of organizing professional work are produced, often melding the demands of a for-profit business with traditional professional prerogatives. This work also focuses on the creation of newer, hybrid professions in finance and management consulting.

Occupations were evaluated on the basis of their conformity or deviance from these traits. Trait models were popular in the 1950s and 1960s (Carr-Saunders and Wilson 1933; Parsons 1937; Goode 1957; Hughes 1958; Wilensky 1964). Later researchers (summarized in Roth 1974 and Abbott 1988) expressed dissatisfaction with trait conceptions of the professions. The lists were inconsistent. It was not clear that all of the traits were necessary to attain professional status, and trait models said little about the actions of professionals themselves in promoting these traits at the expense of others. However, trait models do provide us with some rough guideposts to look for as signs that work life might be changing. This is especially true if specific characteristics of an occupational group start to disappear (as is the case with law school closures in Chapter 6 or the end of licensing requirements). As we will see later on, some traits associated with professional work are changing and, in some cases, drastically.

Liberal/technocratic theories usually emphasize one of two themes: (1) increased skills and sophistication of work under post-industrial capitalism have increased demand for highly skilled workers and that the process of filling these roles has produced a new professional elite (see, for example, Bell 1976; Inglehart 1990; Manza and Brooks 1999) and/or (2) a focus on the link between professionals and other highly educated workers in a "new class" of economically prosperous, post-materialist, socially liberal citizens with distinctive world views and political orientations. The empirical evidence for this "new class" is considerable and (as we will see) the political and social implications are profound. Some researchers (most notably Rifkin 1995; Wilson 1997; Gordon 1996; Massey 1996; Castells 2011) have spoken with some alarm about the increased separation of this new class from everyone else in a highly globalized, highly unequal, highly privatized global economy. Others (most notably Braverman 1974; Edwards 1979; Littler 1982; Form 1987; and Burawoy 1979, 1985) have questioned whether there is a natural and inevitable relationship between new technologies and the organization of work and suggest that professional work can be degraded and devalued just as readily as other labor (see Castells 2011).

More importantly for our argument in this book, liberal-technocratic theories ask us to examine the role that expert knowledge plays in the larger social order. Variations on this perspective either take rising expectations and expertise for granted, suggest that there is a far-from-straightforward relationship between technology and professional work as it is organized now, or express concerns about whether professional groups have become a global, technological elite detached from the rest of us (with the potential backlash to follow, see Mooney 2005; Nichols 2017a).

Power theories of the professions emphasize three themes to different degrees. First, power theories question whether the prerogatives of professional groups arise from the inevitable relationship between technology and complexity or whether these flow from conscious manipulation by the professions themselves. Monopolization of knowledge and the use of mechanisms like extensive educational requirements allow professionals to exercise "social closure," limiting the number of practitioners, harming entrance to the profession by disfavored groups, lobbying the state for exclusive licensing agreements, and driving up prices.

Other variants of power theories talk about inequalities within the professions themselves. These variants point to the massive differences in compensation produced by high-status specialties that are often distant from providing for the general welfare. For example, different types of very expensive surgery command huge fees from paying customers, while basic issues of public health and basic healthcare access are not addressed. The same could be said of corporate law as part of the legal profession. Marxist scholars would point out that professional services are skewed to benefit the rich and powerful, protecting them from everyone else (in some cases, or providing them with exclusive services that only they can pay for). Others (see Larsen 1977 and Leicht and Fennell 2001) suggest that control over professional activities has gravitated away from professionals themselves and toward more powerful groups that seek to control costs and extract financial benefits for themselves (see also Leicht et al. 1995). In this variant, professional work is slowly degraded or "proletarianized" in the name of making someone else very wealthy. In other contexts (Leicht and Fennell 2008a), we have argued that this type of control over professional work has become far more normative than the free-standing practitioner model or ideal that motivated mid-20th-century work on the professions.

Finally, postmodern variants of power theories question whether professional expertise is important or valuable (see, for example, Illich 1982). In this variant, the very existence of professional knowledge is an expression of power and domination. The end result of privileging professional knowledge is the political and social disenfranchisement of nonprivileged groups and the knowledge claims themselves are dubious. This variant of power theory looks very much like free market and neoliberal critiques of professional work (Leicht 2015), and the reasoning used looks very much like the overall questioning of expertise that contemporary professionals face, though postmodern critiques are usually identified with the political left rather than the right (see Nichols 2017b).

As we will see in Chapter 6, especially in North America, the otherwise altruistic yearnings of would-be professionals often come into contact with the harsh reality that (1) professional education is very expensive, (2) one needs to take out massive student loans to pay for it, and then (3) one needs a high-paying job in a well-compensated specialty in an urban area to pay off the debts accrued because of (2).

Finally (and more recently), theorizing about the professions has focused on *hybridization and a focus on institutions*. Much of the recent theoretical scholarship has focused more on how professional work is organized than on what professionals themselves do or how they justify themselves. Much of this work draws from the work of Scott (2008), Friedson (1986), Abbott (1988), and more recently Saks (2016, and elsewhere).

Much of this work originally drew on Scott's classification of professional organizational forms. Scott's perspective focused extensively on the relationship between professionals and the organization surrounding the professional, placing particular emphasis on whether and how standard bureaucratic and managerial prerogatives impinged on traditional concepts of professional autonomy. The three models for embedding professionals in organizations included (1) *autonomous*, where professionals retain authority and control to evaluate themselves as a group (as in, for example, the traditional stand-alone law firm), (2) *heteronomous*, where professionals are subject to more line-authority control (as exemplified by today's managed-care organizations in medicine), and (3) *conjoint*, where professionals and administrators recognize not only their separate domains of expertise and power but also their shared benefits and need for collaboration. As Hafferty and Light (1995) suggest, different organizational forms have implications for changes in the content, terms, and conditions of work, something that we clearly show in our analysis here in later chapters.

Others who draw from this tradition (most notably Abbott 1988) focus on systems of professions, or ways in which competing knowledge claims are resolved. Writings in this tradition focus on work settings where multiple interests are represented and multiple professional claims are at stake. Relative dominance depends on symbolic appeals, social closure, and gatekeeping mechanisms tied to the state.

Neo-institutionalist accounts focus on the ways that different organizational forms develop and slowly become dominant (Saks 2016; Empson et al. 2017). This is especially the case with much of the work on growing professional service firms (see also Saks and Muzio 2018). These firms are often global in reach, employing thousands of professionals from a variety of professional groups – lawyers, accountants, managers, marketing professionals, and management consultants – in an attempt to produce an omnibus, one-stop-shop for global business services. Tied to this are distinctive organizational forms that bring together a myriad of professional activities in multidisciplinary teams to address big business problems. These organizations are very large and very bureaucratic, and their attempt to construct a distinctive brand for the PSF itself leads to unique constraints and opportunities for professional practice. As Suddaby and Muzio (2015) suggest, these organizational forms represent a unique amalgam of established professional projects (law and to a large extent accounting) with newer professional claims (by management consultants, for example), big business reach, and deep pockets. As we will see in Chapter 7, the road to the omnibus professional service firm has been anything but smooth, yet the global reach of these mega-firms is unquestioned and their role in providing institutional models for other forms of professional practice is much debated.

To varying degrees, we will appeal to many of these theories as we provide our analysis of how professional work has changed, who benefits from those changes, and what the implications are for the expert division of labor in the 21st century. Specifically, our book develops cross-cutting themes that tie our examination of changes in professional work together.

Four Cross-Cutting Themes

Our task in this volume is to understand how these changes have occurred, and what the consequences are for those seeking to find their place in this new world of skilled work. We will pursue this investigation by recognizing there are at least *four important cross-cutting themes* that must be examined as we attempt to build our explanation. The first of these is that *change in professional work and professional careers is a multilevel phenomenon* (see Figure 1.1).

The changes noticed by individuals in how they work and what they expect from their work and their careers have an impact on the structure of professional labor markets and the sectors of professional service provision. And similarly, sectoral and societal trends influence the career options and choices of individuals. In other words, jobs, careers, labor markets, sectors, financial systems, global professional markets, and advances in technologies are all interconnected across multiple levels of analysis. We will use this important observation as an organizing theme for our work (Leicht and Fennell 2001), as we move first to describe systemic changes that influence professional work, then to changes in professions and professional training, and then to individuals (particularly younger workers) and their career aspirations and expectations.

In many ways, professionals now find they have increasingly more in common with a new class of worker whose work arrangements are lacking one or more of the seven forms of labor-related security (defined by Standing as labor market security, employment security, job security, work security, skill reproduction security, income security, and collective voice security; Standing 2011; see Box 1.1). Standing coined the term "the precariat" to refer to blue-collar workers and lower-level white-collar workers who find it harder and harder to stay financially above water, despite working multiple part-time jobs, and are thus highly susceptible to class-based conflict and/or unionization. Sociologists of work have focused on "precarious work" and defined this as employment that is "uncertain, unpredictable, and risky from the point of view of the worker" (Kalleberg 2009). Both Standing's work on the precariat and Kalleberg's work on precarious work (among others) underscore the continuing erosion of worker control, the proliferation of short-term employment, and the disappearance of basic job characteristics that had for so long been associated with "good jobs": benefits, advancement opportunities, and loyalty between firms and workers. *The second major theme of this volume focuses on the development of the professional precariat.*

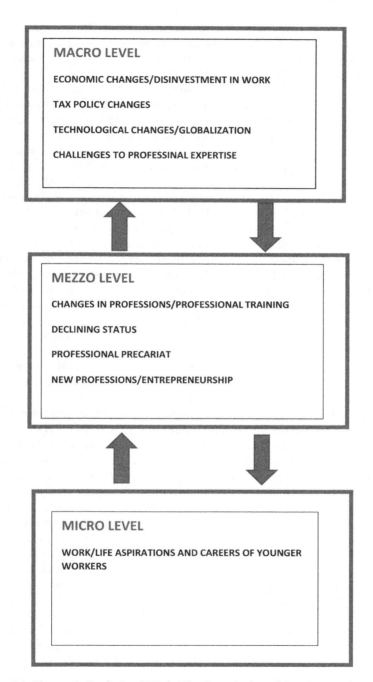

Figure 1.1 Changes in Professional Work: The Organization of Our Argument

There is a third major societal change related to the decline of professional jobs, one that has only very recently become evident. Turning back to the classics of sociological theory, scholars have always defined *expertise* as the foundation of professional power and the basis of all managerial systems and rational order in the modern world. As Freidson reminded us, knowledge is power (1986), and even earlier than Freidson, Durkheim's work (1933) developed the notion that specialized bodies of knowledge can be used as a basis for distinguishing between groups of actors and as a basis for distributing power across groups. Weber linked formal knowledge to the concepts of rationalization and rational action, and the rational-legal bureaucracy became the cornerstone of modern theories of management (1947). Expertise is what gives the professional control over formal knowledge systems, and confers power to those who produce knowledge (especially in science).

In the heady days of the post-World War II United States, the focus on knowledge and expertise was behind many optimistic predictions about the post-War World (Bell 1976). According to Bell and other Liberal/Technocratic scholars of that time, persistent social problems would be subject to systematic analysis and evaluation by experts who came up with evidence-based solutions that would move society forward. Expert analyses and solutions would defy easy political categorization, and disputes about politics, the good society, the just society, and the prosperous society would be solved through expert interventions. The superiority of these solutions to prior evaluations (based on ideology, culture, religion, etc.) would be so obvious that everyone would agree that this was the best way forward. And if some expertise was good, certainly, more expertise was better: these futurists recommended that we populate the labor market with symbolic analysts, scientists, and other experts whose decisions would guide us to a brighter future.

But then, this growing reliance on an expert division of labor to produce the good life for the rest of us ran into the contradiction that the expert division of labor was (by definition) nondemocratic, somewhat elitist, and often manipulative (Foucault 1977; Brint 1994). Thus, the third cross-cutting dimension is the observation that *the expertise of professionals is being devalued and eroded*, and the value of scientific studies, whether about the environment, health services delivery, effective medical treatment, or education are easily ignored; to be preferred are pronouncements based on personal opinion, social media (McAllister 2017; Chamorro-Premuzic 2014), or "alternative facts" (Rutenberg 2017). The *Chronicle of Higher Education* recently published a special report titled "The Post-Truth Issue" (January 2017), which examined the multiple sources of this alarming trend, dating back to the proliferation of grade inflation in American colleges and universities that began in the early 1990s. The term "Post-Truth" had itself been selected by the Oxford Dictionary as their word of the year for 2016, arguing that "a year dominated by highly charged political and social discourse was the driving force that increased the word's use by 2000 percent" (McAllister 2017). And of course, political commentators have noted for

Table 1.1 The "New" Dark Age in Comparison to the "Old" Dark Age

The Original "Dark Age" (Petrarch)	New Dark Age
Time: 100–1000 C.E.	Time: 1980s–present
Decline of the Roman Empire	Attacks on government legitimacy
Fragmenting institutions and feudalism growing cultural	Fragmenting institutions and growing cultural Distrust of established institutions
Knowledge destruction and superstition	Alternative facts, fake news, media fragmentation, and tribalism
Knowledge tied to religious institutions	Knowledge denied by religious institutions
Persecution of free-thinkers	Denigration of expert knowledge

years the proficiency with which the Republican Party has ignored science (and often worked actively to undermine its value and its capacity; Mooney 2005, 2012).

One of the premises of this book is that American professions are entering (or have been in) a new dark age. While this analogy can be overplayed, a comparison with traditional, historical definitions of the "dark ages" might be clarifying (see Table 1.1).

The historical dark ages are a description of the time between the fall of the Roman Empire (or its slow decline from 150 to ~500 C.E. or so) to 1000 C.E., marked by the decline of urban life and the lack of centralized authority in much of Europe. This period was also marked by a decline in traditional institutions (or their fragmentation) and dominance by people usually considered as "barbaric" (Goths, Huns, Franks, etc.). The term also was used as a pejorative term to describe a period of darkness and ignorance spanning 1000 years from roughly 100 to 1100 C.E. Whether the historical Dark Ages were really as "Dark" as observers portrayed them is debated by historians and others, but we are struck by the similarities between how the Dark Ages are portrayed and how our current cultural and political climate devalues or overtly attacks science and expertise as "elitist," "false," or worse.

That part about "elitist" professionals has recently become a very big problem in national politics in this country and in building the new Republican administration. It is important to recognize that the devaluation of professional expertise in scientific work is one thing, but an additional side of this alarming development is that expertise and advanced training have become a political touchstone. Thus, our fourth theme concerns the adoption of "the war on science" (Mooney 2012) by the Trump administration *and the broadening of that war into a full-scale attack on legitimate expertise and training in all areas of knowledge.* For nearly the entire post-World War II era, the federal government was an active partner with universities and other research institutions in ways that built both basic and applied sciences and encouraged growth in knowledge based on facts and the interpretation of verifiable data. The Trump administration had very few (if any) experts in the most important areas of policy development: nuclear proliferation, trade imbalances, medical innovation, global pandemics, global warming, or cybersecurity (Davenport 2018). In later chapters, we will more fully discuss this fourth theme and examine its influence in various forms.

Individual Examples

In our earlier book, we began our examination of professional work with a handful of semi-fictive vignettes about individuals with professional training as they began their careers. These examples served to illustrate then how sectoral and societal trends influence the career options and choices of individuals and how those career patterns come to characterize entire labor markets and sectors. Indeed, as mentioned earlier, one of our goals with this volume is to again stress the inter-connectedness of these changes across multiple levels of analysis: systemic changes in financial systems, globalization of markets, advances in technologies and their diffusion across sectors and societies, jobs and the working conditions that define those jobs, and individuals and their careers, aspirations, and career paths.

To begin our unraveling of these various influences, we offer the following four vignettes. Each is based in a different professional arena, and each young professional is at the beginning of his/her career, struggling with decisions about the best options, given current job market and financial conditions, and their hopes and expectations about what would constitute a strong launch. There are some linkages between these four vignettes and the four young professionals we introduced in our 2001 volume, but their options, what they face in terms of economic uncertainty, and their career hopes are very different.

Box 1.3   Sequestration and the Federal Budget

Sequestration is a budget tool used to impose mandatory spending cuts in the U.S. federal budget in order to reduce budget deficits. These are cuts that are applied to budgeted money that have already been approved and "ear marked" for specific purposes, such as research programs that have been approved through rigorous review. Typically sequestered budget cuts are applied across the board and are permanent.

Sequestration has been used since 1985 as an inducement to focus attention on the federal deficit. It has most recently been applied in 2011, triggering automatic budget cuts to reduce the national debt by $1.2 trillion over 10 years (Murse 2017).

Four Vignettes

Maria is a Latina PhD Biologist, holding credentials from all the "right" places (BS Stanford; PhD University of California – San Diego, which at the time was the #1 biology program in the country) and without any delays in completion along the way. She is now in her third year of postdoctoral studies on the West Coast, focusing on amyloid deposits and beta-cell protein death, an area of research with major implications for addressing the growing epidemic of Type 2 diabetes. When she began her postdoctoral, she was assured that funding would be available for three to five years to cover her salary. But beginning in her second year, she has been pressured by the lab principal investigator to apply for funds from both the National Institutes of Health (NIH) and private foundations. The NIH research budget has been in steady decline after eight years of sequestration (see Box 1.3), and the Trump administration proposed (without success) a budget that reduced the NIH research budget by 20%, as well as major cuts in the federal indirect cost recovery rate. Funding from major private foundations in her area is also in decline.

Maria's career goal is a position in a major pharmaceutical or biotechnology firm, either as a project-area director or in translational science and "science communication." Recent inquiries about such jobs in the private sector have elicited polite interest, particularly given her growing research profile (she has an expanding list of first-authored work in top biomedical journals and has been successful in obtaining her own NIH fellowship and foundation research funds to pursue her work on a gene that has only recently been considered for its impact on the endocrine system). But she has also encountered some words of caution as she is still "only in the middle" of her first postdoctoral position. Two such stints are becoming increasingly common, for both young scientists who hope to become academics or who hope to work in the private sector (Bonetta 2009). In fact, others have commented on the growing period of "servitude" experienced by many STEM PhDs (between completion of PhD and first real job; see Bonetta 2009, 2010), and the development of "permadocs" who continue as postdocs for labs that eventually shut down following senior retirements and lack of research funds. Permadocs are typically stranded without employment prospects (Powell 2015). Further, the average age at which "young" scientists are able to obtain their first independently developed research grant (referred to as the "RO1" from the NIH) has gone from age 30 in 1990 to about age 42 now (Rockey 2015; Barr 2015). So Jennifer, despite doing everything right in her training and research career, is seemingly stuck in a limbo of lean funds, small salaries, and scientific slavery.

Selena, a Hungarian immigrant, is the younger sister of a young professional we wrote about in 2001 who held a PhD in English and teaches part-time at several different small colleges in the Boston area. Like her sister, Selena also holds a PhD in the humanities: in Comparative Literature from

Harvard. She makes a living by teaching courses on a per-course basis for three different colleges/universities in New England (not just the Boston area). She can teach between three and five literature courses every semester, which provides enough combined salary to let her rent one-half of a two-bedroom apartment on the outskirts of Boston. She does not get benefits from any of these universities (since she is only a part-time adjunct appointee at each location), so she has yet to start contributing in any meaningful way to a retirement fund. She is too old to be covered by her parents' health insurance, so she is trying to cover the high cost of an individual healthcare plan through the State of Massachusetts Health Connector plan, an early version of the Affordable Care Act that has been revised to be compatible with "Obamacare." She watched the multiple attempted repeals of Obamacare in 2017 with considerable anxiety, as repeal would have left her with no health insurance options. Selina has won awards for her teaching and has published one book already and has a start on her second major manuscript. Despite this excellent record, she has faced ongoing disappointment in the academic job market: the last two jobs where she applied for a regular faculty position were both "canceled" by university administrators for various budget cutback reasons. Selina sees no prospects for improving her situation and is thinking about leaving the academic labor market entirely. She may relocate to Maine to join her sister Julie, who has opened a daycare facility in Portland. Such a move would mean not only significantly lower income but also lower housing costs, and her income would be low enough to allow her to qualify for Medicaid.

Catalina is an African American woman with an MD from Brown University and a specialty in Internal Medicine. She is burdened with considerable student loan debt and is unable to take advantage of special loan-forgiveness programs by relocating to rural areas with low numbers of healthcare providers. She lives with her parents in Portsmouth, New Hampshire, and provides them with on-site medical oversight, as they are both in their 80s and unable to afford the move into high-quality, but costly, assisted living. Catalina is about to finish her residency in geriatrics but is uncertain of her next move. There are several large HMO-type facilities in the area, but these are known for expecting their salaried physicians to work long hours and see a large caseload of patients each day (with very little time allowed with each patient). She would prefer to stay in New Hampshire and somehow continue the arrangement she has developed to care for her elderly parents (which also covers her own housing needs), but other options are slim. She is considering a position as a "hospitalist" with a large regional medical center in Connecticut, close to the New York state border. A hospitalist is usually defined as a physician who is employed by a hospital/medical center to manage "undifferentiated care" for medical patients in the hospital setting (i.e., all of the patient's care needs; Nelson et al. 2012). This medical center is advertising for someone who is board certified in internal medicine; the position is described as a "day rounder" who rotates through night hours every six to eight weeks and when on night rounds the doctor also takes three to four calls per night at a secondary site. The position is also described as working with an advanced practice support team, being responsible for an open intensive care unit, and responding to all codes. Part of the support team includes a number of specialty nurses and medical scribes, with much of the onerous paperwork being off-loaded to the scribes (Bryan 2015; Gellert et al. 2015). The position Catalina is considering provides a full range of benefits, retirement savings plans, monthly RVU bonuses, and what is described as "generous compensation." A signing bonus is mentioned, and relocation assistance is available, both of which would be needed as Catalina would probably need to set up an apartment close to the medical center and travel back and forth on a weekly basis to cover her parents' care.

Corwin, a white male, is a lawyer who completed his JD in 2015, after majoring in computer science as an undergraduate. He passed the Illinois bar exam on his first attempt. After graduating from the University of Chicago law school, he tried to find work within the major financial services firms in Chicago and interviewed at several firms in Manhattan as well. Unfortunately, his entry into the legal job market came at the beginning of a terrible period for lawyers and law firms, following the collapse of the financial services market in 2008 and the ensuing lengthy economic recession. The demand for legal work nationwide has declined, and after nearly ten years of recession, the issue of law-firm overcapacity has become unavoidable (Olson 2016c). Large law firms are looking for ways to downsize, while in-house counsel positions in many manufacturing and high-tech sectors have expanded somewhat. Common down-sizing strategies include demotions and delays in promotion. Corwin decided to go with an offer from a large local diversified medical services firm. His position emphasizes information management, and he will be pursuing additional certifications in records management and enterprise content management. With this start as a medical in-house counsel, Corwin does not expect he will be able to leave anytime soon for the more preferred option of an associate in a large law firm. Nonetheless, he is happy to avoid the dismal prospects now facing a good friend of his who was hired into one of the top law firms in Manhattan a few years before (2014). She has been at this firm long enough to now be expecting to be made partner soon, but instead, she is being pushed into the option of becoming a "non-equity partner" (a position somewhat below that of a fully equitized partner, with either a fixed share of company profits, or no shares, reduced perquisites and status symbols of a lower rank – smaller offices, lower salaries, and much smaller bonuses). This is an option being adopted by many more law firms in the past few years: among the 200 largest law firms in the United States, the number of non-equity partners has tripled since 1999 (Olson 2016c).

Although these four young professionals represent a variety of disciplines and training patterns, they are all attempting to find well-paying jobs with benefits in a setting where they can practice the state-of-the-art in their chosen fields. Those goals remain elusive for nearly all of them thanks to the impact of changes we began to discuss in our first book: the proliferation of part-time and contract (and subcontracted) professional work (in many ways, the emergence of a professional precariat); the reduction in the size of permanently hired professional staff; the decline of very large organizations composed largely of professional workers and the replacement of such organizations (such as law firms) with smaller in-house departments of corporate counsel; the devaluation of professional training and advanced degrees; the politicization of science and the proliferation of post-truth (McAllister 2017; Nichols 2017) and "alternative facts" (Rutenberg 2017); the globalization of professional work; the changing aspirations and career-confusion of young adults; and the growth of university programs in entrepreneurship to match the popularity of careers in entrepreneurship. And of course, whether professional workers are themselves any more demographically diverse as a group remains to be seen (an issue we will examine later in this volume).

The Organization of This Book

The aforementioned four vignettes provide a good introduction to a number of troubling questions about professional work in the 21st century, many of them generated by the trends mentioned earlier. We have organized this volume into three major sections and will start with the most broad-based view first, focusing on systemwide, macro-level changes affecting professions and then considering meso-level changes in certain classic professions and the emergence of the "Professional Precariat" and a few newly observed occupational categories that cross boundaries between precarious work and professional status. Finally, we will examine the career aspirations of today's young adults and the labor markets they are facing as they begin their post-baccalaureate and post-graduate degree careers. This micro level of investigation delves into the realm of individual motivations and expectations and how these might affect the future directions of professional work (see Figure 1.1).

Part I: Systemic Changes (Chapters 1–3)

Chapter 2 will take a very deep dive into a number of macro-level trends that provide a complicated backdrop to the task of describing and understanding how elite jobs have lost stability and status over the past 20 years. Here we will focus on system-level changes across the economy and across social and political structures in the United States and other western nations.

There are a number of *important economic forces* that have changed how we think about the overall health of our economy and the opportunities available to individuals for upward career and financial mobility. We will include in this discussion observations about the growth of income inequality in the

United States: middle-class earnings have flattened over the past 40 years, and consumer debt has risen as an inadequate (and dangerous) replacement for earnings growth (Leicht and Fitzgerald 2008, 2022); tax codes have shifted to favor the wealthy and corporations and to favor unearned income over earned income (some have described the Alternative Minimum Tax as a penalty paid primarily by employed professional workers; see Burman 2007).

It is also important to recognize that the impact of the 2008 recession is still unfolding in multiple ways. Many have commented on the immediate and mid-term impact of that recession: massive layoffs in finance, the collapse of the legal labor market, foreclosures, bankruptcies, and breakups (Daguerre 2014; Sweet et al. 2014; Schmitt and Warner 2009). But we are still observing second-order effects that include ongoing federal government belt-tightening and state budgetary crises (Gordon 2012) with impending cutbacks to state-related universities and Medicaid programs. Budget freezes in the form of sequestration have taken a heavy toll on scientific funding from all agencies [NIH, CDC, DOE, and National Science Foundation (NSF)] for nearly ten years, and when mixed with conservative political platforms emphasizing "anti-science" the net effect on American innovation and discovery has been crippling (New York Times 2017).

Another observable aspect of financial realignment has been the growth in earnings/income inequality within various occupational groups, particularly within academia and scientific careers outside of academia. The income levels of the most senior levels within academia (including leadership positions such as college/university presidents, provosts, senior vice presidents, and senior deans) have grown steadily, while the bulk of college teaching is now provided by adjunct, part-time, and non-regular faculty appointments (the most glaring example of the Professional Precariat in the United States), as exemplified by Selina in our vignettes. Wages for college teaching tend to be on a per-course basis with no benefits. Within private-sector science, the profits are directed toward shareholders and senior partners; the discoveries depend upon young scientists and posts-doctoral fellows where wages have remained flat at around $50,000 per year (like Maria in our vignettes).

Finally, we cannot leave Chapter 2, our chapter on macro-level changes, without a discussion of what happened to a number of policy areas after Donald Trump was elected president. Immediately following his inauguration, Trump attempted to rewrite policies and regulations in multiple areas, targeting medicine, healthcare delivery, education, environmental science, and STEM fields in general. Early signs two years into the Trump presidency pointed to ongoing trouble ahead for the classic professions: the defunding of science, the de-legitimation of expert practitioners in multiple fields, and the normalization of defunding higher education are good examples. Several writers described all of these issues as examples of a long-standing "war on science" waged by the Republican Party (Mooney 2005, 2012) due to critical differences in conservative and liberal psychologies: a combination of motivated reasoning and personality traits that correspond with political preferences. Another approach is based on observations concerning the overwhelming availability of information on everything: Tom Nichols (2017b) paints the "death of expertise" as the unavoidable result of 24-hour news, Internet access to so-called "facts" about everything, and several generations of college graduates who believe that their opinions are just as important as anyone else's with years of training and advanced degrees and that no one knows more than they do. An inescapable question to be asked concerns truth and evidence in our society: if truth and evidence do not matter, then what is to become of people (i.e., professionals) whose roles have been to make decisions on the basis of evidence, facts, and truth?

Chapter 3 will continue the macro-level focus and look at *technological change and globalization and their influence on professional work.* The technological changes included here are advances in telecommunications, which have had an observable impact on medical work and nearly all interactive platforms in design, entertainment, and banking. The cluster of innovations around the expansion of computational power, analytics, and "big data" has had a boundary-smashing impact on advances in genomics-based cancer care (Fennell 2014), one that has presented significant challenges to the medical delivery system to update systems of health information and patient care to match the promise of genomics-based personalized medicine (Khoury et al. 2012; Fennell et al. 2014). Advances in data analytics have also been linked to changes in legal reasoning (Susskind and Susskind 2017), mathematical modeling in finance, and computer-assisted design in multiple fields. The field of robotics has begun to make significant inroads in medical and healthcare, changing surgical procedures as well as nursing home elder-care.

Regarding globalization, there are questions concerning the increased willingness of professionals to relocate internationally (including graduate students from the United States, international students who used to prefer training in the United States but no longer, as well as postdoctoral fellows and junior-level faculty). The working conditions of faculty at all levels in the United States and abroad have started to blend and merge so that the once famous, once preferred U.S. academic lifestyle is not quite so evident, whereas positions in Europe and Asia are offering more to attract U.S. academics.

The phenomenon of outsourcing professional work in a variety of fields (law, engineering, pharma, science/STEM, accounting, and finance) has shifted the location of nonacademic positions to global markets. A number of examples are possible: medical tourism and medical diagnosis; international postdoctoral positions in STEM fields; legal outsourcing and internationalization of legal practice; and diversified pharmaceutical firms have become globally diversified as well. And of considerable interest in understanding this global picture is the rise of the globalized, omnibus, professional service firm. Financial services are available across time zones, around the clock, seven days a week. And "back office" services can be easily relocated out of major urban areas in the United States, as well as to global locations everywhere (an important result of both technological change and globalization).

Part II: Change in Professions and Professional Training (Chapters 4–6)

Part II will shift our analytic focus somewhat away from macro-level and systemic changes and toward more "meso-level" or mid-level foci on how professional training is changing, how the classic professions are looking more like Standing's description of the precariat, and how new types of professional or elite jobs are emerging that may be eclipsing the former prominence of professional jobs. Chapter 4 will focus on *professions and professional training, examining the devaluation of professional training, and the decline in the status of expertise as the basis of professional authority.* We will consider multiple explanations for this phenomenon including an oversupply of PhDs in various fields, an undersupply of what used to be known as "good jobs," and the impact of overspecialization within specific fields. Additional explanations include technological change and the semi-automation of professional jobs in medicine, law, and some scientific fields. Finally, some have suggested that the cost of PhD training is simply too high, given the student debt crisis, the evaporation of federally funded doctoral training programs, and declining funds for graduate programs in general.

Chapter 4 will also update a theme from our earlier volume on professional work: where are we in terms of the diversity of workers represented in managerial and professional jobs? In our 2001 work, we examined data for law and medicine to see if the representation of women and nonwhites had increased, from 1970 to 1990. We found that there was more demographic diversity, but that diversity had been slow to develop and was not anywhere near parity in any elite profession. For medicine and law (the most diverse of the professions), white males were still the predominant group. In this volume, we will examine the published literature for additional data on diversity within a wider range of professions: law, medicine, science, college teaching, top management, and a newly emerged occupational category: entrepreneurs. In order to more fully develop an updated picture of gender and racial diversity in law and scientific fields, we will turn to data from the American Bar Foundation on recent law school graduates, the NSF's National Survey of Earned Doctorates, and the Integrated Public Use Microdata Series (IPUMS) data from the U.S. Census.

Chapter 5 will follow the *emergence of the "Professional Precariat" and apply Standing's concept to a variety of elite managerial/professional jobs.* Included within this chapter will be discussions of peripheral work (Hill 2015; Bidwell 2009; Elance Desk 2015), contract work and contingency workers (Cortese 2016; Pedulla 2011), the "gig" economy, and "flash organizations" (Scheiber 2017). Examples of precarious professionals will be drawn from medicine (hospitalists, per-diem nurses, data nurses, and medical scribes), academia (adjunct faculty), law (proliferation of legal aids and paralegals, imposition of nonequity partnerships), and the STEM professions (as evidenced by delays in the first job; expectations of multiple postdoctoral positions; delays in lab start-up packages; and increases in age at first independent RO1 grant).

The last chapter in our "meso-level microscope" (Chapter 6) will describe *the rise of new professions and the "new entrepreneurship."* Entrepreneurship has recently emerged as one of the most highly favored career options for new college graduates (Fairlie 2013; Mars et al. 2008; Kauffman Foundation 2016), and for some, the expectation of "make it rich quick with that one blockbuster innovation" has been an effective inducement to forgo one's college degree, based on the popular examples of Steve Wozniak and Michael Dell. It is also believed by some that entrepreneurship provides the autonomy and personal control of professional work without the investment in advanced degrees need by the classic professions. We will examine the growth of university-based entrepreneurship programs. Questions to be examined in this chapter include whether entrepreneurial careers are a comparable substitute for professional careers and in what ways has the proliferation of university-based programs in entrepreneurship contributed to the devaluation of expertise and advanced training?

Part III: Younger Workers and Their Career Aspirations and Expectations (Chapters 7 and 8)

Our last section changes our analytic focus once again and drills down to individual career aspirations and expectations (the micro level). In Chapter 7, we will examine the *work life of millennials*, looking closely at various studies that touch on the question of what do millennials and today's college freshmen want to do with their lives? How do current job expectations compare to the aspirations of college freshmen in the 1980s and 1970s? What do the job markets for young people today look like? And, is there evidence of a shift away from traditional professional aspirations? We will look closely at a study recently released by the Gallup Poll (Gallup 2016), which targeted exactly our questions about millennials: what do millennials want in their jobs? In their careers? How do they define the characteristics of their "ideal job"? And what do they expect from their managers? How would they prefer to structure relationships with managers and supervisors?

Finally, the last chapter of this book will consider *possible future scenarios* that all of these trends might suggest. Chapter 8 is where we paint the picture of the consequences of precarious professional work, starting with Kalleberg's work (2009) and moving forward to more fully incorporate the impact of expanding contract professional work, contingency workers, and flash organizations. The professional precariat has come of age within an era of profound systemic changes, including economic changes, the devaluation of expertise, globalization, technological change, and a confused younger generation of workers. Given this incredibly complex and unstable economic and social context, what do we expect to see in terms of professional work in the future? Will risk in various sectors continue to be shifted to professional workers? What will academia look like in a post-tenure, permanently underfunded university setting? How does a U.S. Congress develop and pass a healthcare plan to replace the ACA, when the experts in that sector (doctors, insurance collectives, the AMA, all of the known institutes and foundations with expertise in health services delivery, and the Congressional Budget Office) are not part of plan development and whose expertise is deemed unnecessary to that process? And how does the U.S. economy build forward and continue to grow when the scientific infrastructure is deconstructed year by year, and permanent declines in U.S. scientific advances become the "new normal." We will review scenarios developed by several leading scholars in this area (Leicht 2015; Daguerre 2014), as well as build our own more comprehensive future model.

2 The Context

Disinvestment in Jobs and Cultural Fragmentation

This chapter addresses two important macro-level changes that have affected professional work and most other Americans too – the widespread disinvestment in the world of work, and the growing cultural backlash and fragmentation that have led to questions about expertise claims. Each change is affecting professional work in different ways by changing how work is valued generally, changing the terms and conditions of what work is performed, or changing how that work is valued.

These big and broad changes are referred to by social scientists as "macro-level," but this does not make them unimportant or distant from our experience. They affect the worlds we live in, the communities where we work, our neighbors, and our fellow citizens. For professionals, some of these changes affect them directly – a robot arm that helps with complicated brain surgery is a directly experienced change to a surgeon's conditions of work. Other changes have come slowly and may affect the clients and patients that professionals interact with, their cultural understandings, and their level of trust. Still, others affect who pays the bills and what those payers expect.

The Biggest Change of the Past 30 Years: Disinvestment in the World of Work

Prior to the 2008–2009 recession, the larger economy was steadily growing, unemployment was relatively low, credit was easy to get, record profits were being made, and the United States was the dominant power in a triumphant world where neoliberal economic thinking was dominant and the "Washington consensus" was spreading to other parts of the world (see Stiglitz 2012). But just underneath the surface, there were serious problems – stagnant wages, rising inequality, job instability, rising poverty rates, and a fraying social fabric (see Leicht and Fitzgerald 2008, 2022).

Then all of the sudden, right on the eve of the 2008 Presidential election, the U.S. and then the global economy collapsed into the worst recession since the Great Depression of the 1930s. It was tempting to view the 2008–2009 Recession as the start of an economic reckoning that could reshape the American economy (cf. Reich 2013), but the recession was

DOI: 10.4324/9781003225485-3

simply the culmination of a series of problems that had been brewing for years. Almost all of these problems affected the quality of jobs and quality of life of the American middle class, that very group which (broadly construed) includes most of the professionals we talk about in this book. Most professionals derive a substantial share of their incomes from earnings on a job, and it is precisely those earnings, and the working conditions that accompany them, that have been under attack for the past 30 years. The technological changes and cultural fragmentation that have accompanied the economic trends we discuss have left professionals in a precarious position early in the 21st century.

The Long-Term Crisis of the American Middle Class

The hidden crisis leading up to the recession and the recession itself were the long-term culmination of a variety of circumstances that all conspired to harm the American middle class (see Hacker and Pearson 2006; Leicht and Fitzgerald 2008, 2022, Porter 2012). The preponderance of long-term evidence suggests the following:

(1) The U.S. middle class experienced an unprecedented decline in real purchasing power.
(2) Gaps between stagnant incomes and consumption aspirations were filled by easily available credit.
(3) This credit appeared at precisely the time that middle-class incomes were stagnating.
(4) Very real productivity gains of the past 30 years were used for the benefit of corporations and the wealthy.
(5) The deregulation of consumer credit markets produced a socialization of credit risk through asset-backed securities and collateralized debt obligations that allowed credit to flow freely (Carruthers and Halliday 2009).
(6) The larger social consequences were real declines in a sense of community and civility and the growth of a general "politics of displacement" where large segments of the political class want to argue about anything except inequality and economic fairness.

We review some of the updated evidence for this argument later using the latest available statistics at the time of this writing (Fall 2021), but most of these trends were present well before the recession and have continued since then.

The Deflated Income Balloon

By any measure we use, *the real earnings of individuals and the real income of families (in 2010 dollars adjusted for inflation) have undergone an almost 40-year period of stagnation in the middle.* Median before-tax family income—the figure that separates the top half of the income distribution from the bottom half—dropped from a high of $52,000 in 1976 to $41,000 in 1992. Median income inches upward again, surpasses the $52,000 mark in 1998 but then dips again with the great recession and does not surpass the 1976 value until 2015 (and then just barely at $52,343. The Washington Post and U.S. Census Bureau recently (September 12, 2018) reported that median family income surpassed $61,000 for the first time in 2017 (in current dollars, $55,400 in constant, 2010 dollars in Figure 2.1) and stands at $63,179 now ($54,873 in 2010 dollars). Regardless, this evidence suggests that family income for those at the middle of the income distribution has not recovered from relatively high levels in the late 1960s and early 1970s, and the 2016–2017 figure still reflects the lingering effects of the 2008 recession.

Stagnant Incomes for the Middle, Rising Incomes for the Top

Income inequality has risen substantially in the United States since 1970. The top 20% of all families went from receiving 43.3% of the income in 1970 to receiving 52% of all family income in 2017. More interesting from our perspective is the change in the relative size of the middle fifth of the family income distribution (those families that made between $41,000 and $62,500 in 2001) whose relative share of the family income distribution has dropped from 17.4% to 14.3% over the past 30 years. In fact, the shares for all families in the bottom four-fifths of the income distribution have declined relative to the top, suggesting that there has been a strong movement of income in the direction of the nation's richer families (U.S. Census Bureau 2018). Equally disturbing is the rise in the top 5% share of aggregate income, the group whose mean household income was above $316,520 in 2018 – their share of aggregate national income rose from 16.6% in 1970 to 23.1% in 2018.

Other evidence clearly shows that family incomes have ballooned for the upper classes and stagnated for the middle class, the group right in the middle of the family income distribution. The ratio of the middle fifth of family income to the top fifth dropped from 42 to 28% from 1970 to 2017 (U.S. Census Bureau 2018). The difference between real mean and median family income increased from under $10,000 in 1969 to almost $34,000 in 2007 and currently sits at $50,000 (Avery et al. 1984; Kennickell and Shack-Marquez 1992; Aizcorbe et al. 2003; Federal Reserve Bank of St. Louis 2017).

The evidence clearly suggests that middle-class purchasing power has eroded as income and earnings have stalled. Income inequality across households has increased and the relative standing of those we label "middle class" has eroded as well.

Figure 2.1 The Organization of Our Argument – Chapter 2 – The Macro Level

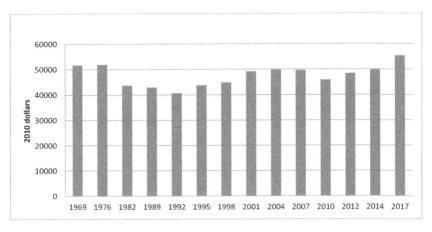

Figure 2.2 Median Before-Tax Family Income (in 2010 Dollars)

Source: St. Louis Federal Reserve Bank (Various Years)

But Not Everyone Is Hurting – The Captains of Industry Cash in

Over the past 30 years, CEO salaries in the United States (already the highest in the world) moved further away from our economic competitors in Western Europe and Asia since the 1980s while compensation for average workers stagnated or fell.

Ratios that started at about 35 to 1 in 1970 (with top CEOs making roughly 35 times what the average worker makes) and 59 to 1 in 1989 mushroomed to nearly 323 to 1 by 2002, 450 to 1 in 2007, and currently stand at 271 to 1 as of 2018, still the highest pay gap in the world. Clearly, the economic landscape for the average worker has shifted and their relative economic standing has slipped (Mishel and Schnieder 2017; Hembree 2018).

If corporate executives are supposed to maximize profits and shareholder value, then plenty of evidence shows that they did just that, especially since 1980. Stock market returns were historically as high from 1980 to 2000 as they were at any time during the post-World War II period, and the Dow Jones Average passed 15,000 in 2013, and 20,000 in 2017. Indeed, it was not until the onset of the 2001 and 2008 recessions that these stock market indices turned away from historic highs and unprecedented returns.

And did all this translate into a good corporate bottom line? Definitely. In the 1990s, corporate profits rose to record levels, dropped a bit during the 2001 and 2008 recessions, and have again returned to record levels as of 2018. These trends left most CEOs compensated with stock options in great economic shape compared to their average employee (Hembree 2018). This move to "pay-for-performance" compensation for CEOs rewarded people with unearned income, and CEOs become a vanguard example of the overall shift in the American economy away from incomes generated through job earnings and incomes generated through rents and capital gains (see Lin and Tomask-ovic-Devey 2013), leaving most professionals on the wrong side of this trend.

Lower Wages *and* Job Instability for the Rest of Us

What happened to this average employee's job? The U.S. government did not start tracking what it terms "mass layoff events" until 1996. Then (ironically) it stopped in 2012 (www.bls.gov/bls/sequester_info.htm). But plenty of anecdotal evidence shows that job instability increased during the 1990s and that middle-class workers were buffeted by the changes produced by globalization. The instability is not only in jobs for individuals, but it is also in incomes for families that rise and fall more quickly than in prior generations. As Jacob Hacker writes: "over the past generation the economic *instability* of American families has actually risen faster than economic *inequality*—the growing gap between rich and poor that is often taken as the defining feature of the contemporary U.S. economy" (Hacker 2008, p. 2).

What Was Fueling All That Consumption? Consumer Credit!

Even though their incomes and earnings stagnated and their CEOs left them in the economic dust, members of the middle class enhanced their purchasing power. They did this by increasing their working hours, reducing their savings, and increasing their debt load. Workers also stopped saving money and started living from paycheck to paycheck, leaving them little or no buffer against the whims of misfortune (see Figures 2.3 and 2.4) (Warren and Tyagi 2003).

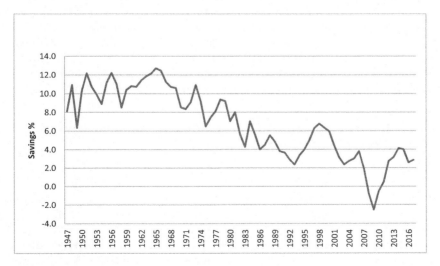

Figure 2.3 U.S. Net Savings as a Percent of Gross Domestic Income, 1947–2017

Source: St. Louis Federal Reserve Bank (Various Years)

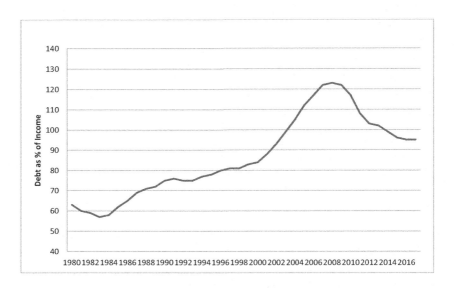

Figure 2.4 Household Debt as a Percentage of Disposable Income, 1980–2017

Source: St. Louis Federal Reserve Bank (https://www.federalreserve.gov/econres/notes/feds-notes/household–debt–to–income–ratios–in–the–enhanced–financial–accounts–accessible–20180111.htm#figure1a)

Not only has real average credit card debt per household risen from just over $4,000 in 1990 to $11,000 in 2003 to $14,991 in 2018—a change in real 2012 dollars of $10,000 in 28 years, but also most of the decline in average credit card debt since the 2008 recession has occurred because credit card companies wrote off uncollectable debt, not because consumers all of a sudden started making big payments on credit cards (Porter 2012; Issa 2018). The overall picture shows that the percentage growth in mortgage and consumer debts has been positive every year since 1970 up until the 2008 recession, and consumer credit growth resumed in 2009–2017 (Bricker et al. 2017).

Some People Got Very Rich From Stock, but Very Few People Actually Own Any

Without question, the overall level of activity in the U.S. stock market has risen dramatically. But how have these gains been distributed? The answer is clear: not very equitably.

Only 22% of all U.S. households have direct stock holdings, and the overwhelming majority of stocks are owned by an extremely small percentage of wealthy people. In 2017, the richest 10% of Americans owned 84% of all stocks (Wile 2017). This is not the only measure of wealth, nor is it the one most Americans rely on, so let us look at broader indicators of wealth and its distribution.

The more complete story is told by looking at changes in family net worth, the total value of the wealth held by different classes of wealth holders. In spite of the spectacular gains in the U.S. stock market since the 1970s, *median net worth for all Americans barely moved*. However, mean family net worth (the average value of all the assets a family has minus its liabilities) increased substantially to almost $600,000 prior to the 2008 recession and surpassed $600,000 in 2016 ($692,100; see Dettling et al. 2017). Since these changes are in real dollars, they represent improvements in the wealth profile of Americans. But since the median does not move, the numbers suggest big wealth gains among those who already possess wealth and not much movement near the middle of the wealth distribution. More ominously, median real net worth *declined* almost 40% between 2007 (before the recession) and 2010 (from $126,400 to $77,300). The median net worth right now (2019) is about where it was in 2001 (~$105,000 2012 dollars). The wealthy lost money as well, but the effects on those near the median were much more devastating.

The Financial Collapse of 2008–2009: The Hidden Crisis Exposed

In the United States and globally, the financial crisis and subsequent recession of 2008–2009 were truly gargantuan by any measure we care to use. Global markets lost $50 trillion in market value in 2008 alone, roughly $8,334 for every man, woman, and child on the planet. (To spend $1 trillion, you would have to spend $34 million every day of your life for 80 years.) So much money was lost that estimates are that it will take around 20 years to recover most of this wealth. The U.S. Stock market lost over $11 trillion in value in just one year. In an eight-day period in October 2008 (one month before the 2008 election), the Dow Jones Industrial Average lost 22% of its value, falling from 10,851 to 8,451. But that drop masks a still larger drop from October 2007 to mid-October 2008 – on October 7, 2007, the Dow stood at 14,164 (Paradis 2009).

By most accounts, there were three major stages to the financial collapse that led to the recession. First, the stock market from October 2007 until March 2008 started to go downward in a more-or-less orderly fashion – no big drops, no big gains, just a steady downward spiral. This is usually a signal from investors that a recession is coming. Investors pull their money out of the stock market and park it in more secure investments (like bonds and U.S. Treasury notes) to wait out what they see as an unstable investment environment. And none of these needs directly affect the "real" economy where jobs and consumption actually occur.

Then in Mid-March 2008, Bear Stearns (a major Wall Street investment house) declared bankruptcy, at the time the largest corporate bankruptcy in the history of the United States (they had already written off almost $2 billion in devalued securities; see Shorter 2008). Investors were stunned but not totally rattled, so things remained relatively calm until around Labor Day, when Fannie Mae, Freddie Mack, AIG, and Lehmann Brothers all declared bankruptcy over a ten-day stretch. Investors panicked and the Dow Jones fell 5000 more points between October 2008 and March 2009 as credit markets froze and fears of another Great Depression loomed. Worse still, from the standpoint of the average American, was the decline in real wealth held in mutual funds whose value dropped from $6.5 trillion to $3.7 trillion in one year (January 2007 to January 2008). Retirement savings accounts declined in value by 17% from October 2008 to 2010 and have only returned to their former levels in 2016 (and by 2018 stood at $6.9 trillion; see Miller 2018).

AIG and Lehmann Brothers were private equity houses worth $712 billion and $639 billion, respectively. AIG was a worldwide insurance company offering mortgage insurance and investment products to hundreds of thousands of customers. Its international division had invested heavily in Credit Default Swaps, some $57 billion of which were designed to cover subprime loans issued to American consumers. The general collapse in confidence in subprime loans created a liquidity crisis in September 2008, and the U.S. Treasury offered to immediately cover AIG to the tune of $85 billion. By the time the government support had ended, the Federal Reserve Bank had loaned $182 billion to AIG and received returns of $205 billion (Swagel 2010). Lehmann Brothers was an investment bank and financial manager, at the time the fourth largest in the United States. When the subprime mortgage market started to collapse early in 2008, Lehmann Brothers lost 70% of its value and was left holding billions of dollars in worthless securities on delinquent home mortgages. Outside investors started to lose confidence in Lehmann Brothers and started dumping stock, driving the overall value of the company down still further. By September 2008 when Lehmann Brothers filed for bankruptcy, they had liabilities of $613 billion. Unlike AIG, Lehmann Brothers was allowed to go through an "orderly liquidation" (meaning that parts of the company were sold off in pieces to other investment banks), and a U.S. Treasury bailout was applied. At the time, this was the largest commercial bankruptcy in U.S. history and led to a general crisis of confidence in financial markets in the fall of 2008.

As with the private investment houses, Fannie Mae and Freddie Mac (major underwriters of American home mortgages) started to lose money as the value of home prices fell starting in 2007 and into 2008. As the value of their holdings fell, their ability to borrow more money and continue normal operations (i.e., buying more mortgages from private banks and mortgage lenders) ground to a halt. The government had to step in in September 2008 to guarantee debt issued by Fannie Mae and Freddie Mac to avert a far bigger catastrophe in the housing market. Both companies lowered the quality of loans they would buy and back, which increased their vulnerability to a financial meltdown as the housing market collapsed. In 2008 alone, Fannie and Freddie lost 80% of their traded value (Semuels 2008).

How did this big crisis affect average people? The average household lost $66,000 in on-paper wealth and almost $30,000 in real estate wealth as a result of the crisis (Swagel 2010). That's enough money to take a second mortgage on a house and finance all or part of college education, save for retirement, buy several nice cars, or retire other debts from wages and earnings that do not grow. The Federal Government (and specifically the Treasury Department) spent roughly $501 billion on the Troubled Asset Relief Program, the major government program to bail out banks and investment houses (signed into law in September 2008 by President Bush and continued under President Obama). Of this, $205 billion went to the Capital Purchase Program to purchase direct stakes in banks to keep them afloat, $20 billion directly to CitiGroup, $20 billion to Bank of America, $70 billion to AIG, $81 billion to the domestic auto industry, $20 billion to Term Asset-backed Securities Loan Facility to securitize new lending in the wake of the collapse of the private mortgage and asset-backed securities markets, $30 billion to Public–Private Investment Partnerships to buy up bankrupt and stressed subprime backed securities, and $50 billion to the Home Affordable Modification Program to forestall massive home foreclosures by subsidizing the re-writing and renegotiations of mortgages that are delinquent or "under water" as housing prices collapsed (more on underwater mortgages shortly). The financial bailout of Fanny Mae and Freddie Mac cost taxpayers $157 billion directly.

As a result of the financial crisis, consumers stopped spending, companies stopped hiring and investing, and investors stopped investing as well, leading to serious drops in national GDP. GDP fell by 5.4% in the last quarter of 2008 and by 6.4% in the first quarter of 2009. Job losses for that 12-month period ran at 5.5 million U.S. jobs costing an average of $5,800 per U.S. household. The value of American family homes for that 12-month period dropped an average of $30,300 per household or almost $3.4 trillion. Total lost wages from underemployment and job loss are estimated at $3,250 per household (Swagel 2010), and (as we have extensively shown already) job quality and earnings were not keeping up with the rest of the economy before all this started.

The credit market collapse was tied to problems with the subprime mortgage market and the aftermarket for mortgaged backed securities. There is plenty of blame to go around regarding the collapse of these markets, and at least some evidence that the entire downturn was avoidable (Chan 2011).

Betting the House and Losing

The availability of subprime mortgages was (partially) responsible for the housing bubble of 2004–2006, though the generally easy availability of credit for everyone else also played a major role. The ability to originate loans, sell them on the securities market, and then do more lending generated profits that were large and almost impossible to resist.

As housing prices rose, more people had an incentive to get into the housing market and those already in it had big incentives to "trade up" and buy newer, fancier, and larger homes. Subprime mortgages offered loans that, in the short term, had easier terms with adjustable interest rates (and low introductory rates for the first few years of the mortgage), interest rate balloons (low rates of interest followed by higher market-based rates later on), low or zero down-payments, and no closing costs. Buyers were lured by these easy initial terms and the hope that they could refinance their mortgages at easier terms in the near future while still maintaining the rising home equity that came from the inflated home values caused by the housing bubble. Between 2005 and 2007, housing prices were moderating and interest rates for home refinancing were rising, making it more difficult to refinance out of subprime loans before the ARM interest rates ballooned.

By 2006, 23% of all mortgages originated in the United States were subprime and a vast majority of those were securitized in the Mortgage-backed securities market. When these easy initial terms expired, mortgage defaults and foreclosures started to go up and investors lost faith in the mortgage-backed securities market. Foreclosures and bankruptcies rose to record levels in 2009 and remained there well into 2012 (Federal Reserve Bank of New York 2016), only recently (as of 2018) returning to rates seen in 2005.

From our perspective, all of these problems were caused by the same underlying dynamic. U.S. middle-class consumers were loaned money they could not afford to pay back in order to fuel the profits driven by a consumer economy that (until the middle of the 1970s) was fueled by rising wages and earnings. But, as we have seen, median earnings and the earnings of most Americans have gone essentially nowhere for at least two decades. In the absence of rising incomes to rely on, easy credit seemed to be the only way to drive consumption forward and secure record financial profits. Once lenders could offload the risks of consumer lending onto investors and the financial markets to make instant profits, the long-standing American desire for home ownership seemed insatiable. Homeowners would benefit from steadily rising housing values as new buyers were continually available. Investors would be assured that housing prices continued to rise and mortgages were paid. The government would see the benefits of a deregulated financial market generating profits and tax revenues. This seemed like a "win-win" on all fronts.

As we will see, the results for middle-class Americans were still more job loss, more income decline, and declines in real assets and wealth. As of 2013, corporate profits recovered, but the middle class has only recently made it back to where they were in 2007 before the recession started, and on some measures (like wealth), the damage appears to be permanent (New York Times, September 10, 2018).

Unemployment, Job Loss, and Collapsing Demand: The New Poor

But the most serious outcome of all from the standpoint of those relying on good jobs that pay good wages has been the near collapse of the U.S. job market. The unemployment rate prior to the 2008 recession was very low

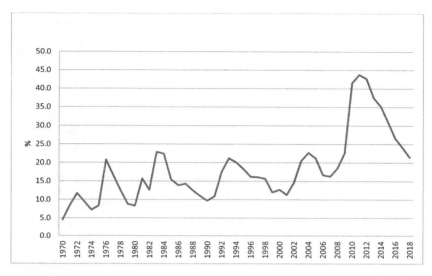

Figure 2.5 Workers Unemployed Six Months or Longer as a Percent of All Unemployed, 1970–2018 (January Estimates)

Source: Current Population Survey, U.S. Bureau of Labor Statistics

(just over 4%, almost the level where economists and other policy analysts declare that we have met "full employment" goals) but almost immediately skyrocketed in late 2008 and 2009 as credit markets dried up, investment dried up, and consumer spending dried up. Unemployment in early 2010 actually rose above 10%, and the percentage of unemployed who were out of work for six months or longer reached record-high levels and has only recently started to dissipate (see Figure 2.5). Even recently, the percentage of unemployed who have been unemployed for six months or longer stood at 21.5%, so one in five unemployed people had been unemployed longer than six months. By contrast, the percentage of unemployed who were unemployed for six months or longer was only 11.3% in 2001 (U.S. Census Bureau 2018). Worse, there is considerable evidence that the long-time unemployed have become "discouraged workers" who have left the labor force entirely. People who stop actively looking for work are not counted in unemployment statistics, even if they have been unemployed for over six months.

What does all this suggest? Our argument is that the indebted middle class has needed ongoing help and support for decades, at least since the early 1980s if not before. But now the situation is worse than it was when we began our analysis. Billions of dollars of personal wealth disappeared. The ability to find a good, steady job is more elusive than ever, and (if you manage to find one) your wages, earnings, and benefits will be a fraction of what they were in the 1970s.

The Rigged Tax System Favoring Unearned Incomes

The results of the supply-side tax cuts and the fiscal policies that followed in the 1980s and early 1990s added further problems to the plight of the middle class. Federal tax rates shifted radically in the direction of providing substantial tax breaks for the already wealthy. But instead of watching the money roll in, the federal government ran record deficits and accumulated unprecedented levels of public debt. Tax receipts, never high as a percentage of GDP by international standards, dipped to a level just above Mexico's. Corporations in particular received huge tax breaks, and in Washington, the number of permanent lobbyists, most of them representing corporate interests, increased substantially.

The middle class saw very little of the Reagan tax cuts, and the effective tax rate change was close to zero for virtually all American taxpayers below the top 10% of income earners. By contrast, wealthy households in the United States saw big drops in their effective taxation. Kevin Phillips describes the net effect of these tax cuts and other changes that came with them as a "capitalist heyday," comparable to the 1890s and the 1920s.

Moreover, the so-called "supply-side miracle" – the increase in tax revenues that would follow from lowering tax rates – never materialized. What did materialize was a sea of government "red ink." The federal debt, about $930 billion in 1980, ballooned to $2 trillion by mid-decade and $4 trillion by the early 1990s, $9 trillion on the eve of the 2008 recession (in spite of a robust economic expansion from 2003 to 2008 and the 2004 Bush tax cuts) and $16 trillion as of 2012 as the Obama administration dealt with the aftermath of the latest economic meltdown.

The Trump tax cut has fared no better. The 2017 tax cut allowed corporations to avoid $200 billion in Federal taxes. Wages increased for some workers but not nearly as much as supporters projected. What did increase were stock buy-backs (topping $1 trillion for all of 2018, a new record) and Federal deficits – $779 billion in 2018, a 17% increase over 2017, and $984 billion in 2019 (Tankersley 2018; Long and Stein 2019). As of January 2020, the total Federal debt has reached $23 trillion (Treasurydirect.gov 2020).

The Federal government's retreat from taxing the rich and its inability to curb budget deficits had another insidious effect on wealth distribution. Saddled with a tight money supply, the United States began financing its government debt with investment income from wealthy Americans and foreign nationals, whose appetite for Treasury Bonds selling at favorable interest rates seemed to be insatiable. The financial payouts from the bonds also went to the Americans who had treasury bills in their investment portfolios, generally the very wealthy. As Kevin Phillips states:

> The underlying problem was the Reagan Administration's need to borrow huge sums of money at high interest rates to fund the 1981 tax

cuts, the defense buildup, and 1981–1982 recession spending. To avert feared inflationary effects, the Federal Reserve Board in 1981 and 1982 raised U.S. interest rates to record high levels. With U.S. Bonds paying 15 percent while equivalent instruments in Germany and Japan were paying 5 percent or 6 percent, capital poured into the United States. As foreigners bought dollars to invest in U.S. debt, the dollar soared against other currencies.

This investment boom in U.S. debt kept the government afloat, but it redistributed wealth to those who were already wealthy. The strong dollar threatened to and eventually did ruin the country's international trade position. The results of this for the manufacturing industry were especially devastating; as U.S. markets were flooded by inexpensive imports in industries like electronics and automobiles, factories that provided steady employment and middle-class jobs were forced to lay off workers or shut down entirely.

The fervor for cutting taxes and the belief that such cuts would raise government revenues and benefit the middle class did not subside in spite of the wealth of evidence that the effects were slanted steeply in the direction of those already well off. Tax cutting by itself seemed to be gaining a momentum that was simply unstoppable: states followed the federal government in cutting their own taxes. As each new piece of evidence suggests that middle-class incomes were stagnant and tax benefits were few arose, the simple response by most politicians of both parties was that the benefits were "forthcoming." The new tax cut passed under the Trump administration is projected to cost $1.2 trillion, add billions to the government's budget deficit, and harm further economic growth (Becker 2018).

The 1980s ushered in a long-term decline in the percentage of tax revenues taken from corporations (on corporate profits, generally a progressive form of taxation) and a gradual but steady increase in payroll taxes and individual income taxes as a percentage of Federal Revenues (see Figure 2.6). Further, a greater share of the federal tax burden was extracted using the regressive payroll tax to fund social security, a tax presently capped at $113,700 personal income. Taxation at the federal level thus shifted toward earned income and away from unearned income.

Evidence shows that corporate taxation was declining and that corporate tax avoidance was rising: corporate tax loopholes grew from $8.3 billion to $119.9 billion annually from 1970 to 1986. The overall effective tax rate for the largest corporations in the United States dropped to 11.8% in 1982 before climbing back to 15% in 1984 and recently stood (as of 2018) at 12.6%. The effect of the Trump tax cut has produced a first in U.S. history – the effective tax rate for the 400 richest Americans is now below the effective tax rate for everyone else (Leonhardt 2019). This long-term trend is unprecedented in any of the OECD countries.

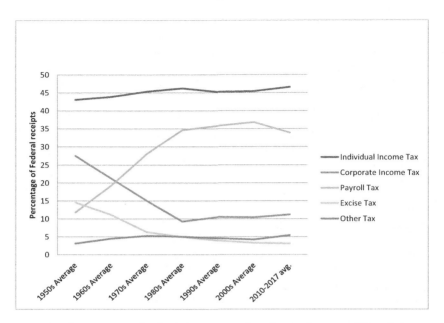

Figure 2.6 Composition of Federal Government Receipts by Source and Decade

Source: White House Budget Office (http://www.whitehouse.gov/omb/budget/Historicals)

The Reality for Everyone Else—Rising Taxes as a Percentage of Personal Income

While corporations and wealthy Americans saw their tax bills fall, average taxpayers (the median family income earner) saw theirs increase. This increase was due to increases in social security payroll taxes and increases in state and local taxes, both generally regressive taxes.

Total taxes as a percentage of median family income in the United States have risen consistently since World War II, peaking at around 40% of family income in 1995 and declining slightly after that. That shift hides a much more serious shift in the sources of these taxes and the relatively progressive or regressive nature of the income source for federal, state, and local governments. Since 1955, the trend has been clear: Federal taxes on income, usually collected through a graduated income tax, have declined as a source of taxation on the nation's middle class. This decline has been more than offset by increases in payroll taxes (since 1955, from under 10% of total tax bills for median income earners to 20%) and sharp increases in state and local taxes as a percentage of total tax bills. Much of this state and local revenue is collected using sales and excise taxes that disproportionately extract income from the middle class and the poor.

In fact, state and local taxation is usually far more regressive in its effect than is taxation by the federal government. For example, the poor and middle class pay a larger percentage of their incomes to state and local governments in taxes than do the relatively well-off. State and local sales and excise taxes explain most of this disproportion: while income taxes are generally progressively administered, the weight of sales and excise taxes falls disproportionately on the poor and middle class.

Box 2.1   What Are Regressive and Progressive Taxes? (Leicht and Fitzgerald 2022)

Regressive taxes take a higher percentage of income from people with low incomes. They are more burdensome on low-income individuals than on high-income individuals and corporations. Examples of regressive taxes are the Social Security Payroll tax, which (as of 2020) is 6.2% on the first $137,700 of income and 0% on any income over and above that. So, for example, someone who earns $137,700 a year owes $8,537 in Social Security payroll taxes, exactly 6.2% of her income, while another making $200,000 still pays just $8,537, in this case only 4.2% of her total income. Sales taxes on food and other essentials also take higher percentages of incomes for families and individuals with lower incomes because these people spend a greater percentage of their income on these items. The same is true of value-added taxes, which are paid by businesses that, in turn, pass costs on to consumers through higher prices.

Progressive taxes, on the other hand, take a larger percentage of income from those with higher incomes. For example, U.S. federal income taxes are progressive, taxing incomes at different rates depending on the size of income. As of 2020, the United States had seven income tax brackets (for single taxpayers):

Income: $1–$9,874T Tax bracket: 10%
Income: $9875-$40,124, Tax bracket: 12%
Income: $40,125–$85,524, Tax bracket: 22% Income: Income: $85,525–$163,299, Tax bracket: 24%
Income: $133,330–$207,349, Tax bracket: 32%
Income: $207,350–518,399, Tax bracket: 35%
Income: $518,400 and above, Tax bracket: 37%

The complicating factor is that individuals owe the U.S. Treasury the listed percentage of income *for each dollar within each range*, so someone making $45,000 would pay 10% on the first $9,874, 15% on the next $30,249, and 22% on the remaining $4,875 of income ($987 + $4,537 + $1,072 = $6,596 in federal tax, before deductions).

Of course, the relative fairness of state and local taxes varies greatly. The ten most regressive state tax systems tax their poorest citizens several hundred times the percentage of income they tax their wealthiest citizens, and many do the same to the middle class as well. Of these ten states, three—Illinois, Michigan, and Pennsylvania—are in the "rust belt," one—South Dakota—is in the upper Midwest, one—Washington—is in the Pacific Northwest, and the remaining six—Florida, Texas, Tennessee, Louisiana, and Alabama—are in the South or Southeast. With the exception of California and Utah, the states with the most regressive sales taxes are all in the South, and almost all of these states collect sales taxes on groceries.

By contrast, the six states with the most progressive income taxes—California, New Mexico, Rhode Island, Vermont, Idaho, and Maine—tax the income of the poor relatively little and even allow tax credits to exceed the total amount of income tax owed (hence, they have negative effective tax rates). All of them have highly graduated tax rate systems.

This evidence overwhelmingly indicates a significant, long-term change in the nature of taxation in this country. We have switched from a system that taxes people on the basis of their ability to pay to a system that taxes unearned income from capital stock relatively little and earned income from work significantly more. Further, we have shifted the relative tax burdens toward earned income below the 80th percentile of the earnings distribution and shifted tax burdens toward regressive sales taxes, excise taxes, and payroll taxes. The result is a government that does less for those who are not already wealthy, extracting more taxes from the have-nots, who do not represent powerful political constituencies whose economic welfare most politicians care about.

Cultural Backlash: The War on Expertise, Brexit, and the Election of Donald Trump

The End of Expertise and the Rise of Post-Modern Reasoning

As if the problems of the economic shift away from earned income to unearned income were not significant enough, and technological changes have not changed the roles of professionals in delivering services to clients and customers, recent cultural developments spell trouble for professional groups who occupy institutional niches based on expert claims. Most damaging is the appearance of a "War on Expertise" and the implications this has for the future of professional expert knowledge.

Where does this "War on Expertise" come from? The United States has always had a love/hate relationship with experts and elites in general. The relationship was baked into the nation's founding as a British colony sought to rid itself of control by a distant monarchy that represented inherited wealth, corruption, decadence, taxation without representation, and limited social mobility. But the founders of the new nation were also worried about "mob rule" as they embarked on their experiment in representative government. The tension between government "by the people" and fears of mob rule (justifying trust in elites and experts as moderators of the people's will) has been a central theme of the American public and public discourse in the United States. To a great extent, Americans have liked their government local, accountable, and transparent.

This dialectic between elites and the masses has fueled periodic waves of populist furor – the celebration of the "common man" (gender intended) as superior in outlook, temperament, and decision-making especially when compared to the claims of high-minded experts and elites who claim to know what is best for us. Closely tied to waves of populist furor have been attempts to reclaim local control from governments and established seats of power that are viewed as distant, clueless, and insensitive to the common man. Worse still, clueless and distant elites are viewed as threats to established local routines and social statuses that emphasize men over women, Christians over other religions, white Europeans over ethic and racial minorities, "honest work" over symbolic work, and self-sufficiency over interdependence and community.

In the United States, waves of populist fervor have defied easy political categorization but are usually associated with right-wing politics (cf. Hofstadter 1963). Populist waves of the 1820s, 1860s, 1890s, and 1950s all sought to limit the reach of the U.S. Federal Government, promote the interests of "real people" over and above economic and cultural elites, or defined traditional elites and experts as disloyal followers of alien plots to subvert the United States (e.g., the Committee on Un-American Activities in the U.S. Senate led by Wisconsin Senator Joseph McCarthy).

The analogous but less strident version of populism has played out in the United Kingdom under the label "Euroskepticism." To a substantial degree, the United Kingdom has a long history of real or imagined Euroskepticism going back to the great wars between Continental European powers. The conflicts between the United Kingdom and Continental Europe in World War I and World War II seemed to mark the end of these conflicts from a military standpoint, but they did little to change the wide gulf of cultural mistrust on the ground (cf. Guardian 2016). In their minds, Continental Europe produced two World Wars tied to the empirical ambitions of Germany and (in the U.K. mind at least) the British "bailed out" the rest of Europe at great personal cost.

The creation of the EU and the European Common Market was met with ambivalence by many in the United Kingdom, and, in the end, the decision to join the trading alliance without adopting the common Euro currency reflects this. The latest populist wave in both countries is part of a larger populist wave that is sweeping through most of the democracies in NATO. These social movements have become political actors by either creating political parties (e.g., Alternatives for Germany, the British and French National Front, Golden Dawn in Greece) or partially taking over established political parties (e.g., the Republican Party in the United States and to U.K. Tory Party). While their party platforms differ in specifics, almost all emphasize the following:

(1) The primacy of local, national cultures over foreign and cosmopolitan cultures;
(2) The celebration of specific ethnic groups as epitomizing the "core values" of the nation so that patriotism has ethnic and racial overtones;
(3) Severe restrictions on immigration, especially from places whose cultures are viewed as "alien" or "different";
(4) The worship of the "common forgotten man," complete with a traditional family tied to traditional gender roles and child-rearing practices;
(5) A preference for the local over the national or international, localism over cosmopolitanism;
(6) A corresponding distrust of "distant elites" and "experts" whose loyalty is viewed as suspect and whose behavior is viewed as distant, unaccountable, and contrary to the nation's good.

At its root the new wave of populism taps into the very real democratic deficit that exists in the 21st-century world (cf. Stiglitz 2012). As Joseph Stiglitz, Anthony Giddens, and Manuel Castells describe it (see also Baker and Leicht 2017), there is a growing disjuncture between what most governments can do to protect their citizens and what the globalized economy can do to those citizens. As Giddens describes it, the nation-state is "too big for the small problems of life" and "too small for the big problems of life" (Giddens 1994). People rightly suspect that they have very little say in how their lives are proceeding and populist ideology is an attempt to reassert control.

The beginning of the latest populist moment in the United States (and the corresponding abandonment of expertise) occurred with the election of George W. Bush in 2000. His election required the intervention of the U.S. Supreme Court to adjudicate between the political parties' claims about the distribution of votes in Florida (Gore won the national popular vote by 500,000 votes and lost Florida by around 500 votes).

The problems with the election itself were many, but the precipitating event was the balancing of the U.S. Federal Budget under President Bill Clinton. The Republicans ran a campaign focused on moral and fiscal responsibility and promptly squandered the label within two years of Bush taking office. The very real horrors of 9/11 put the Bush administration in a serious bind. Their response proved to be the first of many forays into the world of post-truth politics – in addition to declaring war on Afghanistan (a move widely viewed as justified to remove the Taliban regime and their support for Al Queda and especially Osama Bin Laden, the mastermind of the 9/11 attacks), the Bush administration also declared war on Iraq, insisting that Sadaam Hussein was harboring "weapons of mass destruction."

The nature of this claim was exposed in a piece by Ron Suskind for the *New York Times Magazine* in an interview with an unnamed Bush Administration official:

> The aide said that guys like me were "in what we call the reality-based community" which he defined as people who "believe that solutions emerge from your judicious study of discernable reality. That's not the way the world works anymore . . . we're an empire now and when we act, we create our own reality. And while you're studying that reality – judiciously, as you will – we'll act again, creating new realities, which you can study too, and that how things will sort out. We're history's actors . . . and you, all of you, will be left to study what we do."
>
> (Suskind 2004)

As we know now, there were no weapons of mass destruction. The war destabilized Iraq, killing thousands of Iraqis, destabilizing the country, and leading to 31,000 American wounded and 4,400 dead. The claims by administration officials (most prominently Donald Rumsfeld) that Iraqis would welcome Americans with open arms led to an open-ended nation-building operation by the U.S. that has cost billions and has promoted the rise of ISIS. To many, this event was the beginning of the latest bout of post-truth politics in the United States (Suskind 2004).

But it is not just in the realms of foreign policy and anti-terrorism that facts have been ignored or dismissed. There are other examples as well including the following:

- Climate change denial – climate change has been blamed on everything from the earth's wobbling rotation to natural cycles of weather, all in open defiance of scientific consensus on the issue (cf. Anderson 2017);
- Anti-vaccination groups, who spread misleading and false ideas that vaccines cause autism and other health problems and the "herd immunity" is a hoax (Georgiou 2019);
- Claims that evolution is "just a theory" and that public schools need to examine "both sides" of an issue that has been the scientific consensus for almost 100 years (Greener 2007);
- Most recently, the insistence, in spite of overwhelming evidence from the intelligence community, that Russia sought to interfere with the 2016 U.S. Presidential election and largely succeeded in doing so (though probably not enough to sway the outcome). The alternative narrative claims that others were responsible, that the interference had no effect at all, or that Russia had information on Hillary Clinton that they purposely withheld (U.S. Senate Select Committee on Intelligence 2019);
- The clear, present, and repeated cases of Donald Trump ignoring or dismissing expert opinions on everything from the use of Federal funds

to foreign trade to nuclear deterrence (Kinsella et al. 2020). Trump has also dismissed the recommendations of the State and Defense Departments, and the CIA, on how to deal with North Korea, preferring to negotiate a deal with Kim on his own (Walcott 2019).

The most prominent recent version of this argument is by Nichols (2017b, see also Nichols 2017a; Davies 2016; Huang et al. 2021). Nichols suggests that there is a campaign against established knowledge that is dangerous for democracies and their citizens. The traditional role of the expert (in our case synonymous with the professional) is to collect and interpret knowledge for citizens in specific areas. The traditional division of labor as Durkheim described it requires that people defer to professional judgments in specific areas of expertise. The combination of lots of different experts in lots of different areas (and the commitment of professionals to defer to others outside of their area of expertise) leads to an active dialogue where debates center around factual knowledge and interpretation with citizen input. Surgeons are not legal experts. Middle East scholars do not make pronouncements on Japan. English scholars do not do accounting, and so on.

In Nichol's analysis, this dynamic has fallen victim to a pseudo "democratization of knowledge" where everyone's opinion is of equal value regardless of what the conveyor actually knows. Any suggestion that there are factual, scientific, or logical errors in one's argument is met with a direct attack suggesting the critic is "elitist," "out of touch," or worse. This form of "aggressive ignorance" denies that people who have studied a topic for years know anything of value that cannot be Googled.

Nichols points out that the forms of pseudo-expertise this flattened hierarchy has created are elusory and dangerous. Google will confirm any random opinion we have, no matter how fanciful. So-called "citizen journalists" do not do very good journalism. Pontificators and pundits talk about everything from global warming to heart surgery and know next to nothing about any of it. Worse still, the so-called "expert citizen" is never corrected when wrong and their opinions do not change, unlike professionals where there is a check-and-balance system in place that makes corrections (sometimes slowly).

Nichols blames a wide swath of institutions in the public sphere for this problem, from colleges and universities that sell "experiences" that assure that students are never challenged or corrected, to talking heads on news programs, to the general narcissism of American millennials.

Two classic and recent examples of Nichols' argument about expertise (and the accompanying post-truth world it portends; see Rodgers 2017 and Pippenger 2017) are the U.K. vote in support of leaving the European Union (commonly known as BREXIT) and the U.S. Election of Donald Trump as President. Both spell trouble for democratic politics and professional expertise. The nuances of each case differ, but overall these are the same – globalization has produced a "democratic deficit" (Stiglitz 2012) where decisions about people's lives are surrendered to distant cities filled with people who are immigrants or otherwise viewed as "other." Many of these others (foreign and domestic) are skilled professionals who are viewed as out of touch with the "real people" who view themselves as harmed by the prerogatives of experts and the policies they advocate. The politicians' populist voters' champion is viewed as political outsiders, but more directly, they are outside of the conventional corridors of expertise from which elected politicians and policy analysts come from. In the case of BREXIT, voters seemed to be expressing exasperation with globalization and the idea that their lives needed to be tied to a group of "unknown others," many with whom they shared little culturally (see Menon 2017; Koller et al. 2019). In the case of Donald Trump, we saw the revolt of so-called "common people" against "inaccessible and clueless elites" promoting globalization and multiculturalism while paying no attention to the short-term havoc such changes cause. In both cases, campaigns were waged using blatant inaccuracies if not outright lies passed off as truth, often accompanied by derision directed at experts (see Zappavigna 2019). The almost complete free pass granted by the public and supporters to these bogus claims has led many to conclude that we are entering a "post-truth" world (Anderson 2017).

The implications for professional work based on logic, science, knowledge, and expertise are indeed threatening if these analysts are right. But this overall questioning of the value of expertise has a much longer tradition in the form of post-modernism (Anderson 2017), and the latest attacks on professional work and expertise are only the most recent manifestations.

The Overall Result? Professionals Under Attack From All Sides

The overall picture that emerges from these macro-historical changes in the economic and cultural landscape of professional work is especially grim, and these forces have all come to a head in the past decade or so.

- The wholesale attacks on the economic health of the middle class have affected professionals directly and created an institutional environment where their own livelihoods are threatened just as many of their clients and customers are losing the ability to pay for services.
- The substitution of unearned income for earned income as a point of economic and cultural emphasis has fueled neoliberal ideologies that question anything that does not produce immediate economic profit or gain (see Leicht 2015; Leicht and Fennell 2008a). Most professional work involves "system maintenance" functions that keep everything working properly. These activities rarely generate immediate profits and certainly do not produce capital gains or rents.
- The favorable tax treatment of unearned income, and the corresponding "soaking" of earned income, pinches professionals directly as most make relatively high earnings from salaries and jobs (see Phillips 1993).

- The cultural fragmentation, political polarization, and the growth of segmented communications have produced a post-modern world where all claims to expertise are attacked in the name of "real people," "the virtuous," "real Americans," and others with no more knowledge than the web can deliver via a Google search. Why pay for a cancer treatment a cancer specialist recommends if Google says otherwise??

The aforementioned changes have contributed to two other changes that we will discuss in the next chapter – technological change in the tasks and delivery of professional services and a growing globalization of professional work.

3 Technological Change, Globalization, and Professional Work

In this chapter, we focus on *technological change and globalization as they influence professional work* (see Figure 3.1). This chapter makes several interrelated arguments that we will reduce to three big ones – new technologies and artificial intelligence (AI) will produce changes in professional work tasks and protocols; outsourcing of professional work is a growing phenomenon that affects task performance and the labor market for professionals; as does the growing willingness of professionals to relocate internationally as countries around the world compete to lure high-quality talent to their shores. In this chapter, we re-introduce our young professionals and discuss the different ways that technological change and globalization have affected their budding careers in science (Maria), academia (Selena), medicine (Catalina), and law (Corwin). In our concluding section, we will address the broader question of whether the globalization of professional work is diffusing western-oriented models of professional work to other places and the implications this has for global societies and professional workers themselves.

Technological Change and the Professions

The growth in technology, AI, and the gig economy are affecting the professions in a myriad of ways. The predictions of what will happen in the future vary from an enhanced version of professional arrangements now (cf. Frey and Osborne 2017) to the complete destruction of the professions as we understand them (Susskind and Susskind 2017).

The most provocative statement on technology and the professions is put forward by Richard Susskind and Daniel Susskind (2017). They suggest that the monopoly of the professions over professional work historically was based on the following:

- The mystery and overall unavailability of professional knowledge;
- The societal bargain that granted wide leeway to the professions in exchange for the ethical, fiduciary use of professional knowledge;
- Knowledge delivered in an efficient manner and updated in a timely fashion;

DOI: 10.4324/9781003225485-4

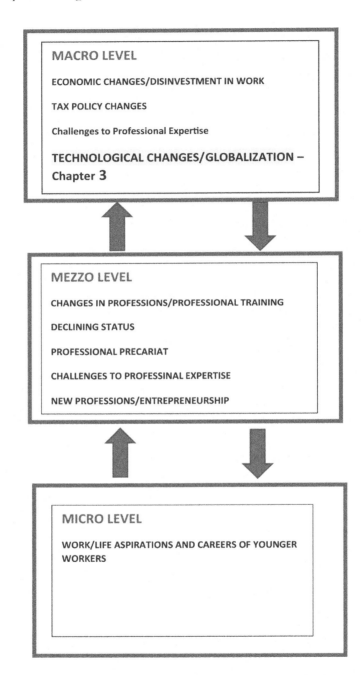

Figure 3.1 The Organization of Our Argument – Chapter 3 – Technological Change and Globalization

- Professions policing their own members and deciding who is to be admitted to practice and who is not.

To the Susskinds, almost all of the bases of the social contract are under siege, so much so that they predict the end of the professions as we currently understand them. Specifically, the bases of the social contract have been changed by the following:

- The growing and widespread availability of scientific and technical knowledge on-line and the general democratization of access to knowledge;
- The growing recognition that traditional, bespoke applications of service delivery are ineffectual or unavailable for many people in the developed world and inaccessible to almost everyone in the developing world;
- The highly visible and publicized ethical lapses in finance and accounting that have led to the questioning of the idea that professions can police themselves;
- The overall velocity of new information, which has gone beyond the ability of individual professionals to keep up;
- Savvy consumers who possess more knowledge going into professional transactions and are increasingly asking for "more-for-less," paying for professional services on an as-needed basis rather than establishing long-term relationships with generalists.

The changes in technology have and will continue to attack the center of the social contract. The changes that will be brought by new technology will lead to changes in service delivery. Many of these changes will attack the task domain of professional groups. Specifically, much work will be *routinized* – routine tasks once carried out by new practitioners "learning the ropes" will now be outsourced or (ultimately) automated. Much profession work will suffer *decomposition*, where the individual tasks of professional workers are farmed out to paraprofessionals and non-professional groups. This either leaves the professional as a supervisor or outsourcer of work they once did or leads to complete replacement by brokers or cheaper intermediaries. Susskind and Susskind also discuss *disintermediation* and *reintermediation* as reconfigurations of professional work. In disintermediation, clients abandon professionals as gatekeepers of knowledge and tasks and directly interact with knowledge aggregators. The knowledge is embedded in either social networks, online self-help, and/or mass communication and customization – the ability to combine elements that themselves are mass produced to create a customized result for clients. In reintermediation, professionals are reinserted into the relationship between clients and professional knowledge but in a different place. This place is a more proactive location usually earlier in the process of providing help – for example, MDs may address general wellness issues with patients, attempting to head off disease by promoting good habits rather than just reacting when people get sick. Lawyers may take a firm's financial position and advise financial officers about how to stay out of tax trouble rather than representing them once they have run afoul of the law. Professional work may be more limited in scope, but reintermediation suggests that professional tasks will be performed at different times than they are now.

How technology and AI affect the professions depends on the susceptibility of professional tasks to decoupling and automation (see Table 3.1).

Table 3.1 Examples of Current and Future Technological Changes Affecting Professional Work (Susskind and Susskind 2017)

Profession	Current/Future Technological Change
Medicine	More sophisticated versions of WEBMD, Betterdoc, and ZocDoc available to patients
	AI-based diagnosis
	Telemedicine
	Medical apps for cellphones
	AI-based hypothesis generation for medical research
	Cheap/free genomic sequencing
Education	Adaptive, personalized learning systems
	Khan Academy-like nearly free online instruction
	Massive Open Online Courses (MOOCs)
	Open-access libraries/knowledge data-bases
Law	Legal process outsourcing
	Automated document assembly systems
	Legalzoom, Rocketlawyer, and other online, self-service legal assistance
	Intelligent search systems
	Virtual courts
	Online referral/ranking systems
Management consulting	Offshoring basic research
	Off-the-shelf data-analytic solutions
	Digital consulting
	Network-based consulting
	AI-consulting systems
Accounting/auditing	on-line tax preparation
	Automated tax collecting/calculation by Governments
	Full-data, "100% testing" audits

The major claim made by Susskind and Susskind is that the customized, bespoke, reactive method of service delivery is inefficient or so expensive that it is inaccessible to most of the population in need of services (see also Sandefur 2016). They place particular faith in the ability of AI systems to sort through digitized stacks of knowledge and render professional advice with little interference by intermediators. The client/patient/customer "cuts out the middleman" and enters their problem into an AI/database system, and a solution is rendered. This type of solution relies on savvy, educated consumers to co-produce the professional services they consume.

Box 3.1   The Promise and Problems of Artificial Intelligence

Artificial intelligence (AI) is intelligence exhibited by machines. The overall purpose of AI (in many cases) is to understand how sophisticated decision-making by humans works, and then improve on it by either (1) increasing the speed at which decisions can be made or (2) increasing the amount of information that can be used when making decisions.

The implications of AI for a lot of professional work are enormous, and the goal of AI is to produce "general intelligence" (the ability to solve any randomly selected arbitrary problem).

Tied to AI are sophisticated statistical models that are capable of taking large amounts of data from different sources and developing decision-making models from them.

Whether people will ever accept direct professional advice from machines is an open question, but realistically the ability of AI to help professionals make decisions for clients is vast.

(1) In medicine, AI has the potential to summarize the latest research and provide guidelines for treating diseases using far more data than individual physicians could use.
(2) In law, AI has the potential to routinize many tasks, allowing lawyers to focus on "big picture" issues and client interactions.
(3) In scientific research, AI has the potential to generate new research hypotheses that scientists themselves may not see.

We are a long way from receiving medical diagnoses directly from a machine, but there is no doubt that AI will change how many professional tasks are done in the near future.

In medicine, the potential for technology and AI to (at minimum) enhance medical practice is vast. More sophisticated versions of WebMD could allow patients to enter symptoms and even blood and urine samples and receive a diagnosis. Doctors could enter patient-specific information into an AI-based diagnostic tool that would scan for relevant medical research literature as well as records from past cases. Advanced teleconferencing tools can spread telemedicine, where the top medical minds are teleported to remote locations to discuss specific cases, and Google Glass allows physicians' notes and visual observations to be recorded and scribed by subordinates on the other side of the world (see Dworskin 2016). Advanced robotics provide a promising way to conduct complex surgeries, making very precise measurements and incisions that are difficult or impossible for human surgeons to make. And, on top of all this, the therapeutic recommendations generated by AI systems could be carried out by nurse practitioners, physician's assistants, specialized therapists, and others at lower prices and with better results. Or at least that's the hope.

In education, the problems that AI and technology can solve do not involve cost (though in higher education in the United States that is a major issue) as much as it is time and learning styles. The standardized classroom can be replaced by customized and adaptive learning systems that gauge the progress of students and tailor lessons exclusively to them. Open-access libraries and knowledge databases will make most of the world's knowledge open to people who live far from traditional libraries and schools. Organizations like the Khan Academy and major research universities are offering "MOOCs" (Massive Open Online Courses) that reach thousands, cover a wide array of topics, and cost relatively little. In all of these scenarios, teachers and professors move from being the "sage on the stage" to a "guide on the side" if a human instructor is present at all.

In the practice of law, the same technologies that allow for telemedicine allow for legal process outsourcing (which we address next under globalization). AI processes can be linked to large legal databases to produce laser-like legal services, eliminating the need for junior lawyers to do legal searches for client cases. AI also holds out the promise of automated document assembly – junior lawyers tell the AI system what documents are needed and the system automatically writes the documents and spits them out, ready to be signed. Online resources and ranking systems will bypass word-of-mouth networks with links to firms that will provide the legal help you need, and this legal assistance will be episodically engaged rather than provided by old established firms paid through long-term retainers.

And, of course, new technologies have the ability to transform management consulting and accounting services too. Not only can basic research be outsourced (much like legal process outsourcing or the outsourcing of diagnostic tasks in medicine) but new technologies can also open the possibility of customized consulting and accounting solutions that are constructed from existing cases and prior rubrics. Clients will log on to these systems and a

Table 3.2 Predicted Probability of Computerization for Different Professional Occupations (Frey and Osborne 2017)

Occupation	Probability of Computerization
Accountants/auditors	High (0.93)
Administrative law judges	Medium (0.64)
Financial analysts	Medium (0.23)
Physicists	Low (0.10)
Chemists	Low (0.10)
Biochemists/biophysicists	Low (0.027)
Physicians/dentists/medical scientists	Low (0.036–0.045)
Pharmacists	Low (0.012)
Microbiologists	Low (0.012)
Biologists	Low (0.015)
Computer and information research scientists	Low (0.015)
Post-secondary teachers	Low (0.0095)

variety of customized options will be available without direct human interaction. For accounting and auditing, AI and technology will provide online "as you go" tax preparation (even for corporations), online tax collection for governments, and automated corporate audits that eliminate sampling and directly audit 100% of a company's transactions.

How likely is all of this? Frey and Osborne (2017) conduct a separate analysis using the O'Net and Dictionary of Occupational Titles to assess the probability that an occupation's tasks can be computerized. Their results for the professions are listed in Table 3.2.

Frey and Osborne use a complex statistical method that combines subjective assessments of the potential of computerization rendered by industrial engineers with several O'Net variables that they see as reflecting obstacles to computerization – finger dexterity, fine manual dexterity, cramped work spaces with awkward conditions, creative intelligence (a combination of originality and fine arts skills), and social intelligence (social perceptiveness, negotiation, persuasion, and assisting and caring for others).

In their analysis, only accountants and auditors, administrative law judges, and financial analysts are in serious danger of replacement by automation. Almost all other professional occupations face relatively low chances of being automated. Why? Mostly because most professional practice activities require creativity and judgment, characteristics that O'Net, Frey, and Osborne do not believe are subject to ready automation (some of the occupations most susceptible to automation in their analysis are telemarketers, cargo and freight agents, title examiners and searchers, and insurance underwriters).

Why does the Frey/Osborne analysis differ from the Susskind analysis? The real difference is that Frey and Osborne focus on and evaluate occupations as they are presently configured. The O'Net takes evaluations from labor force experts on the characteristics required to perform well in each occupation *right now*. They use existing data, data that have been updated regularly since the 1940s, to identify occupations that can be standardized and automated from those that cannot.

Susskind and Susskind start from a different premise and project technology and AI forward in an attempt to describe how new technology could solve some continuing problems of the professions – high costs, poor or insufficient access, and subpar results. They place great faith in the ability of mass databases and AI protocols to conquer what the O'Net would classify as "creativity and judgment." They argue that, at minimum, many professional tasks can be routinized and given to others or (more provocatively) that human creativity and judgment are not all it's cracked up to be and that advanced AI and big data can do a better job of diagnosing problems and constructing solutions. These changes would splinter the occupational groups studied by Frey and Osborne.

The difference between these two portrayals is broad and fundamental. The root of the dilemma for the future of professional practice lies in the roles that human interaction, creativity, and judgment play in the interface between clients and practitioners. Frey and Osborne's analysis implies that human creativity and judgment are not replaceable – that people will want technological solutions intermediated by someone the client interacts with face to face someone who is familiar with the client's problems and is committed to acting in their best interests to construct a customized solution. Susskind's claim (with some evidence to back them up) is that this one-on-one, reactive, bespoke method of delivering customized results is inaccessible to many, costly, inefficient, and produces mediocre results. They believe that clients will accept automated, standardized solutions if the alternative is no service at all. Others will accept these solutions once they see the results produced and the money saved. They imply that government regulation can still control where expert advice comes from without certifying people as professional practitioners (though they don't elaborate on how this would be accomplished).

While neither of these analyses is complete, the Susskind analysis is by far the most radical. While one could argue that Frey and Osborne are tied to what is, the Susskind analysis takes a very real problem (cost, quality, and access to professional services) and eliminates the professional. They suggest that much of the knowledge bottled up in the current system of service delivery could be extracted, democratized, and delivered through other means and that decomposition, disarticulation, and rearticulation are necessary components of doing this.

Our objections to the Susskind analysis lie not in the belief in technological potential but in the light dismissal of the role of human interaction in client acceptance of service innovations (see Lohr 2017). The lack of access to professional services is solved by automation, but this leads to the obvious question of who would be subjected to it and who wouldn't – the poor? Citizens of less-developed countries? The powerless?? Technology is almost never benign. The potential uses to which it is put are tied to powerful economic interests. Are we really to believe that the economic rents collected by professionals won't simply be transferred to another powerful group, and what their interests will be? Scholars in the power theories tradition in Chapter 1 would point this out and would suggest that the solution is not a straightforward "win" for consumers.

In addition to the problem of client acceptance, there are other problems as well. The Susskind portrayal depends substantially on the unmediated flow of information from unevaluated experts to the general public via the Internet. But let us ask ourselves – in what other area of life has the Internet increased the *quality* of information to which people are exposed? (see Nichols 2017). For every WebMD and telemedicine physician, there are a bevy of websites that claim cures for cancer that do not exist, that the earth is hollow and filled with aliens who can cure heart disease, and that most of science, technology, and expertise is a sham directed at "real people" (see our section on the Professions in a post-truth world). Susskinds suggest that regulations can separate out quality information from the fraudulent, but they do not say how this would work without invoking a reaction regarding the censorship of free speech, elitism, and so on.

In addition to depending on an at-best unsteady informational base and platform, the Susskind portrayal has a "before and after" quality to it that does not describe how we get from where we are now to where they see us going. This is far from fatal and the potential of AI and new technologies are vast. But at minimum social scientists and policy analysts who study new technologies would want more assurances regarding how these big transitions would take place. The potential benefits here are not self-evident, and the shifting interests of clients and professional groups would have to be interrogated extensively. A free market run by AI programs is still, at its base, a free market with considerable information problems. AI does not solve those problems, and AI hooked to the Internet has the potential to create many more.

Regarding technology and the future of the professions, it is worth keeping in mind what the history of technological change has taught us about the impacts of new technologies (see Leicht and Harper 2018).

(1) There is the developer's understanding of what the technology will do.
(2) There are evangelists (opinion leaders who are enthusiastic about the new technology) and what they think the new technology will do.
(3) There are buyers of the new technology and what they think it will do.
(4) There are customers exposed to the new technology and what they think it will do.
(5) Then there is what the technology actually does, which usually does not match any of the conceptions in (1)–(4).

Technology and AI will change the professions, but those developments have to deal with existing professionals, governments, institutions, and clients.

Globalization and Outsourcing Professional Work

The phenomenon of outsourcing professional work in a variety of fields (law, medicine, engineering, pharma, and science/STEM) has shifted the location of nonacademic positions to global markets. A number of examples are as follows: medical tourism and medical diagnosis; international postdoctoral positions in STEM fields; and legal outsourcing and internationalization of legal practice. Pharmaceutical firms have become globally diversified as well. And of considerable interest in understanding this global picture is the rise of the globalized, omnibus, professional service firm. Financial services are available across time zones, around the clock, seven days a week. And "back office" services can easily be relocated out of major urban areas in the United States, as well as to global locations everywhere (an important result of both technological change and globalization). We will discuss each of these in turn after providing some general background.

Background: The Growing Global Professional Class and the Rise of the Network Society

Over the past 30 years, social commentators such as Manuel Castells (1998, 2011), Saskia Sassen (2001, 2014), and Richard Florida (2008) have discussed the implications of "societies without borders." There are several implications of their analyses even though each brings a slightly different emphasis to the issue of globalization. First, *the localized, nation-state-based conception of the world's nations and economies that divided the world into clear territories (core/periphery, core/semi-periphery/periphery, developed/semi-developed/less-developed, communist/free-world, etc.) has been de-territorialized.* In practical terms, this means that there are global networks of professionals from diverse racial and ethnic backgrounds (most of whom live in "global cities") that have more in common with each other globally than they do with their fellow citizens in the country they happen to be living in. This means there are networks of professionals not only in New York, London, Paris, and Brussels but also in Kuala Lumpur, Nairobi, and Mumbai. These people tend to share common educational experiences and common, cosmopolitan outlooks. This does not mean they are "all alike" or that there is a global conspiracy to promote expert control by these people. But it does mean that global communications networks and relatively recent technologies allow for continuous contact with like-minded professionals around the world. This, combined with the consolidation of professional services in some fields and institutional pressures to create common international understandings in many content areas (see Suddaby et al. 2007), means that the professional classes in (say) Nairobi may have more in common with those in Paris than they do with their non-professional neighbors down the street or on the other side of town.

The second implication of globalization is that *there is also a de-territorialization of the location of everyone else*. There are big and (in some cases) growing pockets of poverty in developed countries. There are big (and in some cases) growing pockets of affluence in what was once termed less-developed countries. Virtually everyone is attempting to create a middle class. In virtually every place around the world, rural areas are depopulating and being left economically and culturally behind. As Anthony Giddens observed (1991), the contemporary world city is where the first world comes in direct contact with the third.

Third (a point made by both Sassen and Castells), *there are large numbers of people, many desperately poor or downwardly mobile, for whom the global economy has no place*. It is one thing (in a classical Marxist sense) for somebody to need your labor and attempt to exploit you while working. It is quite another thing to not be needed at all. And, as with professionals, the middle class, and everyone else, these "fourth world" people (Castells 1998) are everywhere from the rural areas of developed countries to the inner cities of global metropolitan areas.

Fourth, *the contemporary nation-state is viewed as "too big for the small problems of life and too small for the big problems of life"* (Giddens 1994). In many cases, global professional and cultural norms spread in a segmented fashion within social groups in ways that are out of the hands of local people, local governments, and local communities. Small problems (such as where to dig a water well) are not addressed and big problems (should professional service firms like KPG determine the accounting standards for an entire country?) seem to be imposed by outsiders.

Obviously, these developments are fertile ground for all sorts of social unrest from the rise of cultural and religious fundamentalism to the growth of indigenous social movements, populism of various kinds, and other attempts to reduce the "democratic deficits" (see Stiglitz 2012) that this New World Order has produced. And many of these local cultural uprisings have implications for professionals as science is viewed as an "instrument of Western imperialism," there are growing concerns about who financially benefits from the spread of Western business and scientific practices, growing cultural resentments directed at "global cosmopolitan elites" with their ideas about diversity and gender inequality that clash with local norms (see Baker and Leicht 2017), and politicians and political leaders who fear "brain drain" from the local economy to the centers or metropoles of this global economic order (Castells 1998).

When Alfred Nobel set up what would become the Nobel Prize in various disciplines, he stated explicitly, "It is my express wish that in awarding the prizes no consideration be given to the nationality of the candidates, but that the most worthy shall receive the prize." And that has certainly been the case (see Figure 3.2).

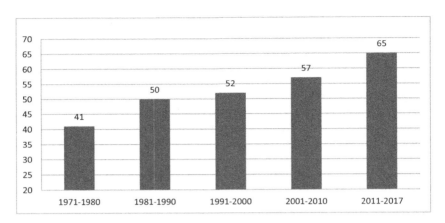

Figure 3.2 Nobel Prize Winners in Physics, Chemistry, and Medicine Since 1970 – Percent Non-U.S. Winners

Source: www.nobelprize.org

Increasingly, post–World War II awards have become less British and U.S.-Centric, both in the national origins of the awardees and in the institutions they represent. Further, the number of Nobel Prize winners who immigrated to the locations where their home institutions are (i.e., were born in one country but work in another) has skyrocketed as well. Overall the Nobel Prizes in science are becoming more diverse in multiple ways.

There is also increased international competition for scientific discoveries that have fueled an "arms race" for the attention of top scientists. As late as the 1990s, the United States and the United Kingdom trained a vast majority of scientists and a vast majority of them worked in the locations they were trained. Young and budding foreign students sought graduate training in the United States in the hopes of securing a permanent position with a U.S. university or in the private sector.

However, numerous observers have noticed that there has been a drastic shift in the locations where new scientists are hired and (in many cases) trained. Universities and private scientific-oriented STEM companies in Singapore, South Korea, China, and the EU are competing for and winning competitions for top talent. In the case of Asian countries, billions of dollars of infrastructure spending have gone into upgrading universities and general research capacity in an attempt to capture the benefits of scientific innovation. Rather than watching top students in science train elsewhere and be permanently lost to the national economy, these countries are assembling attractive packages that lure their own students back upon the completion of their degrees elsewhere or (in some cases) keep them in-country for training and subsequent employment.

On top of this, these same countries and regions have started to lure established scientific talent away from the United States with attractive pay and start-up packages. In the United States, the NSF and NIH fund most scientific research, and their research budgets have flatlined (see Figures 3.3 and 3.4).

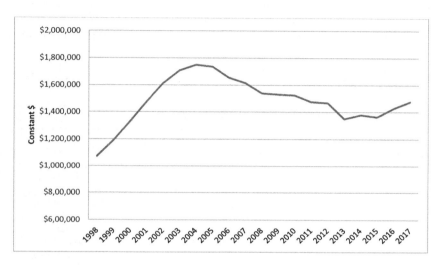

Figure 3.3 Total Funding for Research Grants, U.S. National Institutes of Health, 1998–2017 (Constant Dollars*)

Source: National Institutes of Health, Office of Extramural Research.

*Constant dollars based on the biomedical research and development price index (BRDPI, 1950 = 100).

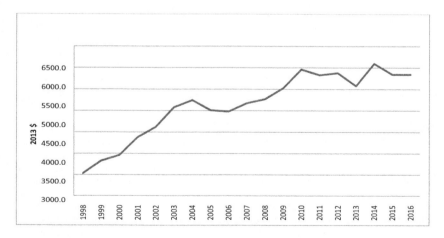

Figure 3.4 U.S. National Science Foundation Funding for Research and Related Activity, 1998–2016 (in Constant 2013 Dollars)

Source: AAAS and NSF Budget Reports. Excludes Funding Under ARRA

And it is not as hard for a U.S. scientist to relocate overseas as you would think. Since most international scientific dialogue is conducted in English, new hires can take their time learning local languages for everyday life while hitting the ground running with their established research programs. Governments are facilitating this process by making visas and immigration papers easy to get as well. The general lack of red tape and the boosterism in promoting science stands in sharp contrast to the suspicions and red tape these scholars face at U.S. universities.

Table 3.3 Examples of Programs and Reactions to Competition Between the United States and Other Countries for Top Scientific Talent

Example	*Implications*
China's 1000 Talents Program	Provides stable salaries, housing allowances and ample research funds for new graduates and established researchers who relocate to China
Canada's Global Skills Strategy	Seeks to hire 150 university researchers and Scholars over the next five years with ample research funding, salaries, quality of life, and amenities
France's "Make our Planet Great Again"	Targeting especially U.S.-based researchers Who are fleeing funding shortages, red tape, poor job opportunities, and political interference
U.S. Federal Funding for Science has Dropped 20% in real dollars over the Past 15 years (Forbes, 2013; see also Figure 3.4)	If funding elsewhere is rising while U.S. funding is falling, the global scientific workforce will move
One in five U.S.-based scientists is considering A move overseas (UPVO report, 2013)	Funding problems and red tape lead people to look elsewhere, and this trend is not limited to foreign nationals working in the United States
46% of U.S. scientists report laying people off recently or will do so in the near future; 55% know a colleague that has lost a job or will soon; 85% believe the United States is giving up its once-dominant position in science (UPVO report, 2013)	Many of these jobs are training grounds for future scientists. If they move somewhere to do their preliminary work, there is a good chance they will stay there
The Chinese are even poaching elite; Ivy League researchers will the lure of steady research dollars (Lambert 2018)	These are the very people who tend to train many of the next generation's top scientists. If they move to China, they will be training theirs and not ours

Technological Change and Globalization for Our Young Professionals

In Chapter 1, we introduced you to four young professionals. Maria, the PhD biologist, is stuck in the limbo of a series of postdoctoral positions, unable to turn her PhD into a permanent faculty position at a research university or a research position at a major pharmaceutical or biotechnology firm. Selena, with her PhD in Comparative Literature from Harvard, is stuck in a series of temporary teaching positions. Catalina, with her MD from Brown University, is looking for a position in geriatrics but is willing to settle for a hospitalist position in internal medicine at a hospital close to where her parents live. Corwin, fresh from the University of Chicago's Law School, looked at the instability of the labor market for lawyers in traditional law firms and opted for an in-house counsel position at a medical services firm. As we will see, all four are having their own struggles with the technological changes and globalized labor markets for their services.

Maria (our PhD in biochemistry introduced in Chapter 1) is increasingly facing a world of global biotechnology where some dimensions of her work tasks can be outsourced if she works for a biotech firm and other tasks can be automated. At minimum, there are too many people seeking too few positions. She needs to look for work in Singapore, China, Korea, and the EU. Funding continues to stagnate in the United States, and the prospects that she has for finding steady work, especially an academic job as a professor, are increasingly remote. On top of this, Susskind and Susskind report that AI technologies may be capable of reading through extant literature, examining different research protocols, and then generating new research hypotheses that researchers do not see (Susskind and Susskind 2017). If this actually happens, then the need for top creative minds could dwindle or be very restricted in the future.

Finally, the spread of telecommunications technologies to all corners of the world has created a "24/7" economy for professional services and a consolidation of those services (see Suddaby et al. 2007). The "Big Four" management consulting firms and the Big four accounting firms have attempted to produce an omnibus model for business-oriented services that are geared toward multinational conglomerates that operate in numerous places at once. All of these firms started in the United States or the United Kingdom. The multinational corporations increasingly demand seamless services to be provided anyplace, at any time, on the spot. This has led to the international branch-office expansion of all of these firms and widespread attempts to find and incorporate locals and ex-patriots in local branch offices.

But the global expansion of services is only part of the equation. The other, in many cases, is lowered costs for back-office operations. The creation of the close-to-paperless workplace means that documents and cases can be worked on by professionals in the home country during the daylight hours and then "virtually shipped" to the other side of the world (to India and other locations) where back-office, non-client-contact work is done while the principals sleep. The project is then "virtually shipped" back to the home country and is in the principal's inbox in the morning when they show up at work.

This shift to 24/7 professional services has profound implications for national labor markets, especially in the home countries where the principals live and work (mainly the United States and the United Kingdom). The back-office work that is now being outsourced used to be the work that young professionals did when they joined firms. This is where beginning socialization experiences took place, performances were critiqued, and people "learned the ropes" from established practitioners. The outsourcing of much of this work would appear to not only cut off these socialization experiences (which now have to happen elsewhere, but where?) but also shrink the labor market demand for new hires in established legal and professional service firms. This is a topic we will return to later in the book (Chapter 6).

How does all this outsourcing, globalization, and technological change play out in different professional environments (see Box 3.2)?

Box 3.2   Globalization and Changes in Professional Work

Medicine

- Outsourcing of diagnostic services
- Medical tourism
- Automated practice protocols

Law

- Outsourced legal research/subcontracting
- Global firm consolidation

Management Consulting and Business Services

- Professional service firm consolidation
- One-stop shopping for accounting, legal services, and management consulting
- Global consolidation

Big Pharma

- Global diffusion of innovation
- Reduced hegemony of U.S. academic science
- Big financial stakes in blockbuster drugs
- Corporate capture of scientific discovery

   Globalization of professional labor markets
   Diffusion of professional organizational forms

Medical Tourism and Medical Diagnosis

This would seem to be a strange place to start. Isn't the relationship between the doctor and patient supposed to be personal, face-to-face, and ongoing?? Don't we go to hospitals and emergency rooms expecting personalized, caring service by local people from our town or city?

Of course, we do. But increasingly, the physicians and nurses we see may be helped by others who not only are not on-site but may also be on the other side of the world. In the growing attempt to cut costs, improve efficiency, and reduce physicians' time spent on mundane tasks, back-office laboratory work and diagnosis can be carried out by licensed physicians and practitioners in other parts of the world where professionals are paid far less than they are in the United States. Need your laboratory results interpreted? Your X-ray, CA scan, or MRI? What about your cancer diagnosis and treatment? Increasingly, the local physician you see may be aided by physicians and specialists in India or Eastern Europe, places where professionals make far less money and work on a time schedule that facilitates getting results quickly through remote telecommunications overnight. In one recent example, Google Glasses allow physician exams to be directly watched by others anyplace in the world. The examinations are recorded, and the viewer (regardless of where they are) sees exactly what the physician sees with the exact angles and visual acuity the local physician has (see Dworskin 2016).

A much older but increasingly widespread phenomenon is happening to U.S. patients and others around the world. And the phenomenon is by no means limited to Western consumers – Asian mothers are traveling to U.S. birthing centers in order to have babies that are automatically American citizens (Robbins and Goldbaum 2018). Patients are traveling around the world to find the high-quality medical care they can afford. This phenomenon (called "medical tourism") allows people to receive high-quality care at prices that are many times less than what one would pay in (especially) the United States and in many cases health insurance pays for it. One especially popular destination is India, where special hospitals and outpatient spas and health centers have been set up to cater to paying customers. Many customers report being very satisfied with their experience and the personal service they receive (cf. Rosenthal 2013). The price differences for different procedures in different parts of the world are quite wide (see Table 3.4), and data on the number of patients engaging in medical tourism are notoriously sketchy. Even the World Health Organization only has rough estimates of how many people seek healthcare outside of their home countries (Rugeri et al. 2015, see Table 3.5). But as global travel has become easier and the quality of care converges, medical tourism becomes an attractive option for lots of people.

Catalina (our physician introduced in Chapter 1) is increasingly subject to automated practice protocols and technology-driven evaluations of the type of care she should be provided, to whom, and when (see Ginsburg

Table 3.4 Relative Prices for Different Medical Procedures in the United States and Medical Tourism Destinations, 2011

Country	Heart Bypass (CABG)	Heart Valve Replacement	Angioplasty	Hip Replacement	Knee Replacement
United States	113,000	150,000	47,000	47,000	48,000
India	10,000	9,500	11,000	9,000	8,500
Thailand	13,000	11,000	10,000	12,000	10,000
Singapore	20,000	13,000	13,000	11,000	13,000
Malaysia	9,000	9,000	11,000	10,000	8,000
Mexico	3,250	18,000	15,000	17,300	14,650
Poland	7,140	9,520	7,300	6,120	6,375
United Kingdom	13,921		8,000	12,000	10,162

Procedure

(Source: Lunt et al. 2011, OECD, in Current U.S. Dollars)

Calculations by Lunt et al.

Costs include surgical and physicians' charges, but not flights and hotel bills for length of stay

Table 3.5 Reported Estimates of Medical Travelers to Receiving Countries (Ruggeri et al. 2015, World Health Organization)

Receiving Country	Estimated No. of Annual Medical Travelers	Year
Australia	13,000	2010
Brazil	49,000–180,000	200517 and 2009
Costa Rica	25,000–150,000	2006, 2007, and 2008
Cuba	200,000	2007
Egypt	68,000–108,000	2003, 2004, 2005, 2006
Germany	50,000–70,000	2008 and 2009
Hungary	1,500,000–1,800,000	2007 and 2009
India	300,000–731,000	2006, 2007, 2008, 2010
Israel	35,000	2009
Jordan	120,000–250,000	2002, 2004, 2009
Malaysia	300,000–489,000	2006, 2007, 2008, 2010
Philippines	100,000–250,000	2006,2009, 2010
Republic of Korea	60,000	2009
Singapore	571,000–725,000	2007, 2008, 2010
South Africa	330,000	2010
Thailand	1,000,000–1,580,000	2004, 2006, 2007, 2008, 2010
Tunisia	10,000–42,000	2002, 2003, 2007
United Kingdom	52,000	2010
United States of America	250,000–400,000	2006, 2007

Note: Reports were identified by Ruggeri et al. (2015) via a non-systematic literature review of PubMed, EconLit, Google Scholar, the World Bank research database, Europe PubMed Central, and EMBASE.

and Phillips 2018). The team with which she works, and many of the people she may correspond with may not work in the United States, let alone in the same hospital she is in. There is some possibility that the basic care provided by the allied health professionals she works with may be automated or done by robots, though she finds such ideas a bit farfetched given her extensive interactions with patients. She finds herself increasingly in conflict with the practice protocols she is expected to follow and believes that these do more to make hospitals and insurance companies' money than they do to provide quality care to patients, especially those with chronic conditions. However, she does appreciate the possibility of having the latest knowledge distilled in a manner she can use since keeping up with the developments in internal medicine is almost impossible given her work schedule and need to care for her parents.

Legal Outsourcing and the Internationalization of Legal Practice

The practice of law has changed fairly drastically as well, especially when it comes to corporate law (Susskind and Susskind 2017). While it is true that you can still write a will, an estate plan, a medical power-of-attorney, file for divorce or bankruptcy, and hire a defense lawyer if you are sued by the local law firm in your city or town (and most or all of this work will be done by the attorney you hire and their legal assistants), the practice of corporate law has changed drastically in the past 25 years.

Several trends have driven changes in corporate legal practice. The same technological changes that have affected all professional groups have affected legal practice in a big way. After all, corporate legal practice is about tasks that can be automated and potentially outsourced – searching relevant case law and writing appropriate documents that represent interpretations of that case law (Susskind and Susskind 2017). The face time with the client can be carried out by local law partners and associates whom corporate clients know and trust, but the temptation to outsource much of this back office work in an attempt to lower costs and increase flexibility is almost overwhelming. This is especially true as corporations hire and rely on in-house counsel more frequently, have law firms compete for business (rather than having a single firm on long-term retainer), and as lawyers move around to different firms looking for a better deal and (in some cases) take their client lists with them.

There has also been considerable consolidation in corporate legal practice, especially in the English-speaking world. The top law firms in the United States and the United Kingdom employ thousands of lawyers and command ever-greater shares of corporate legal business (see Table 3.6).

These law firms have also expanded globally with their multinational corporate clients and are deeply involved in spreading American and U.K. legal norms around the world (Brock et al. 2012). Companies outside of the

Table 3.6 Top Global Law Firms by Headcount and Countries of Origin and Operation, 2017

Firm	Country of Origin Lawyers	Number of Lawyers	Countries With Branch Offices	% of in Country of Origin
Denton's	China	7,445	55	57%
Yingke	China	6.278	26	79%
Baker McKenzie	United States	4,719	47	15%
DLA Piper	United States	3,616	30	32%
Norton Rose Fulbright	United States	3,505	27	21%
CMS Legal Services	United Kingdom	2,719	35	25%
Hogan Lovells	United States	2,609	22	36%
Jones Day	United States	2,523	18	64%
Clifford Chance 30%	United Kingdom	2,466	23	30%
King and Wood Mallesons	China	2.397	16	60%

Source: www.law.com/legal-week/2018/09/24/the-2018-global-100-ranked-by-head-count-378-89154/?slreturn=20180904151701

United States and the United Kingdom that seek to do business there hire these firms because they possess the offices and resources to represent their interests in new markets they wish to penetrate.

But the consolidation of corporate legal practice is only part of the story. Law firms in global cities can and do outsource and subcontract legal work to other firms, especially in India (cf. Wilkins and Ferrer 2018). These subcontractors specialize in doing back-office work with little or no direct contact with clients. They do legal research, write standard documents, and e-mail or deposit their work in virtual clouds where principal attorneys in their home countries can access them. They charge way less than it would take to hire a legal associate in a major metropolitan law firm in the West (currently somewhere between $120,000 and $170,000, see ABA 2018). Most of the lawyers the Indian back-office firm hires are trained in the United States or the United Kingdom, and they are filling a niche in legal services that allows their partners in the developed world to lower costs and increase efficiency and speed.

This is the world that Corwin (our recent law graduate introduced in Chapter 1) faces. Corwin is a victim of the growing ability to outsource legal processing to other countries with lower labor costs. The global oversupply of lawyers and the increasing number of American law school graduates from foreign countries have meant that law firms need far fewer associates to "push the paper" and, in any event, corporate clients increasingly shop around for customized, one-shot legal services rather than retaining big law firms on long-term retainers. The ability to automate some legal work and outsource a substantial amount of the rest means that corporate counsel and other means of making a living as a lawyer are the main avenues for advancement in the 21st century.

Several questions arise from the globalization of corporate legal practice and the outsourcing of routine legal work; what does this do to the domestic, developed-country labor market for new lawyers? There is already a trend toward hiring fewer legal associates from graduating law classes and delaying (temporarily or permanently) promotions to legal partners. The spread of legal services around the world through large law firm consolidation almost certainly reduces demand for lawyers in home countries, and the outsourcing of legal work to India reduces the routine legal work that most new legal associates have traditionally done.

A second question is: where do the lawyers in the peripheral offices of these dominant law firms come from? Most are trained in the United States or the United Kingdom, and we suspect (but do not know) that most are from the nations where the law firm is setting up local branches. Almost all of those international lawyers spend some time in the firm's home country at the principal corporate headquarters learning how the firm operates, meeting with clients, and absorbing the culture of the firm — a culture the partners hope the new hire will spread to their outpost office (cf. Brock et al. 2012).

This is most certainly not the experience of most lawyers who work in subcontracting shops doing back office work (see Brown et al. 2011). These lawyers (though they are often trained in first-world countries) are paid way less, work way more, and have few if any opportunities for advancement. Between the automation of routine legal work, the consolidation of corporate law practice, and the outsourcing of routine legal work to places where costs are lower, the domestic developed-world labor market for new lawyers is in peril.

Management Consulting, Accounting, and Business Services

Much the same thing is happening to management consulting and accounting services (Muzio et al. 2013). The Said Business School at Oxford University in the United Kingdom has devoted much of the past 20 years to studying the development of the omnibus, global, professional service firm (Empson et al. 2017; Saks and Muzio 2018). In fact, they have created a bit of an intellectual movement around studying this phenomenon and (in some cases) promoting it through their yearly Professional Service Firms Conference (www.sbs.ox.ac.uk/faculty-research/tax/events/summer-conference-2018). The omnibus professional service firm was supposed to be a one-stop shop for accounting, legal, and management consulting services. Firms would consolidate and globalize their operations, following their multinational clients to new venues and picking up additional business from local firms seeking to make their way in the global economy through the adoption of "best practices" accounting and management. Governments were supposed to turn to these firms for advice on how to modernize their economies, legal systems, and business reporting practices too (see Hopper et al. 2017).

While the same forces of financial efficiency, technology, and global reach have been working here in the same way as the other professional groups we are talking about, there have been major bumps on the way to creating the omnibus, one-stop professional service firm. The major bumps were the accounting scandals in the United States (Enron, Tyco) and EU (Parmalat), and the financial crisis and accompanying recession of 2008–2009. In each case, big accounting firms had falsified or failed to validate revenue streams, assets, and profits – they certified accounting reports that were fictitious, allowing CEOs and other top executives to pocket big bonuses for reporting big performance gains. In each case, the underlying financial house of cards was exposed, the companies were either liquidated or filed for bankruptcy, and the accounting firms that certified these revenues and profits as "real" either collapsed entirely (Arthur Anderson) or took major reputational hits.

At the root of the problem from the standpoint of professional practice were conflicts of interest. The traditional accounting firms had branched out into management consulting as a way of increasing their revenues. In many cases, firms were providing accounting services to the same people they were selling management consulting services to. This lowered or eliminated the incentive to question revenue and profits reports for fear of losing accounting and management consulting business to competitors. On top of this, the involvement in management consulting meant that multiple professional groups would be singled out as defective if the company's books were not certified as good (see Leicht and Fennell 2008a).

A similar dynamic occurred during the financial collapse of 2008–2009, which started in the United States over doubts about the certification of bonds in the mortgage-backed securities market (see Chapter 2). Rating agencies (staffed by accountants, lawyers, and management consultants) were under enormous pressure from banks and financial houses to certify their bonds as AAA so that bond sales and mortgage lending could continue at a rapid pace. But the construction of the bonds (which the rating agencies did not control) became so complex that it was difficult to understand the underlying financial health of the mortgages the bonds were made of. Further, banks and financial houses could shop for rating agencies that would certify their work as "AAA," putting still more pressure on rating agencies to just give in and trust the financiers.

In both cases, the truth was eventually uncovered, and billions of dollars of assets and wealth disappeared. Many Enron employees lost all their retirement savings. Mortgage lending collapsed, and several financial houses collapsed or had to be bailed out by the U.S. Federal Government. What was less well known and covered were the changes demanded in professional services – accounting was now to be split from management consulting and legal services, ideally in different firms but at minimum in different and non-overlapping branches of the same firm. Bond rating certification has not changed, but accounting requirements have and these make it much more difficult to falsify accounting records.

The overall result of these scandals, from the standpoint of creating the omnibus all-encompassing professional service firm, has been a temporary halt in this type of consolidation as different professional groups and their representatives seek to re-examine how to unite professional service provision without creating conflicts of interest that lead to financial meltdowns.

Big Pharma as a Global Innovation Machine

The production of new drugs used to be pretty easy to describe – almost all new drug discoveries were made in the United States. The NIH and NSF would fund basic research by university scientists and professors. After it was published in peer-reviewed outlets, pharmaceutical companies would contact the scientists about their work and suggest some form of collaboration on a new drug (often aided by a research and development team at the company). A drug would be developed and tested, the FDA would approve it, and the drug would then hit the market, mainly in the United States, United Kingdom, and EU countries.

This once somewhat slow, sleepy, and semi-public relationship between academic and corporate science has changed drastically in the past 30 years. The major drivers have been the globalization of scientific discovery and innovation (see Figure 3.4), the decline in the hegemony of American academic science, the corporate desire to capture more gains from research and development in the form of exclusive property rights to new discoveries, and the growing financial stakes involved in finding new, "blockbuster" drugs that will dominate markets in areas like cancer and heart disease.

The biggest players in this saga are the growth and consolidation of Big Pharma, with an accompanying desire to secure more profits, more property rights to future innovations, and future blockbuster drugs and the accompanying decline or flat-lining of scientific research by the U.S. Federal Government. The overwhelming incentive for Pharma companies now is to (a) find the brightest minds you can wherever they are in the world, (b) sponsor their research in ways that national governments (especially in the United States) will not, and then (c) claim control over everything the scientist produces.

Notice, almost immediately, which phase of the traditional process is missing – public disclosure of scientific findings after peer review. This traditional process (which the U.S. Federal Government has always demanded) means that new scientific discoveries are in the public domain. Anyone can read the papers, derive what scientific value they can from them, and then decide what to do next. Granted, you cannot then create a drug that is just like one someone else has patented (at least not without paying compensation), but the basic science behind the new medications is available for everyone to see and use.

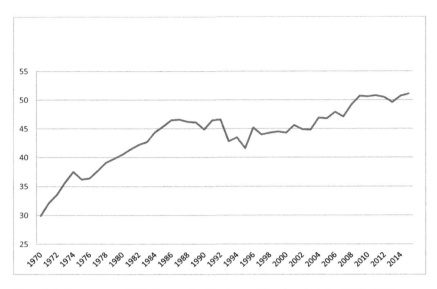

Figure 3.5 Percentage of U.S. Patent Applications of Foreign Origin, 1970–2015

Source: 1970 – Present, Utility Patent Applications: U.S. Patent and Trademark Office (USPTO) Provisional Applications Are Excluded

Increasingly, Big Pharma short-circuits this process by funding the research from the start and then controlling every phase of it. Universities like it because their scientists are funded and there are often agreements with universities about sharing the royalties from marketed products. The Pharma company likes it because they capture all the research and (often) prevent publication of the results, so they control the results the researcher produces.

And even this assumes that the academic scientist is involved in the first place. In many cases, the basic innovation work is done by an in-house Research and Development staff or R&D shops that the Pharma company has outsourced basic research. The value and rigor of the research are not independently checked, and the company controls everything the R&D scientists produce (i.e., there is no publication of results). Clinical trials are arranged at local hospitals, and there is no independent oversight of how the trials turn out (this bypasses a major problem with most clinical trials – effectiveness is not compared to current drugs on the market, but not to taking anything at all, which is not the relevant comparison, see Freeman 2010).

Not only does the academic science occur all over the world, but increasingly the corporate sciences (and the clinical trials) also do as well. Pharma research can be outsourced to or funded in China, South Korea, and Singapore just as easily as it can in the United States. And all of this is done in a massive and desperate search for monopoly profits from the discovery of the next miracle drug (see also Coccia 2012).

On top of this, there have been major mergers and acquisitions that have linked pharmaceutical benefits providers with major health insurers in an attempt to produce omnibus (and concentrated) medical services companies. The most recently announced merger between CVS pharmacies and AETNA health insurance providers would produce a health services company that would control the distribution of pharmaceuticals to the public as part of a global health insurance strategy. This merger (and others like it) have raised concerns among regulators about competition and conflicts of interest that will not go away soon (see Sukel 2019).

And for Professionals Themselves, the Labor Market Goes Global

The labor market for accountants, lawyers, engineers, scientists, college professors, and management consultants used to be easy to describe. The United States and the United Kingdom had the top universities in terms of training and prestige. Most others were nowhere close. The markets for professional practitioners were centered there, and other places were nowhere close. The aspiring student from the global south or global periphery (which had a territorial definition then, see our comments earlier about de-territorialization) tried to come to the United States or the United Kingdom to college and then stayed there since the only effective way to use their skills (and the only people who could pay for them) was there. The environments were, overall, welcoming, and there seemed to be little governments and nations in the global periphery could do to stop this brain drain to the developed world. At most, they would hope that money and resources would return indirectly to them.

But since the 1990s, and especially with the collapse of the global state-socialist system as an alternative to market capitalism, there has been a growing globalization of the labor market for top professional talent. Increasingly, nations are realizing that scientific and professional developments in what was once called the "global north" were not going to trickle down directly to them, nor were they capturing any value from the export of top talent to the global north. Global telecommunications and digitalization allowed for the creation of relatively inexpensive basic infrastructure and allowed more-or-less seamless collaborations with people all over the world. Multinational companies were looking for new markets and new places to locate their research and development facilities, legal practices, and management consulting firms. Local governments started to view the development of higher education institutions as a way of competing internationally and economically and realized that their academics and scientists at home would not be cut off from developments elsewhere.

One of the major driving forces of this new competition has been the opening of China to the outside world and to free-market reforms. China has sought to produce an alternative model of capitalism linked to a one-party political system that can compete extensively for high-value-added scientific discoveries and professional services. The sheer size of the Chinese market and investment in scientific infrastructure are staggering (see Figures 3.6 and 3.7).

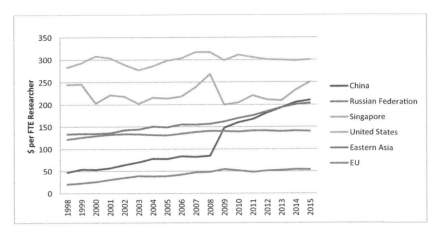

Figure 3.6 Gross Domestic Expenditures on Research and Development (GERD) per FTE Researcher, 1998–2015 ($PPP, 2005 Constant Dollars)

Source: http://data.uis.unesco.org/OECDStat_Metadata/ShowMetadata.ashx?Dataset=SCN_DS&Coords=%5bINDICATOR%5d.%5bEXPRESPPP_CONST_TFTE%5d&ShowOnWeb=true&Lang=en

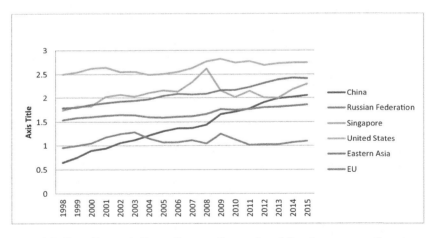

Figure 3.7 Gross Domestic Expenditure on Research and Development as a Percentage of GDP, 1998–2015

Source: http://data.uis.unesco.org/OECDStat_Metadata/ShowMetadata.ashx?Dataset=SCN_DS&Coords=%5bINDICATOR%5d.%5bEXPGDP_TOT%5d&ShowOnWeb=true&Lang=en

The collapse of the Soviet Union has also contributed to the creation of a global labor market for certain types of professional talent, especially scientists. As professionals have won the right to internationally travel and relocate, many have, and this has sparked a competition for them and a competition for Russia and China to poach talent from other places with attractive job offers and start-up packages.

To a great extent, the United States and the United Kingdom have been caught flat-footed by these trends or have done things that have hampered their ability to compete in this now-open labor market. As late as the 1980s, the world's potential graduate students wanted to come here, earn graduate degrees, and then stay in the United States and the United Kingdom to pursue their professional careers. Increasingly, they find crowded labor markets (especially in science and law, see Han and Applebaum 2016; Kolata 2016), they find open cultural hostility to their presence (witness the H1-B Visa debacle under the Trump administration, the Muslim travel ban, etc.), and they find deteriorating working conditions in the academy with postdoctoral studies that last forever, a dearth of available professorships, and open hostility to science and scientific discovery (Nichols 2017).

The net result of both of these trends is that aspiring professionals are looking at U.S. and U.K. labor markets and infrastructure that is sagging or collapsing at the very same time that other countries traditionally excluded from competitions for professional groups are enthusiastically expanding their investments and making relocations attractive. The net result of both trends is that foreign students in the United States and the United Kingdom increasingly want to do work elsewhere and American-based professionals are doing the same thing (see Han and Applebaum 2016).

In the United States, many of these developments are a simple extension of the trends that have harmed the middle class and their connections to prosperity via jobs. Profits are short-term. Universities do not contribute to the "bottom line," and legal services should be cheap and widely available. Further, professionals market in facts, expertise, and best practices, and we do not need those! Markets will determine what's right and the "truth isn't the truth"(!). But, from the standpoint of promoting national competitiveness, these developments could not come at a worse time – as others are investing in the infrastructures of innovation that promote science and professional practice, the United States is disinvesting in them. It is no wonder that international students (and even domestic students) seek their fortunes elsewhere (Han and Applebaum 2016).

In the End, Is Globalization of Professional Work Diffusing Western Norms and Rules to the Rest of the World?

One question scholars are addressing right now is whether the globalization of professional activity and professional labor markets are agents for diversifying professional practice or is simply spreading Western norms of law, accounting, management, and science around the world (see Saks and Muzio 2018).

The answer seems to depend on the area of expertise one is looking at. In science, the spread of science and innovation across national boundaries and from traditional places of strength (essentially the United States and the United Kingdom) to the rest of the world is a welcome development.

People can train where the training is best and then watch as a growing competition for their services allows them to relocate to places that can compete for them. As the would-be STEM worker population diversifies further, the places where they work will diversify as well, and all will be part of a growing cosmopolitan elite that keeps up with professional and scientific developments happening around the world (Castells 1998). Further, as universities around the world start to compete globally, students will be able to continue studying in their own countries and still be competitive in international labor markets. Few would argue that this is a bad development though (from the standpoint of the United States and the United Kingdom) the loss of scientific dominance is viewed as worrisome.

The answer in the areas of business services is not so straightforward. The playing field is dominated by a small number of very large legal, accounting and management consulting firms. All of these firms have their primary offices (and still do most of their business) in the United States and the United Kingdom. They are establishing branch offices and subcontracting relationships elsewhere. In many cases, home office people are temporarily or permanently relocating to set up these branch offices. The professional service firms are beholden to multinational corporations that seek to seamlessly operate anywhere in the world, expecting their service firms to fix their local problems. The service firms themselves appear to be promoting single set "best practices" that are consistent with their prevailing corporate models, attempting to spread those norms and rules elsewhere. To some locals, this can come across as western imperialism. In many cases, there are few democratic or transparency safeguards that examine this type of influence. And these small but growing members of the cosmopolitan professional classes live in global cities that are far removed from the local cultures and environments that exist at the city's border. This could be viewed as contributing to the "democratic deficit" (Stiglitz 2012) that many observers of globalization refer to critically. Whether this will change as more locals from non-western nations are encouraged to pursue professional careers, along with the local labor markets to support them, is still an open question.

Our next two chapters start to examine the implications of technological change, globalization, and the shifting cultural value of professional work on relatively new entrants, focusing on the (in many cases) stalled gender and ethnic diversification of professional groups and the rise of a group we refer to as the "professional precariat" – technically skilled professional workers who have trouble securing stable and steady employment.

Part II

Change in Professions and Professional Training

This section shifts our analytic focus somewhat away from the macro-level and large systemic changes considered in Part I, and toward more meso-level or mid-level foci on how professions themselves are changing, particularly with regard to their value to society, their attractiveness or job quality in the eyes of would-be job holders, and their economic value. The classic professions are looking more like Standing's description of the precariat, and new types of professional or elite jobs are emerging that may be eclipsing the former prominence of professional jobs.

Our first chapter in this section (Chapter 4) focuses on assessing the value of traditional and emerging professions, considering both supply-and-demand side issues. We will frame this discussion using the classic approach of Reskin and Roos (1990) extending the terminology of job queues and labor queues to understand gender segregation and desegregation over time within diverse occupations. We will consider multiple explanations for this phenomenon, including an oversupply of PhDs in various fields and an undersupply of what used to be known as "good jobs." Finally, some have suggested that the cost of PhD training is simply too high given the student debt crisis, the evaporation of federally funded doctoral training programs, and declining funds for graduate programs in general.

Reskin and Roos provide an excellent frame to introduce our second major focus of Chapter 4 which is to update a theme from our earlier volume on professional work: where are we in terms of the diversity of workers represented in managerial and professional jobs? In our 2001 work, we examined data for law and medicine to see if the representation of women and nonwhites had increased between 1970 and 1990. We found that there was more demographic diversity, but that diversity had been slow to develop and was not anywhere near parity in any elite profession. For medicine and law (the most diverse of the professions), white males were still the predominant group. In this volume, we will examine the published literature for additional data on diversity within a wider range of professions: law, medicine, science, college teaching, and newly emerged occupational categories: finance, data science, and entrepreneurship. We will look at "the numbers" of nonwhite non-male practitioners, especially in medicine, using IPUMS

DOI: 10.4324/9781003225485-5

data. Then we will examine data from the American Bar Foundation on recent law school graduates, and the NSF's National Survey of Earned Doctorates in order to more fully develop an updated picture of gender and racial diversity in law and scientific fields.

The second chapter in this section (Chapter 5) examines the emergence of the "professional precariat." We begin this chapter with Standing's classic concept and how it can be used to examine major changes in elite managerial and professional jobs. Then we expand on Standing's core concept to examine a cluster of related concepts: the gig economy, peripheral work/freelancing, and "flash organizations." Finally, we take Standing's concept and use it to examine several significant examples of precarious professional careers within the classic professions: hospitalists and medical scribes within medicine; adjuncts within academia; legal outsourcing in law; and the changing norms of delay in the first job, multiple postdoctoral positions, and competition within the STEM fields for international post-doctoral fellowships and junior faculty positions.

The last chapter (Chapter 6) in this section on the meso level takes a closer look at some of the newer "professions" to emerge recently, especially new careers in finance, data analytics, and entrepreneurship. Here we use the term "professions" quite loosely: these are decent jobs, but they do not require advanced degrees, some provide substantial salaries, some do not, and some provide new options for university program development. All three examples we examine are recently developed occupations that have managed to usurp aspects of professional work that were once the domain of classic professions such as finance or have carved out specialized occupations within classic professional sectors on the basis of technological advances in "big data" and/or computation/analytics. These are relatively new developments that have found prominence as important aspects of medicine, law, and financial planning. Of particular note is the mushrooming popularity of "entrepreneurship" (or e-ship) as a type of new career for college graduates and those hoping to end college studies early and start building one's first multi-million dollar nest egg. Despite e-ship guru's advice that you do not need a college degree to be a successful entrepreneur, many colleges (both public and private sectors) are jumping on board the e-ship bandwagon with new programs designed to take advantage of e-ship popularity.

4 The Value of Professions and Diversity Within Professions

Conflict and Queuing

In Chapter 1 (and again in Chapter 3), we introduced four young professionally trained individuals at the beginning of their careers: a PhD biologist; a Harvard PhD in Comparative Literature; an MD finishing a residency in Geriatrics; and a young lawyer from Chicago. In our Chapter 1 vignettes, each of these young people is contemplating accepting jobs that do not correspond with their expectations of professional work within their sectors; expectations that probably represent the "standard normal career path" for the past 30 years or more for advanced degree holders in each of their areas. Let us take a quick look at how their current choices stack up against the usual career path.

Maria, the biologist, no doubt expected to complete one postdoctoral fellowship after her PhD to pick up advanced training and publications in her area of research specialization. The post doc would normally be followed by a good position as a tenure-track assistant professor of biology in any number of top-ranked research universities, whether elite private schools or flagship campuses of major state universities. Given her excellent early start on publications and research grants, she probably expected to have a choice of such options. But now she has received funding for a second postdoctoral fellowship and can clearly see the handwriting on the wall of "the future of science." Research funds and regular tenure-track positions are declining across the board; universities that do hire junior faculty in the STEM fields are finding it difficult to deliver on their promised start-up packages (typically used to build the labs they need to do their research), which then puts the young faculty member at a serious disadvantage at the time of contract renewal and tenure review. Maria has decided to instead target the private sector for something like a "starter" job that might lead to a more senior position in time or to a more senior position in another firm. She is looking for a position in a major pharmaceutical or biotechnology firm as a senior scientist (if she is lucky and the firm is interested in having her pursue her line of research), or a project director (acting as the "straw boss" for several projects). She is also investigating positions at science-related foundations, where scientists are needed to develop communication projects to bring in donors or to help "translate" lines of research into meaningful clinical treatment regimens. Her job search has required significant realignment of her

DOI: 10.4324/9781003225485-6

academic CV into a resume that would fit the goals of the private sector and highlight her "flexibility," in terms of both skill sets and interests.

Selena has the PhD in Comparative Literature from Harvard and is now one of the legions of adjunct instructors hired by nearly all universities and colleges, to teach over half of the courses offered by American universities, on a part-time, per course, short-term contract basis (Hurlburt and McGarrah 2016; CAW 2012; Rhoades 2014). Contingent faculty now comprises the largest segment of the academic labor market, and the continued growth in this segment has been observed now (with alarm) for over a decade. As will be discussed in greater detail in Chapter 5, the working conditions of contingent faculty are very poor: compensation is low, career ladders are nonexistent, and benefits are not provided.

In the "good old days" of normal faculty recruitment patterns (perhaps as long ago as the 1980s), the number of jobs available was usually defined by departments in negotiation with deans and other administrators so that empty positions (vacated through retirements and exits of various sorts) would be filled through a faculty search within a year or two. These were primarily the standard normal beginning assistant professor line with tenure possible after a 6–7-year probationary period. The area of specialization would be defined by the department pending approval by the dean or provost. New positions have always been rare: without a specific line to replace, a new faculty position must be connected to larger strategic planning goals of the university to grow the faculty in specific disciplines. External economic stresses could delay approvals to run replacement searches, and new searches could be political "hot potatoes" pitting humanities versus social sciences versus STEM, bio-med, and other areas. Thus, successful pursuit and filling of new faculty lines must overcome a number of internal hurdles.

The external hurdles that clamp down on university hiring have been growing since the mid-1980s when state-related universities often became soft targets for stressed state budgets. Accountability to local priorities and interest groups have led state universities to short-change humanities and social science disciplines in favor of hard science, STEM, and business curriculum with a clear connection to improving regional industrial markets. Even the sciences have been under pressure (given recent experience with sequestration; see Chapter 1) which has whittled away at many of the NIH research budgets. But within the humanities and social sciences, the criticisms of local and federal politicians have had withering effects on hiring. These effects are clearly felt in faculty hiring reductions, as both replacement hires are delayed or eliminated, and what used to be a tenure-track position may become non-tenure-line or part-time. As an example, the total number of tenure-line assistant professor searches reported by the Modern Language Association has been falling since 2007, for both English and foreign language positions, reaching a new low of only 851 ads for full-time tenure-track jobs in English, and 808 jobs in foreign languages for 2017. These totals are 11% and 12% lower than the year before (Flaherty 2017). The number of PhDs granted in these disciplines is much higher than that – 1,389 in English and

Literature and another 751 in languages other than English (numbers as of 2015, the latest date available, see www.humanitiesindicators.org). There are many additional reasons, of course, for the decline in the number of searches to fill faculty positions, including fewer faculty deciding to retire, and universities pulling back on searches once begun, which may have been the case for the searches encountered by Selena which closed before candidates were even selected for interviews. The job market in humanities has been stressed for so long now, she has decided to leave academia and start over in her sister's day-care center.

We also met Catalina, the internist looking for a reasonable job that would take advantage of her residency in geriatrics, provide a good salary and benefits, and still allow her to cover the medical needs of her aging parents living in New England. Her best option seems to be as a "hospitalist" employed by a large regional medical center. This salaried position would actually allow both flexible hours and a stable schedule (thus making schedule planning much easier to achieve). Working for a well-resourced medical center as a salaried physician would eliminate all of the uncertainty and stress of attempting to set up a private practice. The advertisement emphasizes internal medicine, but does not state any preference for geriatrics training; that is both a plus and a minus. Geriatricians tend to make less money than internists, and even though the demand for geriatricians is high (given population aging), interest levels of newly minted MDs in that area are fairly low (Meiboom et al. 2015). How this might play out in the long-term for the types of patients Mary encounters is hard to say. She would be working with a medium- to large-size team, which bodes well for some level of specialization within the team, but it is unlikely all her patients would benefit from a geriatric hospital consult.

The hospitalist "movement" within American hospitals has grown since the 1990s (Burleson 2017; Wachter and Goldman 1996), as a way to control costs of inpatient stays, and eliminate the need for primary care physicians to coordinate with hospital attending physicians. The theory behind this model was that hospitalists would be specialists in "inpatient medicine," and their care decisions would be more cost-effective, and would mesh well with the objectives of managed care. Not everyone welcomed this development, and criticisms arose concerning care discontinuity and mandatory use of hospitalists by managed care organizations (Rubenstein 1997; Michtalik et al. 2017; Foubister 1999). Evidence since then has been equivocal as analysts have struggled to accurately measure the effects on care quality and care cost (Maguire 2014). But given the differences between hospitalist training and emphases compared to geriatrics, it is probably safe to predict that Mary may have some level of difficulty making both roles work (we will discuss hospitalists further in Chapter 5).

Finally, our young lawyer Corwin has encountered the worst-case scenario: he has accomplished an advanced degree from a highly ranked law school, at the same time that three major trends converged to create the perfect storm of a bad jobs market for law grads. First, the number of jobs available within law firms (the expected first job for nearly all new JD recipients) has declined steadily since 2010, following the height of the financial recession. Law firms have been cutting back since 2008, and many new grads have settled for part-time and nonpermanent positions outside of the traditional law firm setting, such as in small firms, government work, and various industries (Olson 2016). The "lawyer's dream" was well described by one of the 2010 graduates interviewed by Elizabeth Olson: the plan was to "spend three years at school in New York, then work for a big law firm and make $160,000 a year . . . and someday become a partner and live the good life." Instead, about 40% of the 2010 law school cohort have taken jobs that do not require admission to the bar, have attempted solo practice, or even gone beyond practicing law in order to stay afloat with crushing student debt. The second major trend is the reality of huge law-school student debt levels: average debt following public law school for 2010 graduates was over $77,000 and over $112,000 for graduates of private law schools. The third factor depressing the market for lawyers is the growth in online legal start-ups like LegalZoom and LawDingo. These are now being used to automate and routinize many low-level legal tasks such as patent searches, discovery review, contracts, wills, and so on (Toppo 2017). In the past these tasks provided entry-level jobs for first-year graduates, but now task automation is contributing to making the start of a legal career extremely difficult for all but the most talented graduates of the top ten law schools.

There is some evidence that things will get better for new cohorts of young lawyers, perhaps including the career picture for Corwin. Opting for a private sector legal position in a medical services firm, with additional training in software and enterprise content management, Corwin may have caught the leading edge of a solid wave reported by the *After the JD* multi-wave research project: more lawyers working in the business sector, fewer top law school grads working for a "mega firm" (defined as law firms with more than 251 lawyers), and more law graduates able to pay off their educational debt (American Bar Foundation 2014).

Our four vignettes give "faces" and stories to illustrate the societal and economic changes surrounding the world of work – particularly professional work – in the second decade of the 21st century (see Figure 4.1). Professional work still requires advanced degrees and specialized training which typically stretches for four to eight years beyond one's undergraduate degree. But unlike earlier decades, the job and career value of that advanced degree and specialized training is no longer assured: the job options waiting for new graduates in law, medicine, humanities, and scientific research are no longer clearly defined or available with certainty.

The rest of this chapter will examine in detail why and how that has evolved. *How is it that professional training has lost value*, and has become disconnected from a sure and certain set of well-paid, high-status job options? We will first review assessments of value from both standard economic and sociological literature on labor markets. Then we will turn to an examination of how professional labor market issues of supply and demand are also connected

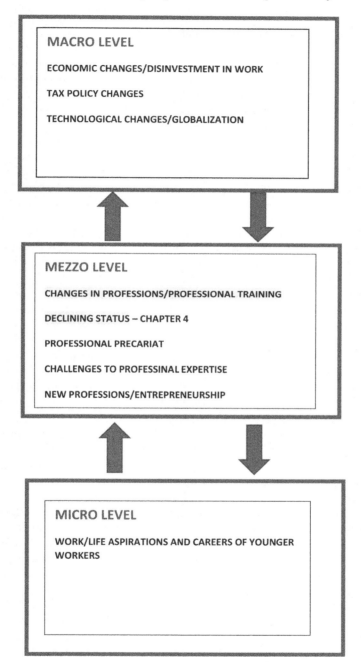

Figure 4.1 The Organization of Our Argument – Chapter 4 – Changes in Professions/
Professional Training

Box 4.1 What Determines Value?

As we discuss here, supply and demand are two key components to understanding value, as are cultural meanings or assessments of importance. While the "supply" component is easier to understand (people gravitate to positions that are valued and that pay well as a result), what constitutes "demand" is a bit more arbitrary.

The position of the professions depends a lot on demand for their services and, more importantly, what economists call "effective demand"– the desire for services with the dollars to back it up. For medicine in the United States, people can pay for services out of pocket, through private insurance, or through public insurance such as Medicaid or Medicare. This gives lots of people (though not everybody) effective demand and keeps the demand for health services robust even though those services are extremely expensive. This "demand boost" renders almost all specialties in medicine at least modestly lucrative.

In law, there is no public provision of law that is paid for via insurance policies or government action beyond public defender services for criminal defendants and legal clinics run by law schools. This means that there are vast differences in the monetary value of legal services based on what the client can pay. Clients with deep pockets are sought-after. Corporations and rich individuals can purchase the legal services they need. The middle class and the poor cannot. Does that mean there is no demand for legal services? Not at all, but many potential clients lack "effective demand."

But the differences here are not as wide as they first appear. In medicine, insurance and effective demand are tied to individuals rather than to some larger understanding of overall public health. This means that certain specialties with paying customers generate more income for practitioners than others, even if their overall assessment of societal value is lower. Does it make more sense at the societal level to spend healthcare dollars on children or the elderly? The answer (usually) is children, but that isn't where most of our healthcare spending occurs. The elderly (via public insurance and private insurance supplements) have a more effective demand for health services than most children do, so they receive more care.

IF this seems a bit unfair, it probably is. In the United States in particular, assigning high value only to professional services provided to those with effective demand is fraught with problems for societies and for the professions themselves.

to gender representation within professions. Thus, we will attempt to update what we reported on gender representation in our first book.

What Affects the Value of Professional Work? A Mezzo-Level Look

In any given labor market, value can be defined in economic terms of supply and demand. A job is considered valuable to the extent that the work to be performed is itself important and is highly valued by others, that not everyone can do this work, that it cannot be completely simplified (routinized or mechanized), that knowledge of how to do that work is typically gained over an extensive period of training, usually resulting in an advanced degree (requiring a considerable investment in time and money), and that access to those doing the work (professionals) is expensive and probably regulated. To economists, professional work combines expensive and competitive access for would-be practitioners (few slots – many applicants), high costs for students selected (because the supply of people for scarce educational slots does not respond to the costs of education), high costs for clients and patients (due to the scarcity of practitioners and the relative value of their work), and high rewards for the practitioners themselves (to compensate for expensive and long training and as a reflection of demand and supply in the labor market).

Another way to think about value, however, is to stress the cultural and institutional meanings of value: the work of professionals is valued because it is important to work (perhaps affecting issues of life and death, freedom or imprisonment, scientific advancement, etc.). Normative value, however, can change over time, perhaps due to important external factors such as economic changes, globalization of markets, and/or technological change in the knowledge base of a discipline. Institutional value is also tied to individual beliefs in the importance of certain types of work: professional work is highly valued because it is more than simply a job; the importance of the work goes beyond what it might cost to pay a professional; the ability to evaluate the quality of that work by people not steeped in professional knowledge is difficult; and professional work involves a "calling" to do work that has special meaning. Thus, whether we prefer definitions of value based on economic or normative factors, it is obvious that assessing the value of professional work is a multilevel problem. The definition of value comes from individual assessments of value, as well as economic systems (Chapter 2), globalized labor markets (Chapter 3), and the role of technologies in changing the work itself or expectations of outcomes (Chapter 3). It also comes from repeated, public, and often unsubstantiated statements made by political and government leaders.

Stepping down a level of abstraction, it may be useful to think in terms of professional jobs rather than the entirety of professional work. Then we can try to assess the value of professional jobs simply in terms of *job queues and labor queues*, concepts used by labor economists (Thurow 1969; Doeringer and Piore 1970) and sociologists (Lieberson 1980; Reskin and Roos 1990) to study the distribution of workers across jobs and the segregation of certain groups across occupations. The strength of this conceptualization is its flexibility to include definitions of value from both workers and employers and to factor in changes in values and norms over time. Labor or worker queues are another way of expressing supply-side factors (Reskin 1993): they represent the attractiveness of certain types of workers to employers. Job queues are linked to demand-side factors, such as the value of advanced degrees, shortages of skills valued by managers, and the attractiveness of certain job characteristics to workers (such as flexibility in work hours). Together, this model predicts occupational composition as the result of both preference orderings: job and labor queues. Reskin and Roos (1990) used this approach to provide the single most important framework for understanding the linkage between gender representation within occupations and whether the proportion of women/minorities in professions is increasing, declining, or stagnant. They also managed to combine both micro-(individual-based factors) and macro-level forces (changes in economies and technologies) as they affect norms and values. For example, Reskin and Roos reviewed several important periods in U.S. economic and labor history: the shift from farm to nonfarm economies; the shift from blue-collar to white-collar work; and the shift from nonskilled to skilled and professional jobs. Each of these periods and historical shifts changed the underlying norms and institutions that determine how workers and employers define their labor preferences.

In the next section, we will take a closer look at supply and demand issues from both economic and normative frameworks, considering factors that influence both the supply of professional jobs, the requirements of jobs, and the role of college and advanced degrees in matching workers to jobs in professional labor markets.

Review of Supply/Demand Issues: Are There Too Many Degree Holders?

Undergraduate Degrees

Before we can attempt an answer to the question of "are there too many degree holders?," we need to be specific about what kind of degree is at issue: college degrees versus advanced degrees of various types (master's, PhD, etc.).[1] Let us first consider the issue of college degrees and whether they have lost value (due to the preponderance of college degrees as a requirement to obtaining a first job, or whether jobs are more likely now to explicitly require a college degree or better). Value in this case is often defined in terms of the ability of the new degree holder to obtain a job post-graduation, and whether that job qualifies as a "good" job (full-time work, high wages). Employment outcomes do tend to vary across types of majors: training in technical fields tends to provide higher wages than training in liberal arts or social science (though there is some debate about whether earnings differences at the start persist, see Humphreys and Kelly 2014). Further, it is generally understood that new college graduates (just out of school, or within five years of graduation) need a little time to become adjusted to the labor market and employment options: recent college graduates are less likely to be employed and are more likely to be underemployed (working part-time or in a job that does not require a college degree) compared to all college graduates (Abel et al. 2014). Compared to young people without a college degree, however, college degree holders fare much better, and this tends to be true regardless of general economic conditions or college majors (Abel et al. 2014; Kahn 2010; Humphreys and Kelly 2014).

Even when we only consider college degrees, there are several issues worth considering. We will focus on three: (1) has the value of a college degree declined as more people and more employers assume the degree is essential? This is the phenomenon of "credential creep" (or credential inflation) and is typically defined as employers setting degree requirements for jobs that never required them before (see Collins 1978), (2) what is the impact (cost) of under-employment on the value of college degrees, both short term and throughout one's career?, and (3) finally, the third issue flips our focus: If "everyone" is graduating from college, and more jobs require the bachelor's degree, then what happens to the job market for folks who do not hold college degrees?

Credential creep sounds as if it is primarily the actions of employers that cause an unrealistic push for college degrees. Some argue that this is essentially the fault of educational systems: such systems are overproducing degree holders, and that employers then face larger and larger queues of applicants. The col-lege degree then becomes a floor-level job "filter," used to help employers narrow the applicant pool to a more manageable size (Vedder 2016; Lederman 2014). But in fact, as others have argued, college completion has become an expected credential, given ongoing changes in technology and the need for more workers who are degree-certified in areas and skills likely to be competi-tive in global markets which emphasize technology and information econo-mies. It may be the case, however, that the failing of educational systems is found more in the quality of the education they are providing, and the impact of that education over time (not so much whether there are too many gradu-ates). A scathing analysis of undergraduates' learning habits and the fundamen-tal goals of higher education was published in 2011 by Richard Arum and Josipa Roksa (with a follow-up published in 2014). This work questions to what extent students are learning what is needed and to what extent universi-ties are providing the type of quality academic and social experiences needed to produce informed, capable citizen-learners. Diverse groups of students are not receiving the kind of pedagogy and skill building we know could reduce what has become a persistent learning gap. And although the United States once leads in the percentage of young people graduating from college, that is no longer true. The United States stopped increasing its college participation rates by the early 1990s, and the ranks of other countries have now passed us by (Arum and Roksa 2011, 2014).

Connected to the assessment of quality education is the *question of under-employment* as mentioned earlier: are degree recipients working in jobs that are less than full-time or that do not require a college degree? Recent work by Burning Glass Technologies and the Strada Institute (Burning Glass Technologies 2018) and from the Pew Research Foundation (Pew Research Center, February 2014) moves us much further in the direction of under-standing the concept of underemployment and understanding how compli-cated it is to measure this accurately. Mastering those two tasks should help us better capture useful data on both the short-term and career outcomes of underemployment.

The Burning Glass Technologies/Strada work has raised the bar on meas-uring and understanding the concept of underemployment. This is a con-cept that requires careful consideration of the expectations of degree holders as well as employers. And each part of this equation involves multiple sets of "logics" or understandings, including the preferences of degree holders and how they define what might constitute full employment versus under-employment, the expectations of employers about what is needed to com-petently perform an open job, and the ability of job descriptions (postings) to accurately capture degree requirements and job characteristics and to communicate comparable information to both employers and job seekers. The BGT/Strada researchers approached this formidable problem by aggre-gating data on American workers over multiple data sources that included over 800 million job postings, a database of over 80 million resumes, and extracted data from at least two government databases (O*NET data on occupation-specific descriptors, and survey data from the American Com-munity Survey). The resulting master database is national in scope, cov-ers multiple decades and generations of jobholders, and has the strength of mixed data collection methods using survey data, administrative data, and population-based data. This is a study that examines multiple levels and paints a broad picture of changes in the U.S. workforce, expectations of employers, and characteristics of job seekers.

Results from the first report from BGT/Strada emphasize that the first job taken post-graduation is critical: those who start out behind tend to stay behind, and this is true at the five-year mark and the ten-year mark. The financial cost of underemployment stays with you over time: the loss starts at an average of $10,000, compared to graduates working in jobs that match their degrees. And there are differences across groups in the effects of underemployment: STEM graduates are less likely to be underemployed, but women are more likely to be underemployed regardless of major.

Finally, *what does the picture look like for non-degree holders*? What is the cost of NOT attending college or completing a college degree? The picture looks rather bleak, as jobs that do not require a college degree tend to cluster in low-paying service industries with limited options for advancement. These jobs typically do NOT have benefits and do not provide a pathway for leaving the hourly wage trap. Non-degree-holders experience an earnings gap when compared to those with college degrees that have increased substantially since the Great Recession (increasing from $7,500 in 1965 to $17,500 in 2014; see also Humphreys and Kelly 2014). A larger percentage of non-degree holders are unemployed, compared to those with college degrees (12.2% compared to 3.8%), and non-degree holders spend on average twice as long looking for work compared to college degree holders (Pew Research Center 2014). *Advanced or Graduate Degrees: Master's and Professional Master's Degrees.*

The master's degree has been afforded hardly any respect or recognition in most disciplines, other than as a "marker" on the way to a traditional research-based PhD. It is common in many humanities and social science disciplines to use the term "terminal Master's degree" to refer to the award of an MA to first- or second-year graduate students who are then weeded out of the doctoral program. Very specific master's programs in business (MBA), fine arts (MFA), engineering, public health (MPH), and others are designed as specific training programs leading to particular jobs; they only require two years (sometimes 18 months) to complete. They combine coursework to provide "mastery" of advanced material, but they are also designed with an eye toward the reported needs of employers. About 20 years ago, the Sloan Foundation funded the first of similarly targeted Master's training programs in math and science labeled Professional Science Master's degrees. These degrees required course work that is similar to PhD level courses, but then in addition, PSM students will take a variety of business courses and special topic courses that are recommended by employers in particular industries (Gitig 2010). The PSM option has grown substantially: there are now well over 300 PSM degree programs within the United States. Access to such programs has been broadened thanks to online coursework and programming.

Traditional Doctoral Education[2]

Most writers now agree that a bachelor's degree is probably a needed entry qualification in most fields, even with arguments and evidence about credential creep. There is also growing awareness and agreement that the production of doctoral degrees has really gotten out of hand, especially in the United States, but also in most European and other highly developed economies as well (Cyranoski et al. 2011). Some of that discussion is unnecessarily critical in tone: for example, graduate degrees are "a waste of money" (Alptraum 2016), while other writers are genuinely concerned that graduate education (especially as part of the biomedical research system in the United States) needs to be rebalanced (Gould 2015). There is an abundance of data available on continued growth in the numbers of PhDs in various fields, while the number of jobs available for those PhDs, within academia and even including jobs in the private sector, does not match.

The value of graduate training and graduate degrees is complicated by cost and especially by loan burden (the portion of monthly income dedicated to student loan payments). Student loans have become more generous, and graduate students have long been considered less risky than undergraduate borrowers (Lee and Looney 2018). As a result, graduate student borrowing has nearly doubled since 1990. But the assumption of "less risk" has started to slip: larger proportions of graduate students are attending for-profit schools, where loan sizes are much larger, and student outcomes are uncertain (probabilities of obtaining a good job, high income upon graduation, loan default rates, etc.). These factors in turn detract from graduate job markets, and a high default rate can discredit both the job seeker and the institution conferring graduate degrees.

Comprehensive numbers on professional degree value recently became available in the 2016 NSF report on "The Survey of Earned Doctorates." These numbers do not paint a very hopeful picture. As mentioned previously, the tightest job markets are for those seeking academic positions in the humanities, education, and social sciences. After many years of increased PhD production, these fields are now witnessing something of a flattening in the number of degrees awarded. Figure 4.2 shows the total number of new doctorates across all fields awarded in the United States by year, from 1957 to 2016, using the NSF Survey of Earned Doctorates. That flattening can be seen in the last three to four years of the graph.

A closer look at these numbers, however, shows that the decline is not spread evenly across all areas of graduate study. Figure 4.3 displays the number of new PhDs in life sciences, physical sciences, engineering, and even social sciences that continue to grow, even as the availability of jobs declines. And as expected, the number of new PhDs in the humanities is growing hardly at all, and in education, it is actually declining.

The NSF report also shows an increase in the percentage of new PhDs with "no definite commitment for employments or postdoctoral study"

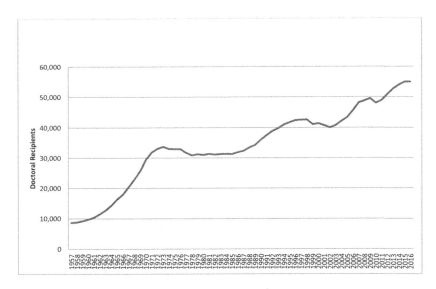

Figure 4.2 Doctoral Recipients in the United States by Year, 1957–2016

Source: National Science Foundation 2018 Survey of Earned Doctorates. https://www.nsf.gov/statistics/2018/nsf18304/data.cfm

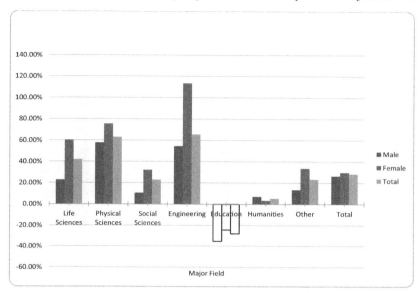

Figure 4.3 Percentage Change in PhD Recipients by Major Field and Gender 2004–2014

Source: National Science Foundation 2018 Survey of Earned Doctorates. https://www.nsf.gov/statistics/2018/nsf18304/data.cfm

(now about 40%), and among those who report postdoctoral plans, many more of those are for specialized postdoctoral study (see Figure 4.4).

This is especially true for new PhDs in Humanities and Arts: in 2016, almost 50% reported no definite post-graduation plans (see Figure 4.5).

The allure of doctoral-level teaching and research in STEM fields continues to attract many very smart and very talented young people, even though the job market is dire. The standard model behind PhD research training and postdoctoral apprenticeship has its roots in the 1800s (Gould 2015), and it still inculcates norms valuing independent research. Thus, the prize at the end of doctoral training has always been a tenured position within a research university, with a lab of one's own, and a squadron of graduate students and post-doctoral fellows working on "your" research program. But the structure of research in the United States (and elsewhere) has changed dramatically within the past 20 years, and this apprenticeship model no longer matches reality.

For decades (since the end of World War II), biomedical research and advanced research in STEM disciplines were built on an infrastructure that assumed a partnership between research universities and the federal government, particularly the NIH, Department of Defense (DOD), Defense Advanced Research Projects Agency, and the NSF. Basic research was valued and assumed would eventually lead to breakthroughs in disease reduction, cures for cancer, and a variety of information and technological innovations with industrial applications that would enhance U.S. stature around the world, and in multiple markets. Universities agreed to support the hiring of junior faculty and the training of graduate

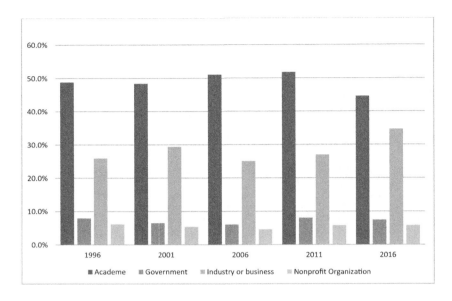

Figure 4.4 Post-Graduation Plans of Doctoral Recipients, All Fields, 1996–2016

Source: National Science Foundation 2018 Survey of Earned Doctorates. https://www.nsf.gov/
statistics/2018/nsf18304/data.cfm

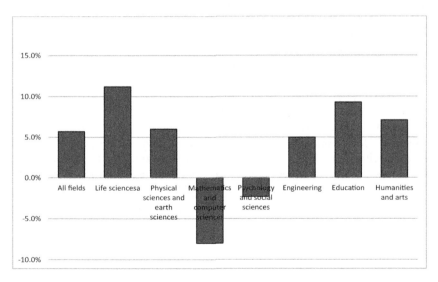

Figure 4.5 Percentage Change in PhD Recipients With No Definite Commitments to
Employment or Postdoctoral Study, 1996–2016, by Field of Study

Source: National Science Foundation 2018 Survey of Earned Doctorates. https://www.nsf.gov/
statistics/2018/nsf18304/data.cfm

students in multiple applied areas, and the federal government would provide the research funds (including indirect costs on peer-reviewed research grants) that would keep those labs active and productive on a continuing basis. Years of reduction in base funds for research through sequestration and other budget restraints have compromised that partnership. And as of this writing, there is a proposal from POTUS that indirect costs on grants should be reduced to only 10% of actual research costs (Kaiser 2017). Indirect costs have traditionally been about 55–65% of direct costs and are intended to cover the ongoing cost of research building maintenance, utilities, lab equipment maintenance, and everything within the university's lab system and research infrastructure that is not directly supported by a grant proposal's budget or the university's budget (for example, tuition money typically cannot be used to build research facilities). Reductions in indirect cost recovery of that magnitude will completely devastate the U.S. research apparatus. At direct risk in this scenario is stable funding of graduate students and postdoctoral fellows.

Back to the question of too many PhDs: there is a flip side to this question posed earlier, but it focuses on the supply of jobs and the structure of labor markets for expertise: are there simply not enough jobs in academia and/or the private sector to absorb the supply of qualified PhDs? This also assumes that there is still an ongoing supply of research questions and applications that require study and development: we know of no one who is arguing that all of the problems in biomedicine, gene editing, or immuno-suppressive diseases have been solved and all the needed applications have been developed: if anything, just the opposite. So how do we match the areas in need of study with the resources and PhDs capable of solving those questions? We've been relying on a system that was developed decades ago, and it now seems to face serious difficulties in carrying out that match. Many writers and analysts prefer to blame universities, professional specializations, and disciplines. There may be a reason to share some blame across those actors, but as with all complicated problems, a number of additional issues need to be considered.

Is the Cost of Advanced Training Just Too High?

If the cost of advanced training was perceived by potential degree students and institutions to be over-priced (i.e., cost exceeds demonstrated value; price no longer rises to meet cost), wouldn't we expect to see fewer students over time, lower tuition costs over time, and fewer students willing to take on debt/loans to cover the price of tuition and fees and to cover living expenses that are not covered by fellowships? We do not readily have data on all of these issues, but as we have seen, the number of students in non-humanities PhD programs continues to grow and part of the answer lies in the relative attractiveness of graduate education versus entering or remaining in the labor market. We should also examine student loan volume for graduate students as an indirect measure of advanced degree value.

Growth in PhD Loan Volume. The most recently available data on student loan volume and burden come from the Digest of Education Statistics for 2017, produced by the U.S. Department of Education. 2017 data reveal a marked increase in average cumulative loan balances, comparing 2015–2016 to 1999–2000, and this is true for all degree types (professional doctorates, research doctorates, master's degrees, and post-baccalaureate certificates; see Figure 4.6; Source: US Department of Education, National Center for Education Statistics 2017, as published online in *Spotlights: the Condition of Education* 2018).

Loan volume for research doctorates doubled during this time period, almost doubled for professional doctorates, increased by 85% for post-baccalaureate certificates, and Master's degree recipients increased their loan volume by 57%. Similarly, NPSAS data reveal how student loan debt is distributed by type of degree and by type of institution granting the degree. Figure 4.7 reveals the highest percentage of students with debt in 2015–2016 was found among students who attended private for-profit institutions, and this is true no matter what kind of degree was achieved.

Finally, a quick note on the debt burden of PhD students of different gender and racial/ethnic groups: as might be expected, the debt burden is not distributed equally (see Figure 4.8). Women carry more debt than men, and Hispanic/Latinos, Native Americans, and Blacks all carry higher debt loads than either whites or Asians (using NSF data from the 2018 Survey of Earned Doctorates).

Similar data have been analyzed specifically to examine how millennials have managed student loan debt. As reported by Lamont Jones (2018), the work by Sarah House emphasizes what was thought to be (at the time) an expanding job market and an improved economy. Looking at millennials who had graduated into a recession, House found that income strengthened considerably by the time these young adults reached their mid-20s. Positive

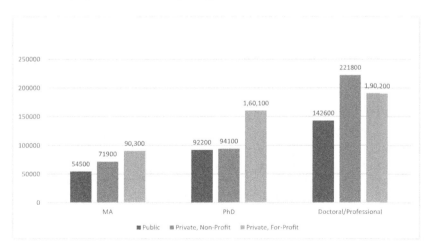

Figure 4.6 Average Cumulative Loan Balance for Graduate Degree Recipients, by Type of Institution, 2015–2016

Source: 2016–2017 Constant Dollars. NCES, Digest of Educational Statistics, table 332.45. Includes undergraduate and graduate studies and excludes students with no student loans

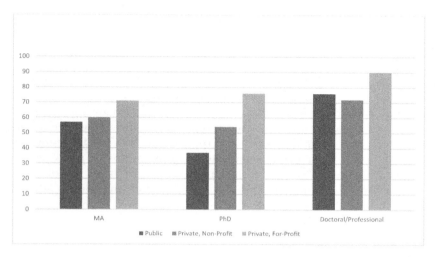

Figure 4.7 Percentage of Graduate Student Degree Recipients With Student Loans, by Institution Type, 2015–2016

Source: https://nces.ed.gov/programs/coe/pdf/coe_tub.pdf

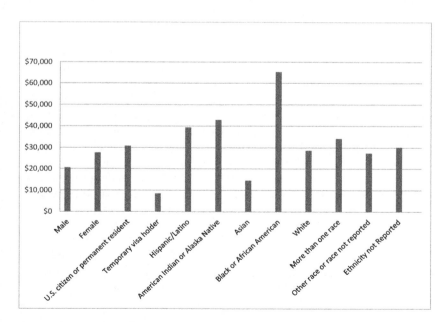

Figure 4.8 Mean Cumulative Debt Held by PhD Grantees, 2016, by Gender, Race, and Citizenship Status

Source: National Science Foundation 2018 Survey of Earned Doctorates. https://www.nsf.gov/statistics/2018/nsf18304/data.cfm

effects included a declining debt-to-income ratio, student loan repayment as a percent of monthly income declined, and loan default rates began to decline between 2011 and 2014.

But these positive effects do not pay much attention to the simple underlying facts that the average annual borrowing of graduate students has nearly doubled since 1990 (Lee and Looney 2018); that default rates are higher across the board, but especially among students who went to for-profit schools; and we are no longer in a bull market with an expanding economy. In fact, the uncertainty facing the U.S. economy at the time of this writing (during the three-week hiatus from the longest government shutdown in U.S. history) is undeniable, thus placing considerable doubt on the somewhat rosy scenario described by House (2018) and re-highlighted by Jones (2018).

Of considerable importance in understanding the dangerous trends we face in the turbulent sea of graduate student borrowing is the report by Lee and Looney (2018) of the Brookings Institute. The trends are numerous:

1) The total graduate student debt has nearly doubled.
2) The average debt per graduate student has doubled.
3) For-profit schools figure prominently in this increase in the debt burden.
4) Larger percentages of graduate students are borrowing to attend for-profit schools, and "the rise in for-profit attendance is larger for borrowers with large balances" (Lee and Looney 2018).
5) Graduate student loan default rates are creeping up.

Unfortunately, for-profit schools are benefiting disproportionately from federal policies to expand credit and extend repayment periods, resulting in slower repayment. Similarly, Public Sector Loan Forgiveness plans remove incentives to search out high-value programs (Lee and Looney 2018).

Among the highest-cost graduate programs are medical schools, and federal student loans are a normal part of paying one's way through an MD. In 2017, the median debt for graduating medical students was over $190,000. Chen reports that the yearly cost of medical school (tuition, fees, living expenses) in 2017 varied from $61,000 to $82,000, depending on the type of school (Chen 2018). Considerable attention has been given to New York University's recent decision to go tuition free in 2018 for all medical students, regardless of financial need. NYU has become the first top-ranked medical school in the United States to do so, citing the hope that this would spur two changes: (1) other top medical schools may follow suit and (2) by reducing debt burden, many hope more medical students will pursue their passions in primary care and as researchers, rather than in more lucrative fields such as highly specialized surgical practices that require multiple certifications and longer training periods (Chen 2018; Singh et al. 2018). Always the innovator, it should be noted that in 2008, NYU's School of Medicine became the first research university to enforce a five-year time limit for postdoc positions: five years total, across multiple institutions. A few other research institutions have followed suit, but many have not, and even places with five-year term limits do not strictly enforce the term limit (Powell 2015).

A Note Concerning Postdoctoral Fellowships

The constraints on federal research funding are significant and not likely to ease in any meaningful way in the near or mid-term future. By 2015, there appeared a number of essays warning us about the coming "storm" or crisis in research funds that would hit particularly hard for postdoctoral fellowships (Howard and Laird 2013; Alberts et al. 2014). Alberts et al. argued that the postdoc oversupply was one of the most urgent issues facing the scientific workforce. The term "permadoc" was mentioned in Chapter 1 and became known as the kind of career "hole" faced by multiyear and multi-institution postdocs who become stranded without a real job, whether in academia or the private sector. This oversupply seems to have mushroomed between 2000 and 2012, when the number of U.S. postdocs grew 150%, to about 40,000 postdocs in 2013 and 43,000 thousand in 2015 (Science and Engineering Indicators 2016).

Although it has never been clear how successful the postdoc model has been in training and mentoring the next generation of STEM scientists, it is very clear that the productivity of most scientific labs is dependent on them. As discussed by Howard and Laird (2013), postdocs are underpaid and do not routinely receive benefits. These are positions with great responsibility and hardly any recognition. They do not easily fit into most academic ladders, even the ladders labeled as "research faculty," and they are definitely outside of the tenure system. What was once considered a temporary stage before finding and accepting the first "big" job, postdocs are now seen as career extenders and sometimes, unfortunately, career-enders. Many science policy writers seem concerned with this problem, but few have come up with any real solutions. In fact, in a job market that lacks jobs, this is a good way to warehouse people with advanced degrees and also a good way to keep the labs of senior scientists productive.

Devaluation of Advanced Degrees and Expertise

At this point in our discussion, we must also consider again the simple fact that the value of advanced training and expertise based on scientific research and advanced degrees is not respected by the highest elected officials in the United States. President Trump waged his own "war on science" during his administration. This has become unavoidably evident in several crucial developments. Early in his administration, it became clear that Trump had whole-heartedly endorsed the "Republican War on Science" (Mooney 2005), which was an extension and refinement of the historic anti-intellectualism of the Goldwater years. Trump's "war" has taken on several unfortunate characteristics beyond the inherent disdain for intellectual pursuits, science, data, and university degrees. With special foci on environmental science, climate change, and deregulation, the Trump war used a special set of weapons: eliminating (or leaving unfilled) scientific advisor positions in nearly all agencies of the federal government, making appointments of friends and political allies who do not have scientific credentials (Rubin 2017), defunding programs focused on environmental improvement and health, and finding bogus reasons to censor scientific inquiry that could inform health and environmental policy (New York Times, September 9, 2017).

Earlier in Chapter 2, we mentioned the war on expertise as it relates to economic changes that privilege unearned income and the "democratization of knowledge," as discussed by Nichols (2017). We have seen this societal-level change in the value of expertise become translated into aggressive ignorance that allows scientific expertise to be devalued, and important advising posts are left unfilled. The extreme danger of this development should be evident in the absence of a senior science advisor trained in nuclear physics at Trump's meeting with Kim Jong-un of North Korea to negotiate denuclearization (Davenport 2018). Similarly, the danger of delegating policy formulation on the environment to non-scientists results in Scott Pruitt's "leadership" of the Environmental Protection Agency, a move that has led to diminishing the role of the peer review process at the EPA, and restricting the voice of established scientists on scientific panels (Davenport 2018; Goodell 2018). Given repetition and translation into policy developments (and important positions left vacant), the message being sent to the general public is pretty clear.

A Reminder: Important Themes Underpinning This Volume

When we started this volume we asserted there were four major themes guiding our investigation of what has happened to "good jobs": specifically, to professional jobs based on advanced degrees and intense training. Those four themes included **(1) a recognition that change in professional work and professional careers is a multilevel phenomenon.** The changes noticed by individuals in how they work and what they expect from their work and their careers have an impact on the structure of professional labor markets and the sectors of professional service provision. And similarly, sectoral and societal trends influence the career options and choices of individuals. In addition, in many ways, professionals now find they have increasingly more in common with a new class of workers whose work arrangements are lacking one or more of the seven forms of labor-related security as defined by Standing (see Box 1.1). Standing coined the term "the precariat" to refer to blue-collar workers and lower-level white-collar workers who find it harder and harder to stay financially above water, despite working multiple part-time jobs. Both Standing's work on the precariat and Kalleberg's 2009 work on precarious work underscore the continuing erosion of worker control, the proliferation of short-term employment, and the disappearance of basic job characteristics that had for so long been associated with "good jobs": benefits, advancement opportunities, and loyalty between firms and workers. **(2) Thus, the second major theme of this volume focuses on the development of the professional precariat.**

There is a third major societal change related to the decline of professional jobs, one that has only very recently become evident. Weber linked formal knowledge to the concepts of rationalization and rational action, and the rational-legal bureaucracy became the cornerstone of modern theories of management (1947). Expertise is what gives the professional control over formal knowledge systems and confers power to those who produce knowledge (especially in science). But now, this growing reliance on an expert division of labor to produce the good life for the rest of us has run into the contradiction that the expert division of labor was (by definition) nondemocratic, somewhat elitist, and often manipulative (Foucault 1977; Brint 1994). **(3) Thus, the third cross-cutting dimension is the observation that the expertise of professionals is being devalued and eroded, and the value of scientific studies, whether about the environment, health services delivery, effective medical treatment, or education are easily ignored;** to be preferred are pronouncements based on personal opinion, social media (McAllister 2017; Chamorro-Premuzic 2014), or "alternative facts" (Rutenberg 2017).

And that part about "elitist" professionals has recently become a very big problem in national politics in this country and in building the Trump administration. It is important to recognize that the devaluation of professional expertise in scientific work is one thing, but an additional side of this alarming development is that expertise and advanced training have become a political touchstone. **(4) Thus our fourth theme concerns the adoption of "the war on science" (Mooney 2012) by the current administration and the broadening of that war into a full-scale attack on legitimate expertise and training in all areas of knowledge.** The Trump administration had very few (if any) experts in the most important areas of policy development: nuclear proliferation, trade imbalances, medical innovation, global pandemics, global warming, or cybersecurity (Davenport 2018).

So far in this chapter, we have reviewed a number of supply and demand issues, from both economic and normative frameworks, that influence the supply of professional jobs, the requirements of jobs, and the role of college and advanced degrees in matching workers to jobs in professional labor markets, and the perceptions of value versus disdain in defining professional jobs as desirable and worthwhile. The last part of this chapter now turns to questions of gender and racial representation among professional occupations.

Where Are We in Terms of the Diversity of Workers Represented in Managerial and Professional Jobs?

In our 2001 work, we examined data for law and medicine to see if the representation of women and nonwhites had increased, from 1970 to 1990. We found that there was more demographic diversity, but that diversity had been slow to develop and was not anywhere near parity in any elite profession. For medicine and law (the most diverse of the professions), white males were still the predominant group. In this volume, we will examine the published literature for additional data on diversity within a wider range of professions: law, medicine, science, college teaching, top management, and a newly emerged occupational category: entrepreneurs. In order to more fully develop an updated picture of gender and racial diversity in law and scientific fields, we will turn to data from the American Bar Foundation on recent law school graduates, and the NSF's National Survey of Earned Doctorates (see Table 4.1).

Table 4.1 List of 15 Occupations of Interest Here (From IPUMS)

Computer and Mathematical Sciences
  Computer scientists and systems analysts/network systems analysts/web developers
  Computer programmers
  Software developers, applications, and system software
  Database administrators
  Network and computer systems administrators
  Actuaries
  Operations research analysts
  Statisticians
  Mathematical science occupations, NEC
Architecture and Engineering Occupations
  Architects, except naval
  Surveyors, cartographers, and photogrammetrists
  Aerospace engineers
  Chemical engineers
  Civil engineers
  Computer hardware engineers
  Electrical and electronics engineers
  Environmental engineers
  Industrial engineers, including health and safety
  Marine engineers and naval architects
  Materials engineers
  Mechanical engineers
  Petroleum, mining, and geological engineers, including mine safety engineers
  Engineers, NEC
Biological Scientists
Life, Physical, and Materials Sciences
  Agricultural and food sciences
  Conservation scientists and foresters
  Medical scientists, life scientists, and all others
  Astronomers and physicists
  Atmospheric and space scientists
  Chemists and materials scientists
  Environmental scientists and geoscientists
  Physical scientists, NEC
Social and Behavioral Scientists
  Economists and market researchers
  Psychologists
  Urban and regional planners
  Social scientists, NEC
Physicians and Surgeons
Lawyers, Judges, Magistrates, and Other Judicial Workers

Gender and Racial Representation in Professional Work in a Rapidly Changing Environment

Figures 4.9–4.14 examine the changing gender composition of the professional groups we are primarily interested in (MDs and surgeons; lawyers, engineers, biological scientists, physical and life scientists, and computer scientists and mathematicians).

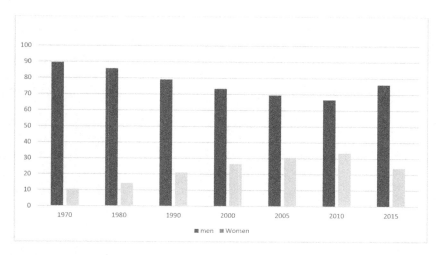

Figure 4.9 Gender Composition of MDs and Surgeons, 1970–2015

Source: IPUMS, University of Minnesota Data Center

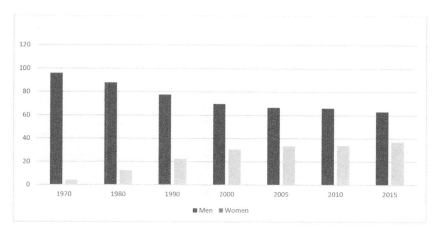

Figure 4.10 Gender Composition of Lawyers, 1970–2015

Source: IPUMS, University of Minnesota Data Center

There is one general conclusion we can reach looking across all of these graphs – the gender diversification of these occupational groups has stalled. For MDs and surgeons and biological scientists (Figures 4.9 and 4.12, respectively), the representation of men has *actually increased* from 2010 to 2015. This is a reversal of the steady, long-term trend toward the greater representation of women in these two professional groups.

Another group of professional occupations (engineers, computer scientists, and mathematicians) has more like a stalled pattern of change – women's

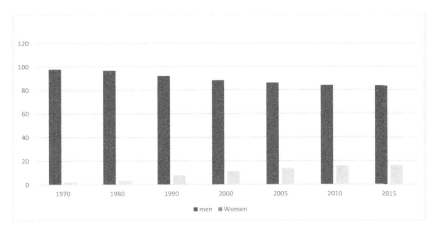

Figure 4.11 Gender Composition of Engineers, 1970–2015
Source: IPUMS, University of Minnesota Data Center

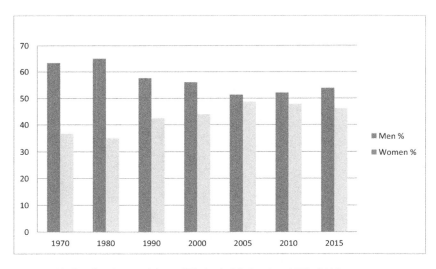

Figure 4.12 Gender Composition of Biological Scientists, 1970–2015
Source: IPUMS, University of Minnesota Data Center

representation increases (albeit from a low starting point) reliably until after 2005. Then progress seems to stall. This suggests that the changes occurring on the ground in these professions (everything from the scarcity of jobs to the overproduction of degree holders to a generally inhospitable environment) could prevent demographic change from advancing further.

It would be tempting to put lawyers in this "stalled" category as well, but, comparatively, lawyers and the physical and life sciences both show relatively

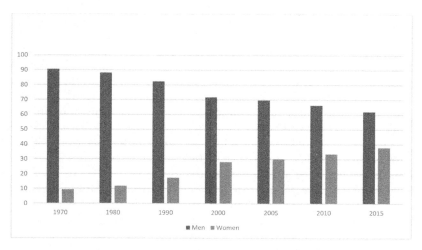

Figure 4.13 Gender Composition of Physical and Life Sciences, 1970–2015

Source: IPUMS, University of Minnesota Data Center

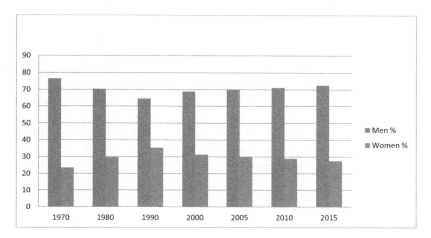

Figure 4.14 Gender Composition of Computer Scientists and Mathematicians, 1970–2015

Source: IPUMS, University of Minnesota Data Center

steady improvements in women's representation over time. The overall progress for women in law slows down, but it does not completely stall or reverse, as we see in other professional groups. The progress for women in physical and life science shows continued and (more-or-less) steady movement toward greater representation.

What does this suggest? It is hard to say exactly since the trend differs across different occupational groups. At a minimum, most of the professional occupations we are interested in show a reduction if not an outright reversal in the trend toward slow and steady increases in women's representation. From the standpoint of job and labor queues, this almost certainly represents a combination of three trends: (1) growing competition in the labor market (as we have discussed), (2) changes in the desirability of professional work for would-be entrants (especially women), and (3) changes in the preferred labor queues of employers (perhaps subtle and unacknowledged).

Greater insights come from examining more detailed changes in the representation of gender and racial groups together.

Figures 4.15–4.20 look at changes in gender and racial/ethnic representation of professionals over time (from 1970 to 2015). Because white men are disproportionately represented in each professional group, we focus on the changing representation of white women, African American women, African American men, Asian Men, Asian women, Hispanic men, and Hispanic women.

In all of our professional occupations, with the exception of lawyers, one trend stands out – *big changes in the representation of ethnic/racial groups are driven mostly by inroads made by Asian men*. Lawyers are the lone exception to this trend (see Figure 4.15). There, white women represent the vast majority of the increase in diversity in the profession, rising from a little over 5% of all lawyers in 1970 to 26% in 2010, declining by 5% between 2010 and 2015. Everyone else is stuck in the low single digits, rising from practically nothing in 1970. This suggests that, in law, there may actually be a racial queue in addition to a gender queue and that women are in the slow process of advancing in that queue.

For the remaining four occupational groups (engineers, physical scientists, MDs and surgeons, and computer scientists), a different phenomenon is occurring – there the representation of Asian men has increased substantially and (in some cases, especially computer science and physical science) Asian women as well. In computer science and mathematics, the representation of white women as a percentage of all computer scientists and mathematicians has actually declined since 1990, and Asian men and women have increased their representation

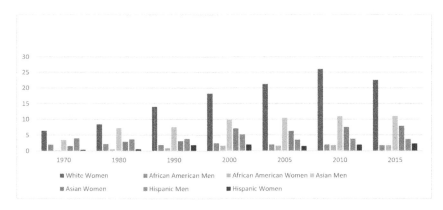

Figure 4.15 Physicians and Surgeons – Race and Gender Groups, 1970–2015

Source: IPUMS, University of Minnesota Data Center

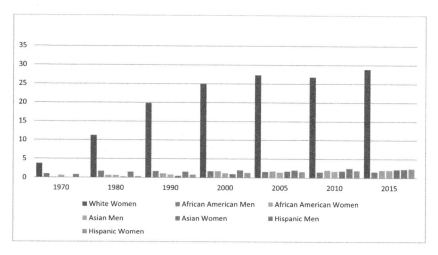

Figure 4.16 Lawyers, Underrepresented Groups, 1970–2015
Source: IPUMS, University of Minnesota Data Center

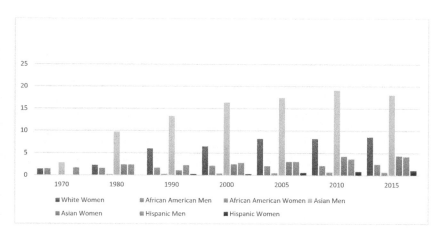

Figure 4.17 Engineers, Underrepresented Groups, 1970–2015
Source: IPUMS, University of Minnesota Data Center

considerably. In Engineering, Asian men's representation has grown out of all proportion to the other underrepresented groups even though the representation of white women has grown too (at least until 2005). Finally, in physical science, white women, Asian men, and Asian women have all increased their representation, while the representation of others has remained basically flat.

What does this suggest? From the standpoint of our theoretical perspective, it looks like Asian men and (in some cases) Asian women are the groups that have risen in the job queue as opportunities have changed and employment

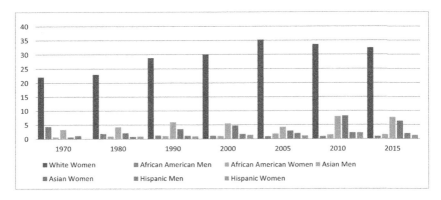

Figure 4.18 Biological Scientists, Underrepresented Groups, 1970–2015
Source: IPUMS, University of Minnesota Data Center

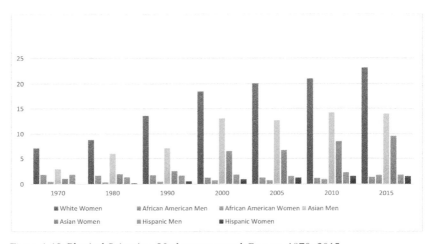

Figure 4.19 Physical Scientists, Underrepresented Groups, 1970–2015
Source: IPUMS, University of Minnesota Data Center

opportunities have diversified. Only in the physical sciences do white women appear to increase their representation along with Asian men and Asian women, and (in law) "diversity" means the increased inroads of white women almost exclusively.

Conclusion – Gender and Racial Diversity in a Rapidly Changing Professional Environment

Let us recap what we have covered in this chapter. The ground underneath many professional work settings has changed substantially – there is a decline in the number of good jobs, which affects their appeal to would-be entrants.

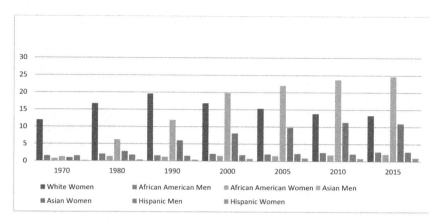

Figure 4.20 Computer Scientists and Mathematicians, Underrepresented Groups, 1970–2015

Source: IPUMS, University of Minnesota Data Center

There is a shifting queue of workers interested in these jobs, recipients of PHDs, MDs, and law degrees. Especially since 1990 or so, this has changed the entrance of people from different gender and racial groups into professional work, increasing the relative appeal of some groups to this work and reducing the appeal to others. We think that the Reskin/Roos framework allows for an analysis of these shifts with some modifications that take into account overall shifts in the labor market for would-be skilled people.

In the classic Reskin/Roos scenario, when job quality shifts in a downward direction, two things are supposed to happen – white men (in particular) and men (in general) are supposed to leave occupations where work is declining in quality, where access to quality jobs is more dubious, where the hope of steady (and rising incomes) has faded, and where fringe benefit availability is unsteady. This is supposed to change the job and gender queues for professional jobs in a direction that favors the greater hiring of women as fewer men are available to fill these positions. The women entering professional jobs are better off than they would be if they didn't pursue this route, but the assumption is that men are leaving for better opportunities elsewhere. In the late 1980s and early 1990s, this assumption made sense.

But this scenario assumes an "all else equal" provision that we would like to suggest may not actually be there, though the overall queueing dynamic is still at work. In particular, professional work may be more precarious (the central theme of this book), but work outside of the professions may be *more precarious still*, as we outlined in Chapter 2. The relative attractiveness of professional work may be just that – relative – leading would-be incumbents (college students and younger people with options) to assess the value of entering the professions we have examined here in relation to other options whose attractiveness is also shifting in a downward direction. If the quality of work not labeled as "professional" declined in quality at a *faster rate* than professional work is declining in quality now, then professional work (even in its reduced form) is *relatively more desirable* than non-professional employment.

This rapidly shifting scenario would bring men back into competition for professional jobs who might otherwise pursue other opportunities, running right into the increased educational attainment levels of (and opening job markets for) women and minorities. If perceptions of potential employers have not shifted or there are now more whites and men available for professional work, then those whites and men will (again) be at the "top of the labor queue" and, combined with the cultural and political backlash against diversity and affirmative action, this will stall or reverse the trend toward more diverse professional occupations.

But, as our results suggest, there is another dynamic happening as well. The relatively stalled representation of women in professional occupations outside of law (where the post-BA educational investment is the lowest in terms of time but not necessarily money) has produced a "backfilling" of professional jobs by principally two groups – Asian men and (to a lesser extent) Asian women. Those who are fleeing professional work appear to be not only white men but to a much greater extent white women whose educational attainment levels are reaching or surpassing white men. The relative void produced by white men is indeed back-filled by people whose place in a gender and racial queue is lower (from an employer's perspective), but those that fill the void are still men and women of Asian ethnicity.

We actually cannot tell exactly if this is happening, just as Reskin/Roos could not tell exactly that their theory of job queues/gender queues was happening when they wrote it, but the clues we see are consistent with this outcome, and our results are consistent with this tentative explanation.

This outcome leads to an interesting question we will address in Chapter 6 – are people who would have entered the traditional professions (law, medicine, and science) gravitating toward the relatively new, would-be professions (data science, finance, and entrepreneurship)? These occupational groups often do not require advanced degrees for entrance, nor do they involve long periods of apprenticeship training at low wages. Chapter 6 will address this question and attempt to address this relatively new part of the skilled-work puzzle.

Notes

1   We will consider medical and law degrees separately in later sections of this chapter and in Chapter 5.
2   This discussion will focus primarily on PhDs; MDs and JDs will be considered in more detail later in this chapter and then in Chapter 5.

5 The Emergence of the Professional Precariat

So far, we have examined the macrostructural trends that have made work more precarious, along with the major technological and global changes affecting the organization of professional work. These changes have come with systematic changes in how labor markets function as well as broad attacks on traditional professional task domains and autonomy.

This chapter looks at the mezzo-level contours of professional labor markets and works (see Figure 5.1). We start with a discussion of Guy Standing's concept of *precariat* and discuss the applicability of this concept to professional work. We then examine the ways that professional practitioners are being sucked into the so-called Gig economy, temporary employment, freelancing, and "flash" organizations that sever traditional employment relationships in exchange for flexibility and "on-demand" availability. We then close the chapter by looking at examples of looming precarity in the professions – hospitalists and expanding job categories in healthcare; the exponential growth of adjunct faculty in the academy; legal outsourcing; and the collapse of labor markets for STEM professionals.

The Precariat – Who Are They and Do Some Professionals Fit the Label?

Social scientists have a long history of addressing overall job quality and the subsequent health of developed and developing economies (see Kalleberg 2011; Bluetone and Harrison 1981; 1990; Gordon et al. 1982). Most of this post-War research focused on deindustrialization and the destruction of high-wage manufacturing jobs. This destruction of high-quality jobs (especially for those without college degrees) has been blamed on falling productivity, growing foreign competition, the shareholder-value movement, and financial deregulation that freed business firms to pursue swift, short-term, on-paper profits. Researchers also point to the destruction of the post-War capital/labor accord (cf. Rubin 1996). The result of this economic tumult was mass unemployment, skill mismatch, and rising income and wealth inequality of the kind we discussed in Chapter 2.

DOI: 10.4324/9781003225485-7

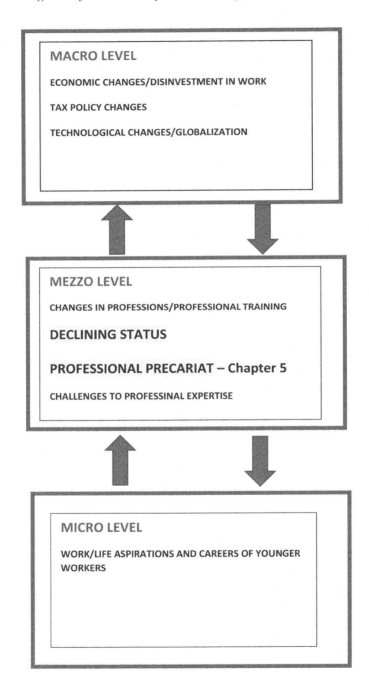

Figure 5.1 The Organization of Our Argument – Chapter 5 – Declining Status and Precarity

But the economic changes produced by the transition to a service economy (as it was called then) did not end with the destruction of blue-collar manufacturing jobs. The growing availability of information technologies (discussed in Chapter 3) meant that the lumbering bureaucratic organizations of the 1970s could shed layers of bureaucracy – legions of middle managers could be discarded with the goal of creating lean and flexible organizations that could respond swiftly to changing market demands. That is the type of workplace reorganization that began in the early 1990s and continues now.

Standing (2011, 2014) and others (cf. Kalleberg 2011) suggest that one result of these shifts is the creation of mass numbers of bad jobs and marginalized, precarious workers. These workers are on the bad end of multiple layers of inequality, low and unstable incomes, and almost non-existent opportunities for wealth accumulation. Standing also points to other nodes of inequality that harm workers' quality of life – lack of control over time, quality space, adequate education, access to financial knowledge, and financial capital. The compounded result of these multiple inequalities is loss of meaningful careers, predictability, and security.

Standing views the current economic class structure in much of the developed world as more complicated than that put forward by 20th-century analysts like Erik Olin Wright (though less complex than that advanced by Grusky and Weeden 2008). In addition to a plutocratic elite that lives mostly on finance capital (similar to the old bourgeoisie but with no actual connection to economic production), Standing talks about a present but shrinking salariat (people with job security, high salaries, and stable corporate benefits) – this group is increasingly tied to the elite through stock options payments and other stock sharing schemes. Beneath them are the proficians, contractors, consultants, and other self-employed members of the semi-professional/managerial classes and the old proletariat or working class.

But Standing claims that there is a class beneath these groups (in the sense that their position is viewed as falling through the cracks of the traditional labor market and social policies of most developed economies) – the precariat. Here Standing discusses the basis of the precariat:

> The precariat has distinctive relations of production, and these are what most commentators have emphasized in discussing the precariat, although they are not actually the most crucial for understanding it. Essentially, their labour is insecure and unstable, so that it is associated with casualization, informalisation, agency labour, part-time labour, phoney self-employment and the new mass phenomenon of crowd-labour discussed elsewhere.
>
> (Standing 2014, p. 6)

In Chapter 1, we introduced Standing's basic thesis about the precariat, and we listed his seven dimensions of "labor market insecurity." Standing sees the precariat as suffering from seven different dimensions of insecurity (only some of which are directly tied to the labor market). Here is a bit more detail on the seven dimensions.

(1) *Labor market insecurity* – in place of a labor market with strong normative sets of expectations and enforceable rules (backed by a political system with commitments to a basic social safety net), the precariat falls through the cracks – rules are non-existent or seem to change very quickly if they exist at all and the entire idea of a stable labor market collapses.

(2) *Employment insecurity* – the establishment one works for has gone from a brick-and-mortar operation with a place and a continued existence to a virtual organization that is difficult to pin down and may employ very few if any people on a continuing basis (see our discussion of "flash organizations" in the following).

(3) *Job insecurity* – many of the same problems afflicting the organizations the precariat works for affect jobs and work security. Jobs last weeks or months, sometimes hours. One has to spend a lot of time "working to labor" – looking for the next job, networking, and performing free labor in order to be a candidate to be hired for the next temporary job. This working to labor is completely uncompensated and sucks up lots of time.

(4) *Work security* – incorporating health and safety regulations, limits on work hours, and so on, to protect against accidents at work.

(5) *Skill reproduction insecurity* – the time and knowledge necessary to stay current with occupation and work trends are obscure or non-existent. Rather than training old workers in new technologies, employers purge their old employees who then must seek new training themselves while employers hire new employees, many of whom they have to train anyway.

(6) *Income insecurity* – As Hacker and Pearson point out (2006, 2008), the result of constantly shifting jobs, work hours, and employers is wildly shifting incomes not only from year to year but often from month to month.

(7) *Representation insecurity* – Not only has private sector unionization been decimated, especially in the English-speaking world, but also unions were not designed to represent people whose labor market contact is not in the same place or same time. The political system represents either investors (almost completely) or steady workers who are part of the salariat, with some bones occasionally thrown to the proletariat. Everyone else is left to their own devices.

The precariat lives mostly on wages (as opposed to investments, or unearned income from stocks, real estate, etc.) and suffers from several forms of relative deprivation – *time deprivation* (the result of continually having to work to find the next job you will perform), *rights deprivation* (there is no political or economic category one occupies that the larger polity cares about), and *security deprivation* (incomes fluctuating wildly, non-existent wealth accumulation, and rising debt loads, see Chapter 2). They are also (and this is critical from our standpoint) *educationally overqualified* because their work situations and status do not match their educational credentials and skills. For members of the precariat, jobs are instrumental and short term, not the basis of an old-fashioned career and not a ticket to a life of emancipatory security.

In Standing's analysis, there are three factions within the group he labels the precariat – *old working-class families* who are largely uneducated and who have lost former rights, privilege, and income granted to unionized blue-collar workers; *migrants and minorities* who are marginalized in the labor market and also possess limited or non-existent social rights; and the *educated young* who cascade from one marginal job to another, over-educated for the work they do, who see and have no sense of a future. It is this last group that we think contains factions of professional groups who are losing job security, steady incomes, and professional status.

A Professional Precariat

Standing's original idea of the precariat was designed to describe extremely marginalized people in the labor markets of developed and developing societies. The people he references are truly desperate and engage in labor market activity that is (at best) day to day, with job and employment instability that makes it virtually impossible to live on the earnings of one job, long hours, with widely variable hours or no hours at all. There is also no collective representation at all – no unions or professional associations – and no way to maintain what skills people have or to know in advance what obscure skills the labor market will reward.

One gets the picture of day laborers standing by the local Walmart waiting to be picked up by people who need help for the day and who pay cash or of a PhD driving a cab in one of the global cities of the world (New York, Cairo, or Paris). On top of this, one finds credentialed workers in places where the production of degrees has far outstripped the creation of skilled jobs. How could professionals in developed countries fall into situations like this?

We argue here that a significant subset of professionals is falling from class locations Standing referred to as the "salariat" or "proficians" to a status that is nearer to the precariat. This is especially true for the subclass of people he identifies as the overeducated and under-placed. In many places, the production of new professionals is totally outstripping the creation of new jobs or the re-filling of old ones. In some cases, the salaried job of yesterday is becoming the precarious job of today. The net result in many cases is a "winner-take-all" labor market where elite practitioners maintain their prestige, prerogatives, and incomes, while younger and newer practitioners are subjected to drastically different labor markets, work arrangements, and incomes. To see this, one needs to look at different segments of the professional labor market to see how this problem is played out (see Box 5.1).

Box 5.1   Examples of Precarious Professional Work

In Medicine/Healthcare

Hospitalists – MDs who work full-time for hospitals, are paid a fixed salary, and manage many patients during their hospital stays.

Per Diem Nurses – Nurses that are paid a flat cash amount on a daily basis as independent contractors.

Data Nurses and Medical Scribes – Nurses and supplementary helpers who take notes and do data entry for physicians and medical providers in order to keep up with documentation and paperwork.

In Law Practice

- Declining law school applications;
- Reduced hiring of new law school graduates by large law firms;
- Legal outsourcing for back-office legal work;
- Increasing use of paralegals and legal aides.

Academia

- Too many PHDs – too few tenure-track positions;
- Increasing use of adjuncts and temporary faculty;
- Growing cost pressures;
- Administrative bloat.

STEM Science

- An oversupply of PHDs;
- Multiple postdocs/permadocs;
- Tight funding;
- Fewer tenure track positions at universities.

Medicine: Hospitalists, Per Diem Nurses, Data Nurses, and Medical Scribes

In medicine, we are seeing the creation of new job categories, almost all of which provide substandard work arrangements relative to elite professionals. Some of these task domains blur into the traditional task domains of physicians and nurses.

For physicians, the free-standing medical practice where a small number of MDs and nurses provide fee-for-service, general-practice medicine is being replaced by the for-profit, corporate-led preferred-provider organization containing hundreds or thousands of MDs housed in multiple locations, and a corporate structure with layers of administrators above them that dictate the speed of service and practice protocols. On top of this, physicians face attempts to speed up work so that more appointments can fit in a workday (the average GP visit has shrunk from over 20 minutes to just 15 minutes in the past 30 years; see Robeznieks 2019), and, in most practices, the MDs and nurses are responsible for electronic paperwork including mandates associated with Electronic Health Records (or EHRs). The average MD spends considerable time at the computer filling out forms – by some estimates two hours of computer time per hour spent with patients. The average MD caseload of 2,500 patients would now require 18 hours a day, 7 days per week, 365 days per year just to keep up (Robeznieks 2019). The confluence of these trends has contributed substantially to physician burnout (Elliott et al. 2014; Michtalik et al. 2013).

Nurses and allied health professionals are not doing much better. They are often considered "administrative overhead," people who do not generate billable hours for the healthcare organization. This is also true of behavioral health professionals and social workers. In effect, the billable hours generated by the physician are supposed to support the growing healthcare bureaucracy that operates to generate profits for shareholders and costs consumers 30 cents out of every dollar spent on healthcare, by far the highest bureaucratic burden in the world (cf. Woolander and Himmelstein 1991). Deviations from organizational protocols lead to reprimands, loss of pay, and eventually dismissal.

The situation of some nurses has improved recently, but the transition to (especially) for-profit hospitals led to a shrinkage in all healthcare job categories except MDs and administrators (see Leicht et al. 1995). Nursing has also morphed into per diem nursing, nurses who work on an on-demand, as-needed basis, and data nurses who are solely responsible for entering data from patient encounters. One of the newest occupational groups is a highly marginalized occupation referred to as medical scribes (see Gellert et al. 2015). Medical scribes are an occupational category created specifically to deal with EHRs. They have their own professional association (the American Healthcare Documentation Professionals Group), but the average scribe earns $13 per hour and has no fringe benefits. They are often paid right out of the pocket of the physicians they follow around.

The other sign of growing precarity in the practice of medicine is the rise of intermediate positions that break medicine into discrete tasks in specific locations. The hospitalist is one of the newer manifestations of this pattern (see Sites 2017; Cook 2015; Lopez et al. 2009; Elliot et al. 2014; Nelson et al. 2012). This is the type of position that Catalina, our young MD with aging parents we were introduced to in Chapter 1, is now considering.

Hospitalists are physicians, but they are physicians who take care of patients in hospitals. They are paid a fixed salary and are employed solely by the hospital they work for. The physician with admissions privileges at local hospitals turns over the care of their patients to the hospitalist, reducing or eliminating the need for independent physicians to "do rounds" and visit their patients in the hospital itself. In some cases, the MD who refers the patient for hospitalization has no further contact with them until they are treated and released for post-hospital care (see Cook 2015).

Hospitalists exist to cut costs for hospitals. By paying a hospitalist a fixed wage while billing for patients' time for hospital case, the revenues from hospital/MD contact are captured by the hospital rather than passed on to the independent physician with hospital admissions privileges. As one might surmise, there is a temptation under this system to increase the work of hospitalists to increase the profit generated from them (see Sites 2017; Michtalik et al. 2013). The hospitalist is under great pressure to follow treatment protocols because they are completely dependent on the hospital for employment. There is also some evidence that increased hospitalist workloads are associated with poorer quality care (Lopez et al. 2009).

Are hospitalist jobs "good jobs"? It would be hard to classify them as bad jobs, but the pressure on hospitalists to do the hospital's bidding (to follow practice protocols and generate profitable care) is great. To some extent, the creation of hospitalists as part of the medical division of labor is a logical outcome of the spread of clinical guidelines as a constraint on physicians' judgment (see Adler and Kwon 2013). Catalina has complained about these clinical guidelines, and for good reason – they seem designed to increase profits and increase the volume of patients she sees rather than improving the quality of care she delivers. But Catalina has student loans to pay and parents to care for and, as an African American woman in a field dominated by people that do not look like her, she is afraid of making waves. Her hospitalist job could not be classified as bad but, compared to what physicians 20 or 30 years ago could look forward to, it is definitely a letdown.

The Stalled Legal Market: Fewer Positions, the Rise of Legal Aids and Paralegals, Legal Outsourcing, and Declining Law School Applications

The legal profession is far from immune to expanding precarity. As we noted earlier in our discussion of Susskind and Susskind (2017), much legal work is susceptible to automation, and much of that work is a vehicle for the training of the next generation of lawyers (see Chapter 3).

The legal profession has suffered from an oversupply of law school graduates, especially in light of the Great Recession (see Figure 5.2).

Granted, most people with law degrees say they have jobs related to their training (American Bar Association 2016), so legal training itself may be an increasingly important component of the 21st-century labor market in the United States. But this shift has masked the not-so-subtle shift away from conventional employment in private, partnership-based law firms (American Bar Association 2016; Jaeger 2016).

Numerous commentators have talked about the collapse of the labor market for private sector lawyers in traditional, fee-for-service law firms (cf. Olson 2016). There are empirical data to back this observation (see Figure 5.3).

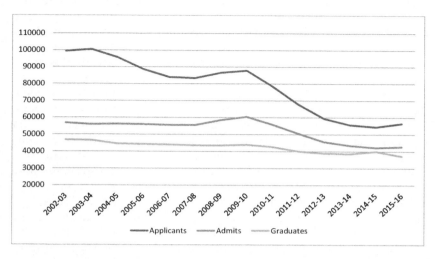

Figure 5.2 Number of Law School Applicants, Admits, and Graduates, 2002–2016
Source: lawschooltransparency.com

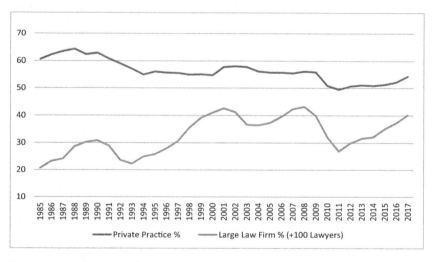

Figure 5.3 Private Law Practice and Large Law Firm Hiring, 1985–2016 (% of JD Graduating Class)

Source: National Association for Law Placement

Not only are fewer lawyers employed in conventional law firms, but there are also major new obstacles to upward mobility. Promotion to partnership has become more difficult and more young lawyers do not "make partner." Many law firms have multi-layered structures full of salaried lawyers and non-equity partners employed either temporarily or indefinitely, all of whom shrink the relative size of the partnership ranks. When Galanter and Palay talked about the *Tournament of Lawyers* in the early 1980s (1991), they laid out the essential truism that the partnership ranks of most law firms depended on the control, replicability, and expansion of Associate attorneys who generate billable hours but do not share in the law firm's profits. If the associate ranks do not grow, the partnership ranks do not grow.

A number of factors have put the squeeze on law firm revenues, including the overall crisis of profitability in law firms, growing competition for legal fees, firm specialization, the decline in omnibus corporate retainers, and the rising influence of consultants and in-house counsel. One logical consequence of this is to shrink or at minimum not expand the full partnership ranks and create a growing number of salaried lawyers and specialists whose time you can bill but who have no expectations of sharing profits in the firm (Richmond 2010). Cameron, our University of Chicago law graduate we met in Chapter 1, is definitely on the receiving end of these trends. Big law firms are hiring fewer associates and are outsourcing much of their back-office legal work to India and elsewhere (work that young lawyers used to do as they were "learning the ropes"), and (as we'll discuss next) there are an expanding set of job titles associated with doing legal work that impinges on the labor market for newly minted law school graduates. He is fortunate to have found his in-house counsel job, but this is not where he thought he would end up at the end of a $300,000 legal education at a top law school.

Among the expanding set of job titles in most law firms are legal aids and paralegals (see Figure 5.4).

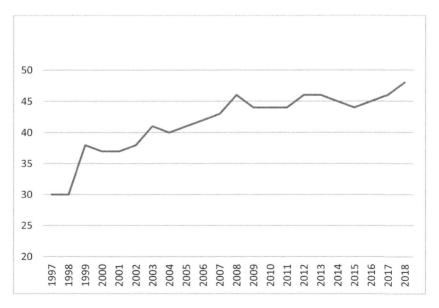

Figure 5.4 Paralegals as a Percentage of Employed Lawyers, 1997–2018

Source: U.S. Bureau of Labor Statistics

Legal aides and paralegals do work for lawyers, but they also do work (especially automated, computer-related work) that junior lawyers used to do. They cost much less, and many of their activities can be outsourced to reduce costs still further (see Chapter 4).

The growing uncertainty in the legal labor market and the increased cost of law school education have led to a decline in applications to law school (see Figure 5.1) and the closing of some schools (Figure 5.5).

State (city)	School	Year founded	Year closed
Arizona (Phoenix)	Arizona Summit Law School,[79] InfiLaw System	2005	Closing 2019
California (Costa Mesa)	Whittier Law School	1966	Closing 2019
California (San Francisco)	New College of California School of Law	1971	2008[80]
California (Anaheim)	American College of Law[81]	1971	2012/13
California (Bakersfield)	California Pacific School of Law	1976	2002[82]
California (Upland)	Inland Valley University College of Law[83]	2003	2012/13
California (Los Angeles)	MD Kirk School of Law[84] (correspondence)	2005	2012/13
California (Carlsbad)	California Midland School of Law[85]	2006	2012/13
California (San Diego)	National University School of Law	1971 (parent school)	2001 (law school only;[86] parent school still active)
California (Sacramento)	Lorenzo Patiño School of Law, University of Northern California	1983	2012/13
California (Inglewood)	Northrop University	1942 (parent school)	2001 (law school;[86] parent school closed 2003)
Indiana (Fort Wayne)	Indiana Tech Law School	2012	2017[91]
Kentucky (Paducah)	Alben W. Barkley School of Law	2005	2008
Minnesota (St. Paul)	Hamline University School of Law	1972	2015
Puerto Rico (Mayagüez)	Eugenio María de Hostos School of Law, Universidad de Puerto Rico	1995	2013

Figure 5.5 Law School Closings in the United States, 1990–present

Source: American Bar Association

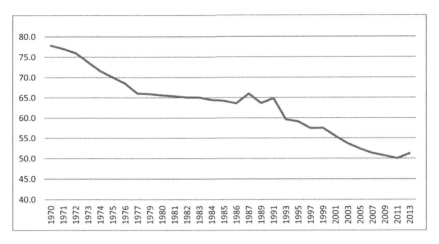

Figure 5.6 Full-Time Faculty as a Percentage of All College Faculty, U.S. Degree-Grant-
              ing Institutions

Source: National Center For Educational Statistics, 2016, Higher Education General Information
Survey, Table 315.10

It looks like potentially bright entrants into the legal profession are turning elsewhere for professional training.

Academia

Of all the professional groups we are discussing in this chapter, the group
with the biggest problems with regard to precarity is the academic faculty at American colleges and universities. College professorships that came
with the prospect of long-term job security have been replaced by temporary, adjunct teaching positions that are paid either for by the course or on
year-to-year contracts (see Figure 5.5). This is the world our Hungarian
immigrant, Selena, finds herself in – there are way too few secure, tenure-
track job openings and way too many PHDs pursuing them. Selena not
only teaches for several universities at once, but she is also increasingly sur-
rounded by colleagues that are doing the same thing. After years of graduate
school, there seems to be no way for Selena to escape the cycle of temporary
and unstable employment in her chosen field.

The issue of the replacement of professorships with adjunct teaching
appointments is especially acute in the humanities (see Figure 5.7).

What has led to this shift? Several things – the financial position of universities and especially the substitution of tuition dollars for state funding –
are part of the equation (Figure 5.8). This has increased pressures for
accountability for university positions, and the hiring of more professors is
usually not viewed as a good use of tuition dollars.

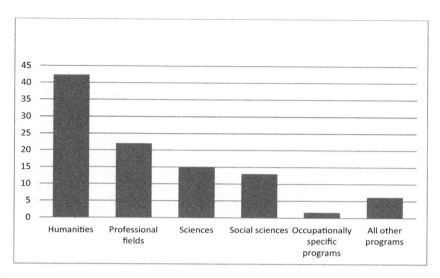

Figure 5.7 Percentage of Part-Time Faculty by Major Discipline Grouping, 2011

Source: A Portrait of Parttime Faculty Members, The Coalition on the Academic Workforce, June 2012

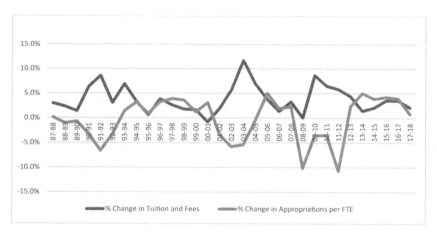

Figure 5.8 Annual Percent Change in Tuition and Fees and State Appropriations Per FTE Student, Public Institutions, 1987–2018

Source: College Board

The other big change that has affected the academy over the past 25 years is the oversupply of PhDs. To put it simply, there are too many candidates chasing too few jobs (see Figure 5.9).

Finally, the ranks of academic administrators and management positions have been growing as accountability pressures have risen

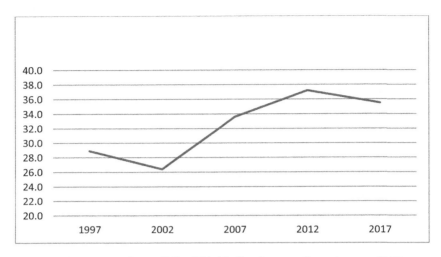

Figure 5.9 Percentage of New PhDs With No Employment Commitments, 2017

Source: National Science Foundation, Survey of Earned Doctorates, Table 42

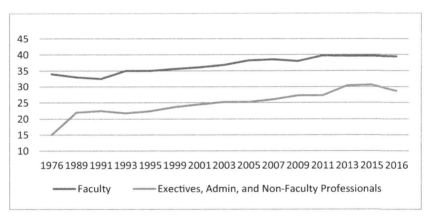

Figure 5.10 Percentage of Total University Employment That Is Faculty or Administrators/
            Executives

Source: Digest of Educational Statistics, Various Years

(see Figure 5.10). There have been major critiques of this trend (see Ginsberg 2011; Leicht and Fennell 2008b), but rising administrative ranks have increased costs and reduced revenues available for the hiring of college professors. Whether this expenditure is defensible is a different story (see Gordon 1996).

Stem Professions

Surprisingly, many of the changes leading to the creation of a professional precariat are happening with scientists as well, especially PhD-level scientists in the United States (see Powell 2016; Kolata 2016). There are several problems here that are very serious from the standpoint of training and replacing a scientific workforce. Almost all of these revolve around the serious delays in securing a first job.

As late as the early 1980s, in most STEM disciplines, a student would finish a PhD in a relatively timely fashion (four to six years) and then proceed to a postdoctoral fellowship to hone their research skills. The postdoctoral fellowship would carry no teaching responsibilities and the new graduate would be apprenticed to a lab, work on their own research there (along with the research of the lab director), and then after a span of two to three years where they made a decent salary, proceed on to their first job in the academy or in industry. The process was relatively smooth and worked relatively well. The person just leaving a postdoctoral fellowship would be well on their way to establishing a research career.

But the economic problems of colleges and universities have combined with the increased short-term perspectives of industry and problems with traditional federal funding mechanisms to put some serious kinks in the scientific pipeline. University tenure track positions have dried up with university positions in other areas, with the additional problem that start-up packages for new assistant professors in many STEM fields run into the millions of dollars. Industry employers increasingly look for people with a specific set of skills that will benefit them right away. If you do not have those skills, your overall research skills are viewed as having little value. Worse still, when they need somebody with a different set of skills, they will lay you off and hire somebody new and you will be gone. There is no way to gauge from a standpoint five to seven years earlier what the industry will want so you can gear your training in that direction.

Federal funding for STEM research has also not grown with inflation (see Figure 5.11). This means that the ability to continue to fund your research in the university if you happen to get a job is increasingly in jeopardy. The average age at the awarding of the first R01 grant from NIH (the standard sign that you have made it in many areas of the STEM funding world) has risen from 32 to 46 over the past 15 years (see Barr 2015). At most universities, once the start-up package is gone, you are expected to fund your own research.

This is Maria's world. She possesses a graduate degree from the top-ranked biology department in the United States. Her postdoctoral fellowship was funded by NIH, but there are many people like her (and many people from underrepresented groups who were encouraged to enter STEM because "the country needs you," "STEM jobs pay well," etc.) who look toward the future and see two or three postdoctoral fellowships and then, perhaps if

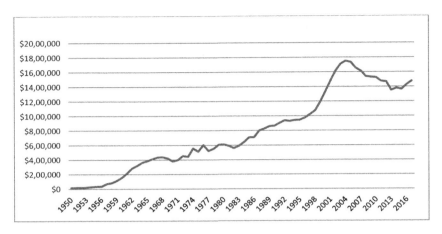

Figure 5.11 National Institutes of Health Grants Awarded, Constant 1950 Dollars, 1950–2017

Source: National Institutes of Health

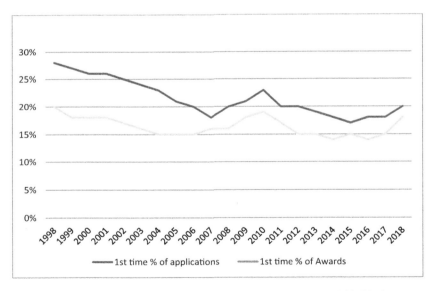

Figure 5.12 First-Time Applicants and Success Rates, NIH Grants, 1998–2018

Source: National Institutes of Health

you're lucky, a job in the industry of you happen to be working on some-thing they are interested in. The overall result of this dammed-up labor market is the extension of the postdoctoral period from one postdoc to two, three, and even four postdoctoral fellowships before somebody secures their first job. This is a lot of time making substandard wages (often in places with very high costs of living like Boston, New York, San Francisco, or Seattle) with little prospect of moving up. In a growing number of cases, the postdoctoral status appears to be permanent as young scientists cling to any chance they have to stay connected (Powell 2015).

The GIG Economy, Freelancing, and Temporary Work: Is This Really the Wave of the Future?

Of course, standing behind all this instability is the new "GIG" or "Freelance" economy where people essentially work for no organization at all and, instead, work as freelance consultants and outsourced technical help (cf. Scheiber 2017; Pedulla 2011; Belew, 2016; Osnowitz and Henson 2016).

The Freelancers Union (a professional association dedicated to freelance workers) estimates that around 53 million American workers (34% of the workforce) engage in some freelance work in a given year (see Freelancers Union 2015; Dokko et al. 2015). Other estimates are somewhat lower (McKinsey and Company 2016). But the general conditions most freelance and GIG economy workers face are not ambiguous;

First, only around one-third of freelance and contract workers want to be in the position they are in (see Dokko et al. 2015; Elance Desk: Freelancers Union, An Independent Study Commissioned By Freelancers Union and Elance-Odes 2015). Most would prefer a more organized employment situation that provided some organizational guidance and a modicum of protection.

Second, freelance and GIG economy workers must spend an enormous amount of uncompensated time keeping their skill setup and soliciting new business (see Osnowitz and Henson 2016; Pedulla 2011). These costs should (in theory) be added to the hourly charges they make to customers, but it is very difficult to do this with any consistency given the competition between providers.

Third, freelance and GIG economy workers may be relatively well-paid (see Dokko et al. 2015), but provisions for fringe benefits and (especially) health insurance are extremely difficult. The ACA's state-level healthcare markets have helped somewhat in this regard, but otherwise, the freelancer is literally "on their own" and needs to pray to not get sick. Further, any sickness leads directly to income loss and lost business as there are no compensated sick days of any kind.

As our section on outsourcing and downsizing in Chapter 4 made clear, the possibilities for slicing up professional tasks and outsourcing them to different occupational and job groups are only growing and show no signs of slowing down (see Susskind and Susskind 2017). But can this type of work, under these working conditions, with the skilled professional assuming all of the burdens of provisioning themselves as the result of a "great risk shift" (Hacker 2008) really provide consistent incentives to invest in professional credentials in the first place? It is hard to see how this will work in the long run. And not all professional jobs involve "back office" work – clients and patients often expect (reasonably) personalized service from somebody they trust. If all or significant parts of that service are outsourced to people and parts unknown, how does that square with the clients' placement of trust in specific professional practitioners?

More to the point, the shift toward freelancing and the GIG economy suggests that we are becoming more reliant on entrepreneurship, personal innovation, and personal marketing as keys to new professional success. That is the subject of Chapter 6.

6 New Professionals and New Professions?

This chapter and the next focus on some of the latest developments that deal with new generations of world-be professionals. Chapter 6 deals with relatively new competition for students' attention – careers in finance, data science, and entrepreneurship. These are small but rapidly increasing career choices.

Chapter 7 moves to the micro level and deals with the occupational aspirations of young people and asks a basic question – have the traditional professions (law, medicine, etc.) lost their allure among young people, and (if so) what occupational choices have replaced them?

Finally, in Chapter 8, we will return to the meat of the argument throughout the book and assess where professional work is heading from here, with a follow-up epilogue on the professions and the COVID-19 pandemic

The Rise of New Professions

Our young would-be professionals Maria, Selena, Catalina, and Corwin represent many of the problems with the professional life that people encounter in established professions – science, academia, medicine, and law. This section deals with three would-be professional groups that reflect the rapid changes in the U.S. labor market and global economy. There have been numerous analyses of the financialization of the U.S. and global economy (cf. Castells 1998; Lin and Tomaskovic-Devey 2013; Fligstein and Roehrkasse 2016; Halliday and Curruthers 2009). With this has come a surge in the hiring of financial analysts and advisors. In many cases, these are glamorous jobs with relatively high salaries in glamorous locations. Data analysts and data scientists are at the forefront of dealing with the surge in "big data," data generated by our Google clicks, card swipes, likes, dislikes, surveys we fill out, taxes we file, places we go, and people we correspond with. The sheer volume of this data is enormous (see Groves 2011, Burrell 2013; Executive Office of the President 2014). Data scientists and analysts seem to be the would-be professional groups that deal with these data and provide analysis for business, government, and nonprofit organizations. And, without a doubt, the surge in interest in

DOI: 10.4324/9781003225485-8

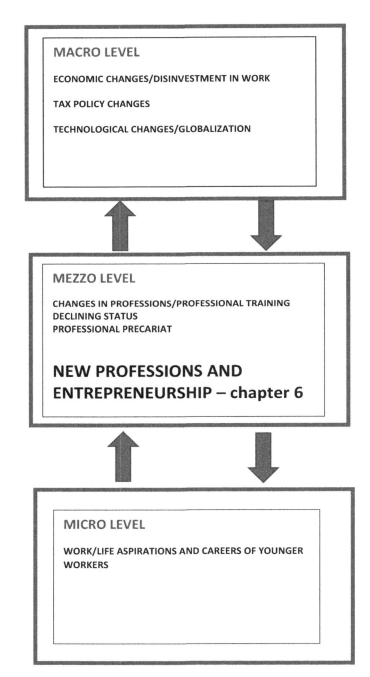

Figure 6.1 The Organization of Our Argument – Chapter 6 – New Professions and Entrepreneurship

entrepreneurship in college has been a major development in higher education. Universities are creating entrepreneurship programs that attempt to bring together interdisciplinary groups in real-world situations to create value and new products. There is some evidence that these programs have increased the number of new ventures created by students (Ulrich 2018; Berkopec 2013).

Financial Analysts – The New Accountancy?

As late as the mid-1990s, students who wanted to enter the business world without getting a law degree would focus on majoring in accounting. One could graduate from an accredited accounting program at an American business school, take the CPA exam and become a certified public accountant, take a job at one of the (then) "BIG 8" accounting firms as an associate, and expect a career featuring upward mobility, relatively high compensation, and eventual promotion to a partnership where you could share in the profits the firm generated. In the process, you would be assured that a steady stream of corporate clients in need of your services to certify their financial well-being would pay the bills, keep you employed, and keep your firm healthy and growing.

But the financial de-regulation that began in the mid-1980s and continued more-or-less unabated since that time was not kind to the accounting profession. Changes in depreciation rules, financial practices, stock options, mergers and acquisitions, stock buy-backs, and other gimmicks were designed by corporate managers and financial officers to generate maximum reward while appearing to generate little or no taxable revenue. The globalization of financial markets that accompanied financial deregulation increased the opportunities to move money and investments to different parts of the world where they were subject to lax financial regulation and taxation or (in many cases) no regulation or taxation at all. In the end, many companies were making financial transactions that were so complex that people inside of the company could not keep track of their money and external auditors could not either. On top of this, there was a tremendous incentive to cheat – simply hide revenues, profits, and losses, keep them from the eye of the auditors who worked with you on retainer, and have them certify that your books were good and the finances of your company sound (Enron and MCI-Parmelat and Tyco were the most notorious examples; see Leicht and Lyman 2006).

Also to be noted: accounting firms were looking for new sources of revenue and expanded into the management consulting business and traditional management consulting businesses were expanding into accounting and legal services. The goal appeared to be an omnibus, one-stop professional service firm (see, for example, Suddaby et al. 2007) where accounting, management consulting, and legal services could be provided under one roof.

Enron, MCI-WORLDCOM, and Royal Ahold: Bumps on the Road to
Professional Omnibus Business Services

The accounting and financing scandals that rocked the American business community in 2005 and 2006 (and the European business community through Royal Ahold, a Dutch food market supplier) point to many of the institutional and technical problems with deregulated financing systems and deregulated financial markets. These scandals also served as a precursor to the Great Recession of 2008 (see Chapter 2). For our purposes, these cases also expose some of the more fundamental problems with the interface between management consulting, accounting, and law that will likely prevent the consolidation of these professional groups into new organizational forms.

In each of these cases (and the case of Tyco International), the problems were highly similar, as were the abuses. Top executives of each company were paid through stock options. These options were supposed to tie the compensation of top officials to the financial performance of the company, but instead, they provided a built-in incentive to report ever-rising profits to Wall Street and the larger financial community so that stock prices would rise. None of this would be problematic if the professional groups (lawyers and accountants) exercised their professional prerogatives to independently monitor the legal and financial behavior of the firms involved. But, in each case, there were significant conflicts of interest that prevented this from happening.

The Enron case is a typical example. Enron purchased consulting and accounting services from Arthur Anderson, at the time one of the "Big Five" accounting firms. Enron also retained external legal counsel that assumed that Arthur Andersen was doing their job of monitoring the financial transactions of the company so that the certified profits of the company were legitimate. Both Arthur Anderson and Enron's legal firm received millions of dollars in fees, fees that rose with Enron's reported profits.

When these cases began to unravel, each revealed a tangled web of financial transactions that (a) systematically misrepresented the financial health of the firm, misrepresentations that were certified by accounting firms with substantial financial interests in the consulting income they were deriving from the firms they were auditing, (b) law firms that were more than content to look the other way as long as legal fees were regularly paid and audits were certified as legitimate, and (c) CEOs and top managers who made millions from falsified corporate profits and backdated stock options (see Froud et al. 2004 for an analysis of Enron as both an example of corporate failure through "financialization" and a firm embedded within a political web of special interests and powerful actors).

All of these situations have led to fundamental questioning of Generally Accepted Practices in accounting and the ability of accountants and lawyers to remain independent from their clients. They have also struck a (for now) fatal blow to the concept of clusters of accounting, legal, and management consulting services (omnibus business services firms) given the likelihood of fundamental conflicts of interest in a deregulated financial environment.

The globalization and deregulation of finance and the change in the business model for big accounting firms led to built-in conflicts of interest, lack of oversight, and dubious financial practices that bordered on and sometimes crossed into the area of financial fraud. Accounting firms often provided managerial consulting services to the same companies they audited, and this put enormous pressure on auditors to certify firm accounting practices as legitimate and to issue good credit ratings. Audited firms often knew that the accounting firms would have to certify their books or risk losing not only the accounting businesses but also the managerial consulting business as well. Also tied to this less-than-ideal situation were credit rating agencies like Standard and Poor's, organizations that were assigned the role of certifying the creditworthiness of corporations seeking to borrow money and float new stock offerings.

Ultimately, the combination of increased complexity, lax oversight and deregulation, and built-in incentives to look the other way contributed to the financial crisis of the 2000s. Entire firms and segments of the U.S. economy collapsed and brought down other nations' economies in their wake. The housing crisis and the crisis surrounding mortgage bonds in 2008 were just the end of a long string of corporate and professional malfeasance that led to bankruptcies, plant closings, and the destruction of accounting firms and credit rating agencies (see Halliday and Curruthers 2009).

From our standpoint, what the financial collapse did was take much of the luster off of accounting as a profession and it also affected the well-being of major accounting firms. This led to mergers among the big accounting firms, and there are now just five such firms worldwide. In the process, the power of accounting as a profession was shown to be only associated with the underlying numbers accounting firms were given (cf. Brewster 2003). Hiring of accountants slowed and students started looking for other avenues of securing a professional life. The rise and expansion of finance played right into this dynamic.

While the accounting scandals of 2000–2006 and the financial crisis of 2008 put the spotlight on the vulnerabilities of the deregulated financial system, only a few financial houses, banks, and accounting firms collapsed (see Table 6.1).

Yet very few people or companies were called out for financial malfeasance, and the overall dominance of the financial sector in the U.S. economy has proceeded without interruption. Finance has shifted long-term from being a facilitating, infrastructural need of a thriving market economy to the main driver of corporate profits and revenues – non-financial firm profits from finance have risen from 26% in 1973 to 43% of firm profits in 2005 (Batt and Applebaum 2013) and up to 40% of non-financial firm revenues (Krippner 2012). Companies are making more money from financial transactions than they are from their core business.

Table 6.1 Top Ten Accounting Scandals of the Past Two Decades

Corporation	Year	Context	Value
Waste Management Incorporated	1998	Reported fake earnings	$1.7 billion
Enron	2001	Using accounting loopholes to hide billions of dollars in bad debt and inflate company earnings	$74 billion
Worldcom	2002	Underreported costs; fake revenue entries	$180 billion
Tyco	2002	Stolen funds and inflating earnings	$650 million
HealthSouth	2003	Inflated earnings	$1.8 billion
Freddie Mac	2003	Underreported earnings	$5 billion
American International Group (AIG)	2005	Counting loans as revenue; forcing clients to use insurers with pre-existing payoff agreements with AIG	$4 billion
Lehman Brothers	2008	Hiding loans, claiming them as cash assets	$50 billion
Bernie Madoff Investment Securities	2008	Ponzi scheme	$64.8 billion
Satyam Computer Services	2009	Inflating earnings	$1.5 billion

Source: Corporate Finance Institute

https://corporatefinanceinstitute.com/resources/knowledge/other/top-accounting-scandals/

The major drivers of this change are financial deregulation (which we discussed in Chapter 2), the rise of shareholder value as the rationale for corporate activity, and the linking of shareholder and managerial incentives via agency theory (see Box 6.1). Shareholder value theories of corporations claim that the sole purpose of the corporation is to increase shareholder value (see Van der Zwan 2014). The ultimate owners of the corporation are shareholders, and their interests are to take precedence over all others. Tied closely to this development is the belief that managers' interests need to be tied to shareholder value, a major tenet of agency theory (see Lazonick 2013). The major way of tying shareholder interests to managers is through stock options that pay for managerial compensation through stock purchases and sales.

The net result of these changes was a huge surge in financial returns for financial service firms and top managers in non-financial firms (see Freeman 2010). Employees of all kinds (including skilled professionals) were squeezed, laid off, or deskilled (Freeman 2010; Batt and Applebaum 2013). Companies started using surplus revenues to manipulate the value of their stocks, which guaranteed big paydays for corporate executives (see Thompson

---

Box 6.1 Financialization, Shareholder Value, and Agency Theory – Facilitating Corporate Deviance?

Financialization refers to the shift in the economic system toward financial transactions and away from brick-and-mortar businesses or services. Financialization has crept into the activities of what one would think of as traditional manufacturing – General Motors, for example, makes more money from loaning money than it does from making and selling cars (see Daily Record 2004).

Shareholder value theories attempt to tie the activities of top firm managers to shareholders, those who actually "own" the company. Because managers are few and shareholders are many (and dispersed), one way to tie the interests of managers to shareholders is to pay managers in *stock options* – either grants of stock shares in the company as a form of payment or, as the name suggests, options to buy shares at reduced prices to be sold at higher prices at a later time.

As the corporate scandals we have discussed suggest, this system was ripe for abuse – granting stock options to managers dilutes the shares of actual stockholders; stock options timing is often manipulated (or changed) so that the profits accruing to managers are large even of the company's performance is poor; there are ways of making company stock prices jump that do not involve producing better products or services; and shareholder value theories have been implicated in promoting short-term thinking at the expense of long-term company financial health (see Lazonick 2013; Thompson 2013).

2013). Financialization was dubbed a "new regime of accumulation" as U.S. companies stopped investing in innovation, stopped investing in employee skills, and oriented themselves toward maximizing profits through financial transactions (see Lazonick 2013; Thompson 2013). Thompson (2013) has dubbed this development "disorganized capitalism." Others have pointed out that this system rests on a type of "private Keynesianism" where people go into debt to fund their own consumption and human capital accumulation (see Streek 2014; Leicht and Fennell 2008a; Leicht and Fitzgerald 2022).

The implications of the rise of finance for young, would-be professionals are pretty clear. As we lay out in Chapter 7 ahead, more students at elite institutions aspire to positions in finance and management consulting rather than the traditional professions of medicine and law. The U.S. Department of Labor ranks financial analysts as one of the fastest-growing jobs in the U.S. labor market for the next 10 years (U.S. Department of Labor 2019). The educational requirements for entry-level positions are modest (a bachelor's degree plus certification from the Financial Industry Regulation Authority). Job growth will be way faster than average for the entire economy – 11%

growth from 2016 to 2026, or an additional 32,000 jobs added to a base of 300,000 jobs. And the median salary is well over two times the median salary in the entire U.S. labor market ($85,660 in 2018; Occupational Outlook Handbook 2019).

The question this change suggests is far reaching – why should an enterprising student who is looking at years of educational debt invest in extensive professional training that stretches for years beyond a bachelor's degree, leading to an uncertain payoff, with little occupational control and mountains of bills to pay? With the shift toward the financialization of the economy, a career in the financial industry looks like a better alternative.

Data Science – Who Will Manage All Those New Data Resources?

By far the fastest-growing would-be professional occupation in the United States right now is in the category of "data science." Data science incorporates elements of statistics and computer programming and does not exist as a distinctive occupational category in itself just yet (BLS 2019), but it will soon.

Big data encompasses an array of potential data sources that overwhelm existing data storage and analysis infrastructure. It includes everything from the output of surveillance cameras to the continuously collected vital signs of hospital patients, to credit card transactions and Google searches. All of our social media data on Facebook, Twitter, Snapchat, and Instagram are included, as are the GPS signals from our cars and cell phones, satellite feeds, remote sensor readings, and weather reports. In short, just about anything that can be collected is being collected. The ability to collect these data, make them useful, and analyze them to answer important questions is the essence of what data science is about.

There are big ethical, scientific, and practical issues surrounding the collection, analysis, and use of big data (Davenport 2016; Federal Trade Commission 2016; Japec et al. 2015). One of the biggest scientific issues is that the data are "organic" – they are a byproduct of our everyday lives in an electronic and interconnected world. They are not collected as part of a deliberate attempt to answer a scientific question and that leads to a number of questions about their usefulness for answering these questions; who is the population represented by these data? (People with enough money to engage in a specific activity, with computer skills, and spare time? Everyone with a cell phone? Customers interested in a specific item? etc.); are there people who are systematically excluded from these data whose preferences and behavior are important for answering important questions? (Minorities? Immigrants? The elderly? etc.); does the data measure things that are important or things that are superfluous? And what types of questions can be answered with these data that cannot be answered otherwise?

A second set of questions deals with the ethical and moral implications of these data and their potential use – Who owns the data and has the rights to use it? Can the data be bought and sold by third parties without the permission of those whose behavior has been recorded? Do individuals have a right to privacy and to assume that their data won't be misused? Do we have a "right to be forgotten"?

These questions and others are big issues for the data science community. One thing is certain, the sheer volume of data we are generating dwarfs the amount of data governments and corporations are intentionally collecting for analysis purposes (see Figure 6.2).

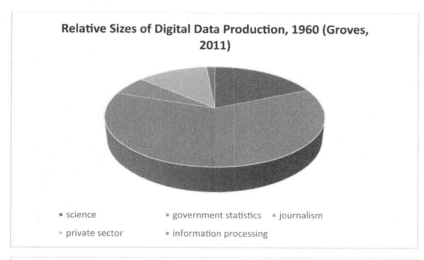

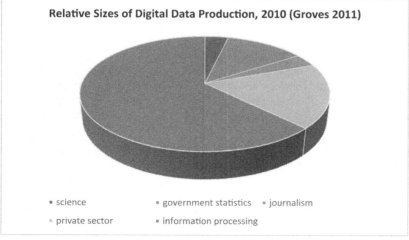

Figure 6.2 Relative Sizes of Digital Data Production, 1960 and 2010 (Groves 2011)

In fact, there is so much data being generated that most of it is not used or analyzed (see Groves 2011). And "big data" does not just drop into our laps and tell us what is happening. A substantial amount of time and energy is spent cleaning and reformatting our clicks, posts, and likes into something that can be analyzed and used.

There are at least five steps to the data analysis process, all of which require considerable care and skill on the part of the data scientist. First, the data have to be *collected*, which usually means downloading reams of activity from a collection server. Then the data need to be *compiled* and *consolidated* – not every piece of data is useful and much of the data needs to be scanned with A.I. and optical character recognition software to look for an activity that is important for the specific question the data scientist is answering. Then the data need to be analyzed statistically using software packages such as "R." Then the results are ready to be presented to the agency or client that is asking the question.

So how much data are we talking about? In 2010, U.S. businesses generated seven exibites of data. One exibite is 4,000 times the amount of information stored in the entire Library of Congress (Manyika et al. 2013). And the labor demands are enormous. In 2018, data science employment reached 300,000 people and that still left 150,000 jobs unfilled. In the next ten years, the U.S. will need 1.5 million data-savvy managers as well (Manyika et al. 2013). The BLS projects strong growth in data science occupations (Computer programmers and statisticians) with median annual wages around $75,000, double the median wage for the average U.S. worker. The future demand is so high that in 2012 the Obama administration dedicated an additional $200 million to the NSF, DOD, and Department of Education to stimulate the training of data scientists and the use of big data. Colleges and universities have responded by creating over 100 data analytics programs at the undergraduate and graduate levels.

University Entrepreneurship Programs: Can Everyone Be an Entrepreneur?

The third trend in occupational choice that is affecting young people is the new university-based focus on entrepreneurship (cf. Mars et al. 2008). Kuratko (2005) states that, as of 2005, university entrepreneurship programs went from essentially nothing in 1970 to 1,500 in 2005. Now there are over 2,100 courses, 1,600 schools, 277 endowed positions, and 44 academic journals devoted to entrepreneurship research. There are over 100 formal centers as well dedicated to promoting entrepreneurship and entrepreneurial research. Much of this research is devoted to the personal characteristics and contexts that promote success (cf. Kalleberg and Leicht 1991).

A central question we have is whether this focus on entrepreneurship is a genuine new trend or is simply a compensation for the destruction of conventional labor markets (see O'Shea et al. 2008). The statistics here are troubling (see Table 6.2).

Table 6.2 Bureau of Labor Statistics Projections of Most New Jobs by Occupation, 2016–2026, With Median 2017 Yearly Earnings

Occupation	Number of New Jobs 2016-2026	2017 Median Annual Earnings
Personal care aides	777,600	$23,100
Food preparation and serving workers, incl. Fast food	579,900	$20,180
Registered nurses	438,100	$70,000
Home health aides	431,200	$23,210
Software developers, applications	255,400	$101,790
Janitors and cleaners (ex. Maids and Housekeepers)	236,500	$24,990
General and operations managers	205,200	$101,410
Laborers and freight, stock, and material Movers – hand	199,700	$27,040
Medical assistants	183,900	$32,480
Waitstaff	182,500	$20,820
Nursing assistants	173,400	$27,520
Construction laborers	150,400	$34,530
Cooks, restaurant Accountants and auditors	145,300	$25,180
Market research analysts/ marketing specialists	138,300	$63,230
Customer service representatives	136,300	$32,890
Landscaping and groundskeeping workers	135,200	$27,670
Medical secretaries	129,000	$34,610
Management analysts	115,200	$82,450
Maintenance and repair workers, general	112,500	$37,670

Median U.S. pay in 2017 = $31,099
Poverty line for family of four = $24,600 (Medicaid eligibility = $33,948)

Source: Occupational Outlook Handbook, 2018 (www.bls.gov/ooh/most-new-jobs.htm)

The fastest-growing occupations in the U.S. economy do not require a college degree; 36% of young people between the age of 25 and 34 have a college degree, but only 25% of all jobs require one (see Fuller and Raman 2017). Median real wages for college graduates have been stuck at $52,000 since 2000, and almost all of the income gains for the past 20 years have gone to the top 1% of the income distribution (Congressional Research Service 2019; Pew Research Center 2018).

The combination of declines in job quality for new college graduates and the frightening increases in the expense of going to college contrasts mightily with the "rock star" status of a few young entrepreneurs who make millions or billions of dollars in winner-take-all labor markets. This contrast, and the uncertainty it has produced, has contributed to the development of university entrepreneurship programs (McMurtrie 2015; Kuratko 2005).

What does the average university entrepreneurship program entail?

- An interdisciplinary, product-based focus that uses teams to solve problems and pilot new products;
- University support through dedicated space in entrepreneurship centers, the provision of equipment and dedicated faculty in business, science, engineering, and liberal arts;
- The support of prominent alums, many of whom made their fortunes as entrepreneurs and developed new products or services;
- A university that fears their graduates are "unemployable" and that seeks to provide hands-on business experience, especially to liberal arts and STEM students.

Some have pointed out that commitment to entrepreneurship or "built-it-yourself" careers has happened precisely in the wake of declines in stable professional career paths in law and medicine (McMurtrie 2015). Others have claimed that the new platform economy has stimulated entrepreneurship as the strictures of traditional employment are loosened and people learned to market themselves and their talents (Han and Applebaum 2016). Others suggest that poor labor market conditions (and especially high unemployment and lower labor force participation) spur entrepreneurship and that the effect of bad economic times is especially salient in areas where home ownership is common and housing values are high (Farlie 2013).

But stimulating entrepreneurship is much more difficult than just kicking the stool out from under conventional labor markets and employment, and there is considerable disagreement about what makes for a good entrepreneurial education (see Rideout and Gray 2013). Few, however, disagree that the entrepreneurial process involves a set of distinctive steps once an initial idea is developed. These include:

1) A commercialization decision – the initial belief that an idea has market value;
2) Prototype generation and establishing commercial and technical viability – can we make it at a reasonable price and can we sell it?
3) Founding team formation – deciding who will be part of the venture and what their specific roles will be;
4) Determining a business and commercialization strategy;
5) Finding funding to sustain new activities.

At their best, entrepreneurship programs bring students together, help them to develop their ideas in an interdisciplinary environment, and then give them the opportunity to develop their ideas and present them to experienced people who may act as investors and facilitators. The end results can be dramatic as we have seen with the likes of Microsoft and Facebook. But more realistically, the average student is exposed to the way new business ideas are developed and marketed as they learn to work in teams to solve problems.

Just how important is this? The *Princeton Review* ranks university entrepreneurship programs every year. The top 10 are listed in Table 6.3:

While these could not be construed as the "average" entrepreneurship program across 1,600 schools in the United States, the students enrolled, start-ups launched, and funds raised by students to support their ventures are impressive. The entrepreneurship track is definitely an alternative to conventional employment for ambitious students and especially those that might have pursued conventional professional careers in the past.

There are several problems with university-based entrepreneurship programs that critics have alluded to. First, there is a debate about whether

Table 6.3 Top 10 U.S. Best Undergraduate Programs for Entrepreneurs, 2019

School	# of entrepreneurial related courses	Start-ups Launched by Grads, last 5 yrs	Students enrolled in entrepreneurship classes	Funds Raised by Students, Last 5 years	Year Established
U. of Michigan	68	807	4,554	$20 million	1999
U. of Houston	34	475	2,268	$57 million	1991
Babson College	38	334	2,342	$40 million	1978
Brigham Young University	49	361	5,823	$733 million	1989
Northeastern University	37	657	1,537	$100 million	2012
Baylor University	31	1,095	1,800	$678 million	1977
Washington University/ St. Louis	28	84	584	$329 million	2003
U. of Maryland	80	226	9,754	$49 million	1986
U. of Utah	36	266	882	$33 million	2002
North Carolina State University	42	104	3,433	$ 365 million	2008

Source: www.entrepreneur.com/slideshow/322898

entrepreneurship can be taught (cf. Rideout and Gray 2013). Clearly, there are a few skills associated with making good business decisions that can be taught, but creativity and innovativeness might not be those skills. Second, the track record of success for most entrepreneurial ventures is dismal – almost all fail within the first few months and practically none last longer than five years (see Kalleberg and Leicht 1991). The new would-be entrepreneur has to be prepared to fail repeatedly in order to finally succeed, and even then, millions of dollars are not forthcoming – the average entrepreneur does not take home more income than the average worker. Third, most entrepreneurial ventures create very few jobs, almost no wealth, and little in the way of innovations or patents (see Shane 2009). Further, there is too much focus on gurus and unusual success stories – in fact, one cannot discount the possibility that universities are involved in entrepreneurship programs to find the next "winner-take-all" entrepreneur who becomes a billionaire before the age of 25. The hope is that our new captain of the industry will remember where they came from and shower the university with donations! Finally, entrepreneurial programs at universities can be critiqued for caving into the collapse of the conventional labor market for professionals rather than pushing back and demanding better for their charges (Hanauer 2019; Leicht and Fennell 2008b).

In short, we would not suggest that learning teamwork and teamwork skills is a bad idea, but the idea that entrepreneurship is a substitute for middle-class professional jobs is not a viable long-term idea. The very best of the e-ship programs within universities include several important dimensions: (a) they teach individuals to gain team skills, but they also provide teams with opportunities to learn and produce as teams; (b) they impart work habits at both the individual and team levels that encourage discipline and responsibility; and (c) they teach teams and individuals how to recognize and nurture new ideas and creative approaches. In other words, it is not just teamwork.

Finance, Data Science, and Entrepreneurship: An Alternative to the Traditional Professions?

So where does this leave young and ambitious students looking for professional careers? Table 6.4 provides a side-by-side comparison of data science and financial analysts compared to medicine and law.

There are several issues this table brings to light.

- *Demand for workers in the traditional professions is still strong – physicians and lawyers are not going away anytime soon.* However, as we documented in prior chapters, rising income inequality and threats to professional prerogatives and traditional sources of revenue affect the choices that young people make. This is especially true with post-secondary teaching where the growing use of adjuncts and non-tenure track faculty has jeopardized the research careers of scientists and scholars.

Table 6.4 A Comparison of Financial Analysts and Data Scientists With Lawyers and Physicians: Current Position and Future Employment Prospects (U.S. Department of Labor 2019)

	Computer and Information Research Scientists	Statisticians and Mathematicians	Financial Analysts	Physicians	Lawyers
2018 Median Pay	$118,370/year	$88,190	$85,660	$208,000/ year	$120,910/ year
Entry-Level Education	Master's degree	Master's degree	BA degree	Professional degree	Professional degree
Number of Jobs, 2016	27,900	40,300	296,100	713,800	792,500
Job Outlook, 2016–2026	19% growth	33% growth	11% growth	13% growth	8% growth
Employment Change, 2016–2026	5,400	13,500	32,200	91,400	65,000

Source: Bureau of Labor Statistics, Occupational Outlook Handbook, www.bls.gov/ooh/

But this is not the only place where professional work has been parceled out. As we stated earlier, law and medicine have witnessed the growth of cheaper substitutes for certain job tasks. The Department of Labor claims that the market for physician assistants will grow by 37% in the next decade (around 37,000 jobs) and the market for paralegals and legal assistants will grow by 12% (around 39,000 jobs) over the next decade (U.S. Department of Labor 2019).

To be sure, these would-be professional groups are not necessarily treated badly in all cases, and the educational requirements are far below those required for the traditional professions (professional degrees and PhDs).

- *The educational requirements of these relatively new professional groups are far less than the regular post-graduate and professional degrees needed in the traditional professions.* Many can enter with only a bachelor's degree, with earnings well above the median in the U.S. labor market, and demand is growing rapidly. With college costs out of control and students going into debt to finance much of it, the opportunity to make good money with considerably less education has got to be appealing.
- *The median earnings for financial analysts and data scientists are quite favorable considering the relatively short time spent in training.* Median earnings are about two-thirds of what doctors and lawyers make, but again one has to consider the additional debt in current to attend medical school or law school. If a substantial chunk of the earnings of new doctors and lawyers is going to pay student loans, then the difference in earnings is not as wide as they seem.

- *The lack of scrutiny and interference has to be appealing as well.* Especially in medicine and science, the "war on expertise" is taking a toll. Financial analysts and data scientists (not to mention entrepreneurs, who are highly valued in our neoliberal world) do not have to deal with arch conservatives who believe the U.S. should return to the Gold Standard and that whites are genetically superior to other races. They do not have to deal with creationists or religious fundamentalists either. If nothing else, the continual exposure to media portrayals of this kind has to have some influence on what young people decide to do with their work lives.

A final question we raise has to do with the future of these new professionals and would-be professional groups. We already know that the entrepreneurial track is a hit-or-miss/winner-take-all endeavor where many will try but few will succeed. Will the other competitors for young people's attention move in this direction too? Financial analysts who work for big investment houses already make millions of dollars, but this does not seem to be tied to the consolidation of the profession into a few high-visibility firms. For every high-roller who needs the services of J.P. Morgan/Chase, there are hundreds of people who simply want to save enough to retire and sent their kids to college.

The same may not be true for data science. The companies that collect social media data are very concentrated and function as oligopolies. Much of the financial data are collected or consumed in the same way. These companies have enormous, built-in incentives to maximize the value they can derive from the data they collect. They employ lots of data scientists now and will in the future. Where does that leave everyone else, and what does that mean for a society where a few private firms control a vast swath of the data on our public and private lives? The dystopian potential here is enormous.

In the end, it would not be surprising if bright and ambitious students looked for alternatives to traditional professions. We've presented three alternatives, but there are others too (Management consulting being one). But what do ambitious young people actually aspire to do now? Chapter 7 addresses this issue.

Part III

Younger Workers and Their Career Aspirations and Expectations

In our two concluding chapters, we address the likely future of professional work and professional workers. So far, we have described how and where professional work is changing and how this has affected established and new entrants to these occupational groups. We have looked at some likely replacements or new would-be professions, many of which are a product of automation and the deregulated global economy. We have also addressed the small but growing trend of would-be professionals not finding a place or gaining an economic foothold (Chapter 5 and our discussion of the professional precariat).

Chapter 7 takes a micro-view of professions, examining what new, young and ambitious labor market entrants believe their work lives are like and (more importantly for the future) what they think their lives will be like (see Figure 7.1). At least at elite institutions, the lure of work in the traditional professions has lost its appeal. We will also see that the typical millennial worker is not engaged with their work and that levels of workplace alienation, non-engagement, poor income streams, and debts are harming the labor market debuts of many young people. We then discuss the implications of these results for professional work specifically before we turn to our conclusion.

The concluding chapter lays out a series of scenarios for professional work in the 21st century. Some of these scenarios seem more likely than others, and we will be sure to emphasize that in our presentation. We will also make a series of modest policy recommendations that we think would improve the recruitment of new professionals and (more importantly) more adequately use the human capital and enthusiasm of new, ambitious workers with professional credentials.

DOI: 10.4324/9781003225485-9

7 The Worklife of Millennials and Other Generations

In this chapter, we seek to understand what is known about the millennial generation, and how this generation may differ from earlier generations in terms of career aspirations and the perceived value of professional work. To do this, we explore the major models for understanding generational differences in careers and how individuals come to "aspire to" or prefer certain professions and careers, especially in their young adult years. We will briefly review the two major models that have been used to do this: (1) the traditional model (also called the "corporate view") and (2) the "new career model." In this chapter, we will focus primarily on the individual or micro level of analysis, and many of the meso- and macro-level processes we have already discussed will come into play as environmental or contextual variables that can influence that individual decision-making. We will focus on three questions: (1) what was valued about work by earlier generations? (2) what is valued about work by millennials? and (3) has there been a shift away from valuing professional work? In our quest to answer these questions, we seek to understand what is known about millennials compared to earlier generations, and we explore the two major models used by analysts to understand careers and how individuals come to "aspire to" or prefer certain careers over time.

Definitions: A Generational Perspective

So far, we have examined both macro-level changes and meso-level changes that have influenced the nature and shape of professional work. Macro-level changes have included major economic trends, technological trends, and globalization. Meso-level changes focused on the various ways professional work has gained and lost value: cultural value; labor market value; value as defined by job queues and labor queues; value connected to the supply and demand for advanced degrees; and value as measured by the cost of professional training. We have also examined recent changes in demographic diversity within selected professions, the emergence of a "professional precariat" and the rise of new "professions" (or highly valued new jobs), such as entrepreneurs and venture capitalists. These same systemic changes provide

DOI: 10.4324/9781003225485-10

the context in which young adults make decisions about their first jobs and careers. Changes in these contexts influence the aspirations and labor market behaviors of multiple generations.

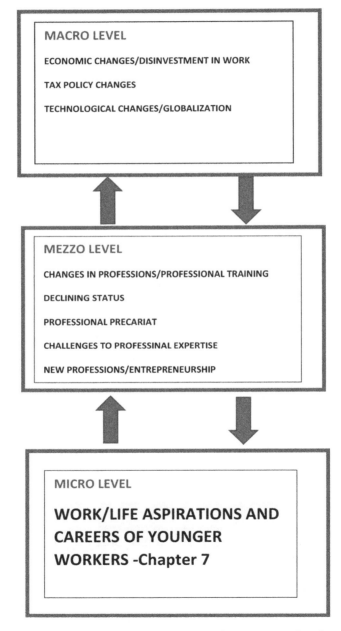

Figure 7.1 The Organization of Our Argument – Chapter 7 – Work/Life Aspirations and Younger Workers

Box 7.1   Some Terms Used in This Chapter

Generational Terms

Generations – Usually defined as (a) a group of people in a population born at the same historical point in time and (b) the time it takes for these individuals to be born, grow up, mature, and have their own children.

Millennials – The generation born between 1980 and 1996, who reached maturity at the turn of the millennium (the year 2000).

Gen-Xers – The generation born between 1965 and 1979, the group immediately following the post-World War II baby boom (1946–1964). Referred to as "X" because the group defied easy categorization by commentators.

Baby Boomers – The immediate post-World War II generation born between 1949 and 1964. An uncharacteristically large generation because of delays in marriage and fertility produced by the war.

Traditionalists – The generation born between 1900 and 1945, identified as "traditionalists" because their employment experiences and expectations set the norms for the 20th Century workforce. This group is either deceased or mostly out of the labor force at this point.

Careers: The work-life biographies of individual labor force participants. Individual careers may be organized or disorganized, "orderly" or "disorderly," and may include stints out of the labor force.

Career Paths – Established progressions of jobs that are structurally established and through which many labor force participants pass.

Job Mobility – Movements from one job to the next, where a job is defined as a cluster of tasks. Job mobility can be upward, downward, or lateral.

Organizational Mobility – movement from one work organization or firm to another. This change may be accompanied by job mobility (either to a better job or to a poorer one) or represent a lateral job move.

Generations are themselves social and historical phenomena. Traditionally, the notion of "generation" has been defined as all of the people in a population who were born at about the same historical point in time. Another common definition focuses on the measure of a generation as the standard period of time needed for individuals to be born, grow up, mature, and reach the stage of having their own children, typically about 30 years. Generations tend to experience historical events in ways that influence their maturation and life histories in distinctive and similar ways. The classic studies of generations who grew up during the Great Depression, (Elder 1974) or matured during World War II (Brokaw 1998), have provided riveting accounts of cohort differences in attitudes about job stability, wealth, and socio-economic change (Elder 1974). In this chapter, we are particularly interested in comparing contemporary young adults and how they approach career and/or professional training choices – those referred to as millennials – to prior generations. This includes the cohorts of young people who were born between the early 1980s and the early 2000s.

There are three generations who "share space" in the contemporary labor market with Millennials: Gen-Xers, Baby Boomers, and Matures. These four generations are all part of the current professional labor market. However, how they perceive and experience that labor market is filtered and shaped by their dissimilar career histories, norms, values, and age/maturation effects. For example, the impact of the Great Recession varied across the four generations even though they all felt the impact of declines in the stock market and the closure of major financial, consulting, and law firms.

"Matures" probably have the least in common with Millennials. Members of this generation were born prior to 1946, so are the most chronologically distant group from Millennials. These workers have been studied by demographers and labor force economists. An excellent study of four generations of Canadian workers showed interesting differences in the career patterns of Matures compared to other generations (Lyons et al. 2012). Matures tend to show career patterns of upward movement within single organizations, but low rates of cross-organizational mobility, and most of this generation has now aged out of the labor market.

"Baby Boomers" (those born between 1946 and 1964) benefitted the most from the post-World War II economy, and their early careers were blessed by favorable employment conditions and an expanding economy. Unemployment after World War II was low, and this cohort was very large; thus, early career stages provided almost across-the-board benefits in promotion rates. Later career stages for boomers, however, told a different story. Many boomers with early career promotions found themselves stalled: continued promotion was subject to intense competition with younger generations who are more facile with new technologies. The Boomer generation needed to change employers in order to continue their career advances.

Following the Boomers and preceding Millennials were the cohorts born between 1964 and 1979: referred to as "Generation X." These cohorts were entering the labor market by the early 1980s, when unemployment rates had nearly doubled compared to 20 years earlier. The Gen-Xers faced recessions and corporate downsizing, as well as a labor market saturated with displaced Boomers (Moses 1997; Lyons et al. 2012). These cohorts pre-dated the Millennial cohorts and were the first cohorts known for job hopping and the pursuit of lateral moves, rather than the steady ladder climbing of their parents' generations. In part because of the precariousness of the labor markets they entered, Generation X is known for a greater focus on monetary rewards and security relative to Baby Boomers (see Leicht and Harper 2018).

Careers and Career Paths: Two Models in the Literature on Careers

In our earlier work (Leicht and Fennell 2001), we used the concepts of "career" and "career paths" to understand how professional work and the organizations in which professional work happens have changed over time. As we explored then, professional careers provide a useful window for studying both change in professions and change in organizations. Careers are orderly progressions of jobs that represent changes in responsibility, status, and authority. Career paths trace the training outcomes (degrees, location of the first job, and choice of specialty) and job transitions of individuals over their working lives. The career paths of professionals have been exceedingly orderly until recent years. The standard path of most classic professions was represented by simple, unidirectional ladders with only one path: upward. This was the visual symbol of the earliest model for studying the movement of individuals across jobs: the "traditional model." This model assumes an orderly progression of positions leading up the career "ladder" from entry level through positions with authority and high status. Internal ladders and firm-based training and skills are paramount. The traditional model also assumes a base of loyalty to the organization and stability of the firm's structure and of the model itself. Individuals, then, are tied to a "corporate view" of jobs and careers that support the corporation, and of the firm's loyalty to the employee (Baruch 2004; Capelli 1999).

More recent studies have found that the traditional model is losing relevance: careers do not follow orderly progressions. The "new career model" emphasizes the acquisition of portable competencies that do not fall within organizational boundaries. Employees do not identify with the firm so much as they identify with "meaningful work," which requires on-the-job action learning. Connections are based on strong social networks of professionals that span organizational boundaries, and individuals are responsible for their own career management. In fact, the "new career model" shares a considerable interest with the classic model of control over professional work. What matters most to professionals is autonomy on the job and control through the expertise of other professionals. Organizational controls were less important and connections between professionals carry more weight than organizational hierarchies.

The change in emphasis between the traditional model and the new career models is particularly important in understanding the basic model of the "career ladder." Careers are no longer straight vertical progressions: the unitary ladder is now replaced by models that resemble "chutes & ladders," with multiple off-shoots, and lateral diversions that sometimes deliver the employee back to the same level. The more recent career literature has also been helpful in distinguishing between processes of job mobility (in which the employee changes jobs in an orderly sequence over time, usually within the same organization), versus organizational mobility where job changes occur along with firm changes, or firms change but the job does not. One can experience organizational mobility by changing firms but keeping the same basic job (i.e., no job mobility).

Our earlier review of systemic meso-level changes from Chapter 4 is of special relevance in understanding how and why individuals make decisions about their careers. Those systemic changes (economic, technological, and global) are themselves factors that influence the different generations in different ways. For example, the influence of the financial recession of 2009 may have seriously hurt the savings profiles of the mature generation. However, the impact of that recession on professional organizations and their plans from 2009 to 2016 to hire and/or build their professional workforce has negatively influenced the job mobility and career patterns of thousands of Gen-Xers and millennials. This includes young people who (such as Maria, Selena, Catalina, and Corwin) spent enormous time and resources training for degrees that will now be less relevant to their job careers.

What has not been clearly defined by the careers literature, however, is the extent to which the changes represented by the new career model are pervasive across the multiple generations represented within any labor market for professional jobs. Clearly, millennials are probably influenced the most by these recent changes, but in any study of a single generation, there are problems with confounding age and period effects (see Box 7.2), as well as untangling the effects of various changes in context.

We are also lacking a clear picture of how jobs become valuable to young people. What is the process that constructs the social meaning of jobs over time? How do those aspirations and values differ across genders or across race/ethnicities?

Box 7.2   What Are Age, Period, and Cohort Effects?

In most analyses of change in people over time, social scientists and others talk of age, period, and cohort effects.

Age is something you are probably most familiar with. Age effects are linked to biological and social processes that affect specific people as they grow older and are simply products of the aging process.

Period effects refer to external factors (famine, war, recession, and depression) that affect all people at a specific point in time. The trauma or boost that results from exposure to the external factor affects everyone, regardless of age.

Cohort effects are external effects that affect specific groups of individuals as they move across time. Generations, and our descriptions of them, are great examples of cohort effects. The coming-of-age young adult group is exposed to a specific set of experiences, cultural changes, and turmoil that affects them more than other age groups.

As you might guess, it is hard to pull these apart in actually analyzing what happens to actual people. In our case, exposure to severe recessions (as in 2009) affects everyone and could be called a "period effect." However, the effects were especially disruptive for young people just starting their work careers, an example of a cohort effect. The same could be said of the Great Depression of the 1930s (see Elder et al. 1974).

Many sociological and psychological models of career aspirations tackle one side of what is, essentially, a multifaceted problem. Early "functionalist" models followed economic models of wages and job seeker demand. Blau and Duncan (1967) emphasized the importance of background (family, class, race, etc.). And many have studied the links between entry into college/universities and labor market outcomes (Brint 2013; Stevens et al. 2008). Most of these, however, emphasize person-level factors in educational achievement. Binder et al. (2016) shine a clear light on what they have labeled the mechanisms of "career funneling," where students are channeled into certain jobs due to interaction with others in local campus contexts, especially on elite campuses. Student clubs, career guidance offices, and recruitment fairs are all mechanisms through which students "collaboratively construct ideas about desirable jobs or how universities serve as pipelines to a narrow band of professions" (Binder et al. 2016, 22). As of this writing, that narrow band is particularly full with positions in finance, consulting, law firms, and high-technology fields. Binder and colleagues drew a small sample of students from Harvard and Stanford, which were heterogeneous with regard to gender, race, ethnicity, major, and socioeconomic status. And from this non-representative sample of 56, they engaged in qualitative in-depth semi-structured interviews to determine how these elite students viewed their career ambitions and how their views of status attached to different careers. Figure 7.2 provides bivariate breakdowns of career impressions and student demographics. Of considerable interest are the results displayed in the three-column area for "traditional professionals." There are no bars shown for working-class students, or for upper-class students, and only 15% of the middle-class students in this sample demonstrated any interest in traditional professional careers. These numbers are fairly low, and there is much more interest in consulting, finance, impact professions (education, public service, and nonprofits), and high-tech fields. An illustrative quotation describes these results:

high tech had become a strong competitor as a high-status job destination on their campus and that law had receded in prestige. Our interviewees' impressions aligned with recent campus surveys of graduating seniors (e.g., those published by the *Harvard Crimson* each year) that lists entry into first jobs.

(Binder et al. 2016, 25)

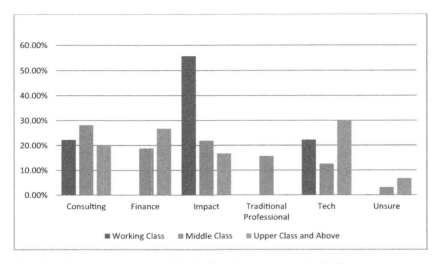

Figure 7.2 Career Aspirations of Elite College Attendees, by Social Class
Source: Binder et al. 2016

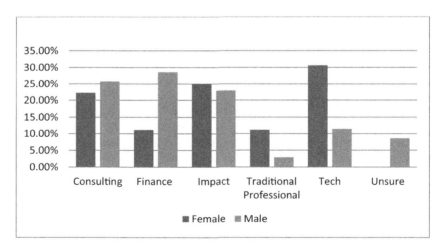

Figure 7.3 Career Aspirations of Elite College Attendees, by Gender
Source: Binder et al. 2016

Figure 7.3 is also based on Binder et al. It shows men and women in the sample and compares their career preferences. Men and women are not far apart in preferences for careers in consulting and impact professions (nonprofits). But many more men prefer finance and technology careers compared to women. And the bulk of students with an interest in traditional professional careers are women: 11% are women compared to almost 3% men.

From the work of Binder and colleagues (as well as earlier work on how university experiences of young conservatives have shaped their political development; see Binder and Wood 2014), we can be fairly certain that universities, particularly elite universities, are central to the process of career funneling. To the extent that university officials and parents understand the central role played by elite student bodies in defining and spreading shared cultural logics, it is not difficult to understand why the recent admissions scandal has so upset the world of college admissions. The bald-faced dishonesty involved in this scandal and the range of lies packed into the application process were astonishing. From cheating on SATs (in multiple ways), through phony athletic star profiles, the entire spectrum of career definitions and job value is thrown into the garbage can when those definitions can be bought and sold via admissions consultants and parental checkbooks.

One final note on constructing the social meaning of jobs: these constructions do not always remain stable over time. The Pew Research Center recently found changes in how men and women value a high-paying career compared to being a good parent or having a successful marriage (Patten and Parker 2012). Women have made great strides in labor force participation, although a gendered wage gap remains, especially for older workers. For many years, fewer women placed a high value on committing to a meaningful career, compared to valuing a family and a strong marriage. Women seemed to value family more than men, and men valued career success much more than women. But now, the latest Pew Research survey data show young women valuing career success more highly than young men (Patten and Parker 2012), an astonishing reversal of traditional gender roles.

Career Stories and Career Aspirations

Let us return to our four young professionals and examine which aspects of societal trends have been most influential in their decisions to opt out of the traditional professional career paths that have been historically connected to their advanced degrees. Given their similar ages, we can probably assume some similarity in their experience of economic changes. All four completed their advanced training around 2010–2012 when various job markets (and the country as a whole) were struggling to climb out of the Great Recession.

Catalina the Internist

Our young physician has opted to go with an organizationally structured, salaried position as a hospitalist within a good size regional medical center. Although in prior decades internists could look forward to very impressive salaries and reasonable patient loads, corporate medicine has changed that description in many ways. Lack of certainty about lawsuits, startup costs, and malpractice insurance have eaten away at those enviable salaries. Catalina is quite happy to be pulling in a salary in the low $100K range, with benefits, a reasonable workload (at least for now), and the ability to frequently travel to her parents' home in northern New England and provide for their medical care needs. Of course, the corporate partners of the medical center could always change the policies on benefit packages for medical employees or demand hospitalists take on much larger panels of patients. Either of those two policy changes would have severe repercussions on Maria's career.

Corwin the Lawyer

Corwin has stopped searching for a dream job in a high-powered law firm and has instead opted for additional certifications in medical software and enterprise content management, making him competitive for a position as in-house legal for a medical services firm. His salary will start lower than it would be as a junior associate in a mega-legal firm (which is reported as just under $200,000; Randazzo 2018), but it will be sufficient to start paying down his college and law school tuition debt. This is a reasonable response to the crash in the labor market for newly trained lawyers and the rise of online legal startups (see Chapter 5). His in-house law position in medical services will provide stability and another ladder outside of corporate law.

Maria the Biologist

Similarly to Corwin, Maria's presumed first job has become harder and harder to reach. Assistant professorships in the tenure line at reputable universities are considerably less available than ten years ago. In addition, guaranteed start-up funds from the university to launch her research program are no longer certain. Luckily she has one more year left on her second post-doctoral fellowship, and she has just received word of positive funding for her NIH career award application. This good news gives her an additional two years of salary and the flexibility she needs to continue searching for an appropriate private sector job in big pharma or biotech. Although she has decided to abandon the quest for a tenure-track position in academia, she now does not need to "settle" for a starter job.

Selina the Comparative Literature Adjunct Instructor

Selina has been totally compromised by the declining role of humanities in academia and their nonexistent role in the private sector: leaving the discipline is one of the very few choices left to her. Universities have been losing ground for nearly 20 years, and the prize of academic tenure is slipping away. As described in Chapter 5, reducing tenure lines only matches the trend in corporate employment toward "precarity": great gaps between starting wages and high-level positions, low and unstable incomes, and low quality of life. Her continuation as an adjunct provides no opportunity for advancement, no real connection to tenured lines, and pushes by most universities to keep those per-course wages as low as possible. The longer she stays an adjunct, the worse are her chances for any academia-related position. It is time to leave and start over.

These four vignettes are not entirely fictive: they are more common than most people think. Three of the four young PhDs have been swept up in overpowering changes in the markets for traditional professional jobs in the fields of law and academia in general. Within academia, the loss of regular tenure-line faculty positions is ravaging the humanities and the sciences; social sciences are only in slightly better straights. Corwin the lawyer is opting for a position akin to in-house counsel for a private sector firm outside of law. Catalina the physician made a decision to forgo a completely changed "medical industrial complex" that shares little with traditional dreams of practicing medicine in ways that benefit one's patients. But she will still be a practicing physician, and she will still have full benefits and some work flexibility.

Millennials Up Close

In Chapter 6, we examined the rising appeal and popularity of alternatives to traditional professional work – data science, finance, managerial consulting, and entrepreneurship. Earlier in this chapter, we discussed research from top U.S. colleges that suggested that traditional professional work had lost its luster among young people at very selective institutions. But what do millennials want and how are they faring in the workplace and in the rest of life?

One of the most impressive studies of the millennial generation has been produced recently by Gallup (2016). Titled *How Millennials Want to Work and Live*, this extensive report covers work issues and life outside of work for samples of millennials across the United States. The results suggest that millennials are expecting a different type of work experience than prior generations of workers, though not all of these differences suggest that millennials are poor candidates for traditional professions. The report suggests that there are six overarching changes in orientations that define millennials and the world of work. Several of these changes are interlinked, and several sound like classic professional traits (similar to the early literature by Carr-Saunders and others). These include the following.

(1) *Millennials want purpose and not just a paycheck.* Unlike prior generations (and especially traditionalists born before 1945), millennials want their work to have a mission and purpose and not simply provide a roof over their heads (though, as we will see, money is not completely unimportant). Ideally, work is meaningful in itself and not just a means to an end, and millennials want jobs and companies whose missions they can identify with. This sounds a lot like the early description of professions as motivated by a sense of mission, or a calling to do work that is important

and of value to society. What is different, however, with millennials is the desire to find work and companies where "they can relate"; whose missions they can identify with (emphasis added). There's no real connection to the values of the profession or of the larger society: the work needs to be important to the individual millennial.

(2) *Millennials are looking for workplaces where they can develop their skills.* Development is (to them) more important than satisfaction. They seek to expand their skills and purpose as companies and jobs grow and change. But again, the emphasis here is on the individual's growth and expanding skill set.

(3) *Millennials want coaches, not bosses.* Managers and supervisors should value workers as people and work to build on the strengths the millennial worker brings to the job. This is very different from prior notions of the workplace and the value of supervision: the emphasis of the organization and of supervisors, bosses, and managers is to deliver value to the millennial workers, not the other way around.

(4) *Millennials want ongoing, preferably continuous, conversations with superiors and others to engage in continuous learning and growth.* This contrasts sharply with traditional ideas (especially in professional settings) that people engage in an annual performance review where strengths, weaknesses, and plans of action are laid out that move workers closer to team goals and to organizational goals. All the emphasis (in the millennial's view) should be on what the worker needs.

(5) *Millennials want to focus on their strengths rather than focus on fixing their weaknesses.* Millennials have a tough time admitting they might have weaknesses; it is usually "all about their strengths." This suggests the need to find better job fit and/or alter job activities to better match employee skills to job requirements.

(6) Finally, *millennials see their jobs as an integral part of their lives rather than "just a job."* They are looking for workplaces that value their contributions and that allow them to integrate work into a continuous stream of life instead of being a means to collect the resources to pursue life meaning outside of work.

One possible response to these differences might be "so what? We all want something out of work we probably aren't getting, why should millennials be any different?" But that would overlook some important generational differences in what millennials actually are getting from the workplace now and how those potential disconnects play into the evolving world of professional work. There are some 73 million members of this generation to which we now look for new ideas, energy, and vitality.

So what does Gallup find from their extensive investigation into the work and personal lives of this generation? The overall results are not a pretty picture for them or the rest of us. On measures of workplace engagement, only 29% of Millennials feel engaged and some 55% are not engaged or "checked out," not putting any passion or energy into work; 54% have full-time jobs and they have the highest rates of unemployment (7%) and underemployment (10%) of any generation studied. They also have lower earnings than other generations at similar times of their lives, higher poverty rates, and are more likely to be overqualified for the jobs they can find. They are also highly constrained by student loan debt, and 3 in 10 of those under 35 still live with their parents.

While initially this looks bad, the proportion of Millennials that are thriving at work is not much different from their parents (33%). They tend to view life and work as one seamless endeavor and are attracted to companies that focus on the whole person. They report that "opportunities to learn and grow" are very important to them when applying for new jobs, and (compared to prior generations) they spend a lot of time job hopping (21% changed jobs in the past year). Perhaps surprisingly, given the importance millennials place on work and the integration of work and the rest of life, six in ten millennials say that work-life balance is very important to them; 87% value professional or career growth, but they do not want to devote their whole careers to one company (Gallup 2016).

For the rest of life, millennials are postponing other markers of adulthood such as marriage and child rearing in favor of career development and advancement. This is a trend other social scientists have pointed to (cf. Cherlin 2018). They are most likely to report being under intense financial pressure and very few report that they are thriving in all five areas of life satisfaction Gallup taps (a purposeful life, social engagement, financial stability, community engagement, and physical well-being), though it is debatable whether their evaluations are worse than their parents at an equivalent stage of life.

The implications of the Gallup analysis for engagement with labor markets for professional workers are somewhat ominous. The professions themselves are being changed radically by the globalization of labor markets, technological change, and growing cultural skepticism about the salience of expertise. Many niches of professional work that once provided an avenue for growth, job mobility, and stable career paths (things millennials claim they value in the Gallup analysis) seem more distant and transitory for new incumbents to professional occupations. However, millennials appear to value organizational stability less than prior generations and the ability to move from one work location to another is something new cohorts of professional workers need to be able to do in response to rapid changes in professional service environments.

The other area where millennials may thrive in new professional work environments involves the recognition that teamwork is important, and most project work, especially, is organized in a team setting, as opposed to sole or "lone wolf" practitioner settings. The ability to engage in multidisciplinary teams to solve common problems and the need to interface with people from a variety of professional and personal backgrounds are activities that millennials generally like and appear to be ready to do. In fact, the lack of such stimulation contributes to job mobility by millennials themselves. Also, keep in mind that not all team-based skills are valued by all professional workers. For some, the emphasis on growing teamwork skills represents a way to better understand team processes and possibly undermine those processes to promote self-interests.

The real question for this group, and the generations that follow, is how professional workplaces will fare in comparison to other ready and available work choices. This is tremendously hard to gauge. Binder et al. suggest that new would-be professional groups are drawing young people who might in other contexts aspire to traditional professional occupations. These occupations usually require less education and provide more ready access to relatively high-quality labor markets. In many cases (but by no means all), compensation relative to the time and money invested in education is favorable as well. Professional training, involving years of post-graduate education at great time and expense, could once be justified because the costs were relatively modest and the rewards all but certain. In some cases, what one traded off in terms of salary was compensated for by steady employment (especially in the academy). In others, high compensation and steady employment were all but assured. The price one often paid in this traditional world was a relatively rigid and unchanging workplace culture with orderly pathways that took years if not decades to navigate. New work environments, including those that millennials claim they look for, promise growth, change, and engagement while not necessarily offering stability or long-term careers. If new professional careers head in the same direction while also requiring much more extensive credentialing, at the incumbents' expense, we can expect traditional professional occupational groups to continue to have problems recruiting the best and brightest incumbents to their ranks.

8   The New Dark Age

Rediscovering Knowledge as the Proper Basis of Authority

Conclusion and Implications

Professional work (as we have defined it) has become less fulfilling, less desired, and more precarious, especially in the United States and (to a lesser degree) in other English-speaking countries. In many cases, professional work has lost status, financial rewards, and job stability. Our analysis developed four themes that sought to highlight different dimensions of these changes across professional settings:

1) *Changes in professional work and careers are and have been a multilevel phenomenon*, spurred on by everything from changes in the broader economy to cultural changes in the valuing of expertise to changes in the relative desirability of traditional professional careers.
2) *Many of these changes have led to the creation of a "professional precariat,"* a group of would-be professionals who are stuck in limbo in various positions that are relatively poorly paid, unstable, and transient.
3) *Expertise of the kind professionals provide is being culturally devalued* and the general status of experts is being eroded by cultural fragmentation and the so-called "democratization" of knowledge.
4) *A lot of many professionals have been under further attack by the political "war on science"* and accompanying attacks on experts and expert training.

Throughout our presentation, we have returned to the individual working lives of four young professionals, a physician, a humanities academic, a lawyer, and a biologist. Each is based on biographies of real people and their very real struggles to develop a professional career and coherent professional identity even after years of post-graduate training and study.

Chapters 2 and 3 took a macro-view of the status of professional workers. Chapter 2 discussed the long-term move toward favoring unearned over earned income as a major driver of wage stagnation and declining job quality, especially in the United States. These changes have left middle-class and many upper-middle-class people (those whose primary source of income is earnings from a job) with stagnant incomes, unstable jobs, and rising

DOI: 10.4324/9781003225485-11

consumer debts. The financial crises of the 2000s (the early 2000s recession and the 2008–2009 Great Recession) exposed these problems as serious and systemic, yet in almost every case, corporate profits have recovered, while wages and on-paper wealth for most people below the top 10% have not.

As if this were not enough, Chapter 2 also addresses the growing war on expertise and science as part of the growing plight of professional workers. If science and empirical inquiry of various kinds form the basis of expert knowledge, then the current cultural fragmentation and political attacks on this expertise spell trouble for those whose labor market standing relies on those very features of public discourse. American political discourse has always contained an element of anti-intellectualism and populism within it, but the current wave of post-truth politics and facts-free argumentation (focusing on emotions and identities rather than evidence and argumentation) has been made much worse by media and cultural fragmentation that separates professionals and their knowledge from ordinary people and provides avenues for opportunistic politicians to impose their will and ignore the long-term implications of denying reality and professional consensus.

In Chapter 3, we examined the role that technological change, globalization, and outsourcing plays in changing professional work. AI promises to fundamentally disrupt the aggregation and use of professional knowledge in very unpredictable ways. Our analysis emphasized two relatively extreme positions, one suggesting that professionals themselves would be displaced to different parts of the professional service pipeline as a result of AI (cf. Susskind and Susskind 2017) and one suggesting that AI will mostly supplement the creativity and personal contact that clients expect from professionals in most settings (ourselves and Frey and Osborne 2017). Globalization and the global movement of skilled workers, combined with the almost instantaneous ability to communicate with those workers anywhere in the world at any time, have and will continue to disrupt local labor markets and contribute to the production of a global, networked professional class that has more in common with other professionals around the world than with people down the street in their home location. In both cases (AI and the globalized labor market), traditional avenues for training and entry-level work have been disrupted and the replacements for this work for young practitioners are far from clear in many cases.

In Chapter 4, we move to the mezzo level and examine what affects the value of professional work and how the U.S. professional labor market is faring in terms of the inclusion of traditionally underrepresented groups. The growing use of adjuncts, the creation of "perma" postdocs, hospitalist positions, outsourcing, and automation have affected the value of professional work. PhDs appear now to be in chronic oversupply, even in the STEM fields, and there is considerable debate about whether the American university system is overproducing BAs relative to what the labor market will support. We also find that the diversification of professional groups which we documented in our 2001 work (Leicht and Fennell 2001) has stalled and, if anything, gone backward. The main new-group beneficiaries of the last 20 years have been Asians and white women – other underrepresented groups have not made many inroads into professional work, including the practice of law. We suggest that this reflects a case of gender/racial queuing "running backward" – professional work may have its luster, but other forms of skilled work have also lost status and earnings as well, stalling the departures of white men from the professions and reducing the inroads of traditionally underrepresented groups.

In Chapter 5, we discussed the creation of a professional precariat, a small but growing group of professionals that are educationally overqualified and suffer from time insecurity, work rights insecurity, and income insecurity. The growth in outsourced jobs, collapsed labor markets, temporary employment, and freelancing, combined with "winner-take-all" labor markets at the top of professions, has led young people to look elsewhere for career and job opportunities as the rewards to advanced education seem more precarious and costs to individuals rise.

Finally, Chapters 6 and 7 looked at new would-be professional groups that are growing and drawing the attention of young people and (at the micro level) what those young people aspire to in their working lives. Finance, data science, and entrepreneurship offer new and promising alternatives to traditional professional credentials with their extensive graduate training and long terms of apprenticeship. This is especially true in cases where the apprenticeship appears to be permanent or lengthening. Universities are spending more of their resources on these career choices and (given the expanding demand for these skills) with good reason. Further, as Chapter 7 shows, the lure of professional labor markets has lost its appeal with the young – old corporate career models are losing ground to new career models that emphasize growth, change, and organizational transience. Millennials in particular do value teamwork but they do not really value hierarchy, and their unwillingness to address weaknesses leads to questions about their growth as practitioners in a new economy that rewards change.

A simplified way of recapping our argument is presented in Table 8.1.

While some of the differences presented in Table 8.1 are somewhat exaggerated ideal types, these differences in many professional endeavors are real and troubling for the future of professional work. Later on, we discuss possible futures for professional work and suggest a few modest reforms.

Is Our Current Intellectual Environment a "New Dark Age"?

One of the premises of this book is that American professions are entering (or have been in) a new dark age (see Table 1.1). In our rendering, the "new dark age" is not as dark as the old, but it might be just as ominous, and it is focused mainly in the West and especially the United States. It involves widespread hostility and questioning of expert opinion on everything from

Table 8.1 The Before-and-After Summary of Our Argument

Before (Post-World War II–1980s)	*After (1980s–Present, Especially Post-Millennium)*
Credential-based social closure	Winner-take-all labor markets and job fragmentation
Local and national labor markets	Global labor markets
A grand cultural bargain – professional autonomy, prestige, and rewards in exchange for guarding the public good	Cultural mistrust and "alternative facts"
Post-industrial society (Bell, 1972)	Post-modern society (Beck, Giddens, and Lash)
Stakeholder capitalism	Investor capitalism
Public research	Private, patent-oriented research
Professional stability	Professional precarity

medicine to law to foreign policy and the replacement of that opinion by emotion and "alternative facts" (opinions that have little or no empirical knowledge to back them up). There are a variety of reasons for this phenomenon, many of which we covered in Chapter 2 – cultural fragmentation, rising inequality, perverse professional incentives, media and information fragmentation, and the traditional American mistrust of experts and elites.

The problem with this questioning is threefold: (1) the populist political elites that take advantage of cultural mistrust to question expert knowledge place more impediments in the way of would-be new practitioners in an attempt to deprive experts of the resources to generate new knowledge. That knowledge often contradicts politicians' emotions, value commitments, and identities; (2) this questioning is only happening here and the accompanying disinvestment harms our international competitiveness at the very same time that India, China, the EU, South Korea, and others are increasing their scientific and technological footprint; and (3) individual consumers are left with no reliable knowledge base to confront the big decisions of their lives.

As our discussion in Chapter 2 emphasized (and as emphasized by Nichols 2017 and others), this is a wider cultural and political phenomenon that transcends the current Trump administration in the United States and the Johnson administration in the United Kingdom. In prior work (Leicht 2015), we viewed the post-fact/post-truth reasoning as a long-term outcome of the marriage of neoliberal thought on the primacy of free markets (sometimes referred to as market fundamentalism) and the critiques of scientific reasoning put forward by postmodernists (see also Sanbonmatsu 2003; Antonio 2000). One group (market fundamentalists) champions economic autonomy, individualism, and individual decision-making as the key to prosperity and success. Attempts to control professional practice and knowledge aggregation limit individual consumer choices and drive up costs. The other group (postmodernists) champions cultural autonomy and suggests that professional claims to knowledge based on science stifle dialogue and undermine cultural diversity. Both ask a lot of individual agents to guide and make sense of their lives. At worst, neither perspective (one identified with the political right and the other with the political left) seems to acknowledge the role that material economic inequalities have in creating exclusion and limiting choice. Simply attacking professional-based collective action in the name of cultural autonomy and markets does not provide a vast majority of the population with a way forward in an increasingly complex, consequential, and fragmented world (Leicht 2015). In the next section and the rest of our conclusion, we take up the plight of consumers and discuss where the professions may continue to find a niche.

Where Do the Professions Go From Here?[1]

Attacks on professional work are part of a broader attack on the concept that an occupational community should be the primary focus of livelihood, meaning, and upward mobility (see Webb 1999). Yet the claim that professional work in all its forms is doomed seems premature at best. Change does not imply disappearance. If knowledge-based claims are losing their cache' and if commitments to professional norms are as well, what's left?

We would argue that a culturally decentered, anomic and marketized world needs professions as much or more than the culturally homogeneous, 20th-century world did (Reed 2007). The major shifts have been (and will be) in the rationales used to justify professional work and the organizational forms used to deliver professional services. Here we will focus on a few themes mentioned by prior literature as a way forward for scholars of the professions and for professional and would-be professional groups.

Professions as Systems of Social Closure

Undoubtedly, one continuing avenue of contestation will focus on attempts by professional groups to engage in social closure through controls on recruitment and task domains (Abbott 1988, 1991; Muzio and Ackroyd 1999). This is a long-standing theme in scholarship on the professions. The major reason this will happen is the result of a basic observation in behavioral economics – *free markets are an aggregate good and not an individual one. They are inferior good people will not pick for themselves.*

This observation applies to the would-be provider of professional services (who needs a coherent explanation of how one becomes a professional and how/when one is rewarded for doing professional work) and to the consumer of professional services who is looking for reliable advice.

This is far from a new mechanism for the continual existence of professional work (Larsen 1977; Hughes 1958) and is totally consistent with the power perspectives on professional work discussed in Chapter 1. An occupational group works to gain control of a specific task domain over and against potential competitors. At the same time, the occupational group seeks to control training and the supply of new practitioners. Occupational groups that succeed in both areas control supply, create shortage, and reap reward and (in many cases) social prestige.

Will any new occupations make it up this steep hill? The most likely candidates are occupations associated with interpreting markets, making or creating markets, and providing financial services (Muzio et al. 2011; Kipping and Kirkpatrick 2013; Reed 1996). These entrepreneurial occupational groups service the needs of corporations and investors seeking to maximize unearned income in political environments where unearned income receives special favors. Not only do the earnings of these financial service occupations derive from the new dominance of profits, dividends, and other capital rents but also the compensation systems provided these would-be professionals with direct benefits from the unearned income they generate for others (cf. Leicht and Lyman 2006). This is a far cry from the social service professionalism of the liberal or bureaucratic professions (Webb 1999; Reed 2007), and the growing concentration of firms associated with these entrepreneurial professions turns professionalism into a "brand" that the firm exploits for reputational purposes rather than a label used by occupational groups to exert professional autonomy (Muzio and Kirkpatrick 2011; Kipping and Kirkpatrick 2013).

Unfortunately, for others' claims over task domains, training, and earnings from a job, the new management and financial occupations generate short-term profits for their clients by marketizing and disarticulating others' work, outsourcing and downsizing back office activities, and otherwise attacking protected sources of earned income (something closer to the proletarianization perspective discussed in Chapter 1). The current political and economic climate directly rewards them for doing so (Khurana 2007). An extreme form of this is management consulting as it is applied to higher education (ex. McKenzie and Associates) that defines professors as impediments to managerial control and not part of the technical core of the university system (cf. Ginsberg 2011). The same dynamic seems to be operating in the overall push to professionalize management (see Skaggs and Leicht 2006; Leicht 2013). In this case, managers and management consultants push for the autonomy to employ professionals at will, mixing and matching the right technologies and people to maximize profits and revenues right now (see Reed 1996). At worst, the professional turns into a "faceless technocrat" loosened onto the anarchic world of free markets to line their pockets with consumers' cash where issues of trust and control are left totally to markets (see Reed 2007).

The attack on middle-class job stability and the attack on professional work are components of the same dynamic. In a system skewed toward rewarding and favoring unearned income (and generating still more unearned income by destroying reliable sources of earned income), the entrepreneurial occupational groups that transfer money and make markets are at a distinct advantage to assert their prerogatives and control task domains (Hanlon 1997, 1999; Leicht and Lyman 2006; Skaggs and Leicht 2006). Other than a brief political backlash (exemplified by Occupy Wall Street and some segments of Tea Party politics), the basic dynamic has not been altered by the global recession or its aftermath.

Professions as Risk Managers in a Risk Society

A second, more constructive possibility broadens the scope of professional practice by casting professionals as risk managers in a risk society (see Beck 1992; Beck et al. 1994). This perspective recognizes (as critical and post-modern scholars do) that the cumulative result of the global commitment to hegemonic science, technology, and rationalization is a series of unintended consequences and externalities that need to be managed. This perspective also recognizes the full-scale assault on individual life worlds that result from these commitments (cf. Beck et al. 1994). This perspective acknowledges that there is more to professionalism than either maximizing one's income (as social closure discussions of professionals emphasize) or passive accept-ance of social trends without any corresponding action or agency (see Muzio et al. 2013; Daudigeos 2013; Scott 2008).

Here professionals mediate and interpret the gap between an impersonal, rational, scientific, and technologically infused world fraught with manufac-tured risks and contradictions and the personal project of producing indi-vidual well-being. This mediation occurs in an environment where choices are abundant and contradictory and every choice has a trade-off. The pro-fessional's claim to prestige and earnings lie as managers of this risk. The fact that the risks are manufactured by the same rationalist, hegemonic forces that provide training and an ideological rationale for professional work (as Illich 1982 and others suggest) does not change the fundamental dynamic for consumers. Risks must be managed and those who can reduce risks for individuals in their personal life worlds will be rewarded regardless of the source of those risks.

This is the area where individual consumers could use the classic liberal professions and the professionals they produce or (in a different context) bureaucratic professionals conferring the services of social citizenship (see Webb 1999). The inherent problem with combining the need for indi-vidualized advice with services from risk managers is to find a risk man-ager that does not also profit from the creative destruction and mayhem caused by unfettered global markets and cultural fragmentation. Corporate organizational forms put the need for profits (and more directly, immediate profits) ahead of the welfare of individual practitioners and the clients too. The direct fee-for-service liberal professional may represent a profession, but the professional is at least somewhat bound by a code of ethics to serve clients and the bureaucratic professional is as well. The corporate employer of professionals is not. Worse still, individual clients would be forgiven for distrusting the hybrid or corporate organization form, the very form that outsources their job, lowers their incomes, and puts corporate profits ahead of community welfare (see Khurana 2007). But professionals have the capacity to exercise embedded agency in many organizational settings, using a combination of network contacts and normative exhortation to manage client risks in environments that appear inhospitable to professional concerns (see Daudigeos 2013; Muzio et al. 2013).

Professions as Trusted Interpreters of Information

Related to the concept of professionals as risk managers is the concept of professionals as trusted interpreters of information (Evetts 2006; Kuhlmann 2006; Olgiati 2006), here the professionals in the 21st century (and would-be consumers) are bombarded with information from a variety of sources, all made widely available on the Internet (cf. Castells 1998).

But this unmediated access to information does not put the consumer in a better position than they were prior to the Internet. The information is provided by individuals, corporations, interest groups, political parties, think tanks, and a myriad of other organizations. All have specific agendas. Customer and individual well-being are not one of them. In fact, the Internet represents the type of globalized market and the cultural free-for-all that market fundamentalism and post-modernism embrace (Castells 2011). The consumer is placed in the position of telling good information from bad, which information applies to their specific situation, and which information will make their situation worse if acted upon.

As Evetts (2013) points out, professionals stand in task domains where disembodied information needs to be interpreted for the benefit of specific clients in their life worlds. The embodied professional becomes not only the voice for the information but the negotiator of the relevance for the client in active interaction with them. Far from being a passive recipient of professional expertise and interpretation, the client is in active dialogue with the professional and may co-interpret the information the professional provides, bring forward new and independent sources of information for consideration, and actively steer intervention in directions that are consistent with their personal circumstances and life commitments. Obviously, a fair amount of the dialogue here involves the interpretation and management of risks ("should we go to court or settle out of court?". . . "should I do more radiation treatment or shift to palliative care?" etc.).

In this situation, access to information and access to other professionals to help interpret that information is critical for the individual client. The individual liberal practitioner is not in a good position compared to bureaucratic and corporate organizational forms that link a variety of professional groups in omnibus professional service firms (see Suddaby et al. 2007; Greenwood et al. 1990; Reed 2007). This conception comes close to Reed's (2007) conception of professionals as "merchants of morality" where professionals act as purveyors of ethical meaning and personal identity in a distrustful world where almost everyone needs reassurance and help. If the client has an omnibus point-of-contact that navigates the information system in the professional service firm, and the relationship between the client recommendations and the products or services marketed by the PSF is clear, the promise of the aggregation of professional services into new organizational forms can benefit individual clients as well as corporate clients.

Professions as Values and Ideology

Tied to the concept of professionals as risk managers and interpreters is a larger issue for societies and cultures around the world. This issue is tied to the values and ideological role professionals are expected to play and the wider acceptance of that role by policymakers and publics (Evetts 2013; Reed 2007).

Do the publics need this role and the aspirations that come with it? We think they do. The aspirations to dignified, meaningful, and well-compensated work embedded in these values are imperiled by the widespread attack on stable employment generally. The larger issue at stake here is whether working for a living has meaning beyond just promoting survival. More basic still is the larger question of whether work and earnings will provide a decent living at all (cf. Rifkin 1995; Hacker 2006; Kalleberg 2011; Leicht and Fitzgerald 2008, 2022).

At a basic level, a global economic system that has disinvested in high-quality jobs in favor of higher profits probably produces a public longing for some triumph of professional values and ideology tied to meaning and public service. This is what people strive for and wish for themselves.

But publics have aspirations as consumers too. The world of competing risks and information overload has consumers looking for those that will exercise fiduciary responsibility toward them in the areas of health, well-being, finance, and so on. Individuals are not likely to believe that unfettered free markets and unfettered cultural anarchy will deliver the best outcomes for them. Instead, they will look to expert labor for help. The nature and training of these experts may change, but the basic idea will be there.

The general value placed on professionals as values and ideology transcends specific organizational forms and heads in the direction of the larger institutional environment. Corporate and bureaucratic organizational forms can provide clients with the right information in a complex risk society and ways to interpret that information to promote individual health and well-being. Liberal professions can do the same thing. The big issue is not organizational form so much as intentions, ideology, and discourse (see Reed 2007). This is another case where professionals as merchants of morality, conveyors of ethical meaning, and personal identity against an impersonal, technocratic, and anomic world can play a decisive role. The ideology and discourse of professional work may be wide-ranging window dressing, but (as an old Rabbi once said) "Window dressing makes you look at the house."

The ideology can survive anything except short-term profits hoarded by non-professionals or elite professionals controlling professional work.

Professionals as Promoters of Endogenous Institutional Change

Finally, professional work helps to aggregate information in different task domains and provides "voice" to larger institutional forces that may be ignored by clients and publics. Professionals can bring best practices to different locations and promote endogenous institutional change (cf. Suddaby and Viale 2011; Sutton et al. 1994; Scott 2008). This is closest to Scott's (2008) conception of professionals as institutional "Lords of the Dance" – embodiments of institutional stability and change that provide clients with stable referents in an unstable world.

This conception of professional work is easiest to see in business services where tying specific firms to larger institutional practices is crucial. These institutional practices may have a nomadic base spread through the activities of the profession itself (as was the case with HRM, see Sutton et al. 1994). Or professionals may play a substantial role in interpreting coercive and mimetic institutional pressures ("The new parliament law says . . ." or "Similarly situated companies have generated new revenues by . . .").

Researchers and critical observers could question how much of this institutional change is truly necessary or whether the promotion of change lines the pockets of professionals more than clients. But in the business case, it is becoming harder to interpret what markets want and what the political and regulatory environment is like. Strategically placed entrepreneurial professionals can provide concrete "voice" to these environmental influences and engage in active dialogue with clients regarding their responses (Scott 2008).

To a great extent, the professions as a source of institutional change compliment the view of professions as trusted interpreters of information. We expect professionals (liberal, entrepreneurial, and corporate) to collect information, interpret it, and then come up with a plan of action that maximizes client welfare. This includes affirmative recommendations ("buy 100 shares of British –Leyland now . . .") and negative recommendations ("you need to lose a few pounds or your blood pressure will get worse" . . . "In light of the new wage and hours laws you need to revise your hiring practices . . ."). We expect professions to enact change, we cannot enable ourselves. The fact that some of these changes are individual and others are cultural or corporate really does not change the expectation very much. But there is one caveat to this – professionals must be increasingly mindful of who is at the table making demands for professionals to solve. Most professionals make ethical commitments to promote the general welfare and the cultural and economic fragmentation of the 21st century will push this capacity to the limit (see Trainor 2000).

Some Modest Reforms

It is entirely possible that none of these new professional roles will materialize and the world of professional work will dissolve slowly and change into
a fragmented, less respected, more idiosyncratic undertaking. But it is not
very likely that people will abandon the core values that professional work
addresses – progress, good health, long life, technological comfort, legal
rights, and help in crisis (among others). In short, somebody will need to be
geared toward these issues because clients, patients, and publics will be geared
toward those issues. Whether this happens as current professional occupations are structured and tasks are allocated is an open question we have no
answer for it. All we have done is highlight some of the changes affecting
professional work, its practitioners, and future would-be incumbents.

There are many obstacles to overcome and reforms that are possible. The
role of AI in areas of professional expertise will undoubtedly grow and the
possibilities there are vast. Given our discussion throughout this book, we
have serious doubts about AI's ability to completely replace professional
workers with AI programs that make decisions for us. We will still, in many
areas of deep crisis, want a personal touch, warts and all.

But there is one problem AI and its advocates (see Susskind and Susskind
2017) point to that is a very real problem that is harming the cultural legitimacy of professions in the United States – *inaccessibly high costs for consumers.*
For example, the United States leads the developed world in medical bankruptcies, and such bankruptcies are almost unheard of anyplace else. The
price of getting sick and being treated here is often your life savings if not
your entire stock of whatever personal wealth you happen to accumulate.
This is clearly not acceptable and harms the legitimacy of professional claims
to be guardians of the public good. Nor is this really acceptable in other professional realms such as tax preparation and legal assistance. If only the rich
can afford justice and low taxes, then the professions associated with these
injustices are rightly held up as groups that cannot be completely trusted.

A second but related problem has to do with market distortions that result
from the costs associated with attaining professional credentials. The accumulation of debts and the need to pay them off steer new practitioners to
areas of the country (cities) and lucrative areas of practice (corporate law,
surgery, investment finance, etc.) that are not necessarily associated with
public goods. Instead, they are associated with relatively well-off customers. If new practitioners flock to such places and market niches, leaving
vast swaths of the population behind, what type of message does this send?
A decision that makes individual sense (finding the best compensation to
pay off debt) becomes a decision that leads to the collective questioning of
legitimacy ("why aren't there any doctors and lawyers here?" etc.).

The other market distortion involves the now chronic oversupply of PhDs
in most disciplines and what to do about it. In spite of all the claims about
credential creep involving Bachelor's degrees (an area where there is some

truth and some bluster), most observers believe that there are too many PhDs produced relative to the labor market's ability to absorb them. The situation in the STEM sciences (with one postdoctoral fellowship required, then two or more required to a seemingly indefinite period of limbo waiting for a job to materialize) is not optimal at all and, especially when combined with the growing demand for STEM scientists in other parts of the world, threatens to harm the competitiveness of the country and the recruitment of the best and brightest new incumbents. The attempt to limit the postdoctoral fellowship period to five years might be the start of more sweeping reforms, and the move by New York University and others to abolish tuition for professional training may be another, but other profound changes are necessary if our scientific infrastructure is not going to be permanently compromised.

Conclusion: What Are the Chances?

In this book, we have argued that professional work and professional workers have been buffeted by technological, economic, and cultural changes that have rendered professional work less secure, less rewarding, and less desirable. We have also suggested that the implications of this are especially ominous in the United States and have the potential to affect the competitiveness of the United States in the global economic race for technical and scientific supremacy. We have further suggested that average consumers need professional practice and professional services as much or more in the culturally fragmented, free-market-driven, globalized world than they ever have before. Given the power of the forces arrayed against professional work and professional workers, what are the chances that consumers and clients will get the types of trusted professional help they need?

Regardless of the agendas of those who point to cultural fragmentation as a victory for the local and specific over and above the modern and cosmopolitan (cf. Sanbonmatsu 2003; Antonio 2000), students of professional work could admit that cultural fragmentation is very real and probably a permanent condition of the modern world no matter how it is labeled. This means that professionals and would-be professionals will have to work extra hard, and in culturally sensitive ways, to communicate with their publics (cf. Trainor 2000). While some scholars have questioned whether the growing racial and ethnic diversity of professional groups will fragment the professions themselves (see Leicht and Fennell 2001), the interest in professional work and professional practice by those who are traditionally underrepresented in professional ranks can only be a positive development in light of the cultural fragmentation that post-modern scholars highlight. The inclusion of traditionally excluded groups provides a golden opportunity for professionals to learn how to address the well-being of groups that are not like themselves and may have drastically different values. If professionals can act as the active agents of their own institutional frameworks (see Reed 2007; Scott 2008), then this is certainly possible.

The final reason professionalism will survive in a modified form is that consumers and clients demand it. And at some level, we need it. Most of us are not about to fix our heart valves ourselves, invest our money without any advice, sue a corporation that has wronged us without any professional representation, or self-medicate beyond drinking our pint in the evening to relieve job stress. The institutional form in which services are delivered may change, but as Scott points out, we will still look to professions and the institutions they create to deal with the complex issues that advanced modernity hands our way.

The real question is whether professional life will be so constrained that professionals are not up to the task that consumers and clients give to it. Dystopian outcomes are possible (see Reed's 2007 discussion of the faceless technocrat among others) – our science fiction cinema is filled with dystopian futures where professionals in various guises no longer represent clients or customers; they control them or exploit them for their own ends or to serve some corporate Leviathan or false political ideology. What most of these movies lack is a mechanism for turning professionals with active agency into automatons who do not realize they are destroying humanity. It is that active agency and action by professional groups that customers and clients depend on and deserve. The real question is what type of institutionalized world will deliver professional training to bright and deserving would-be practitioners and where customers and clients will go to receive those services.

Note

1   Much of this section is taken from Leicht, 2016 ("Market Fundamentalism, Cultural Fragmentation, Post-Modern Skepticism, and the Future of Professional Work." Journal of Professions and Organization, 3: 103–117).

Epilogue – "This Is Not a Drill . . ."

Fall, 2022

WHO chief Dr. Tedros Adhanom Ghebreyesus said on Thursday (March 5 2020) that although public health authorities across the globe have the ability to successfully combat the spread of the Coronavirus, the organization is concerned that in some countries the level of political commitment does not match the threat level.

"This is not a drill. This is not the time to give up. This is not a time for excuses. This is a time for pulling out all the stops." Joshua Berlinger, CNN, March 6, 2020

Today, the total number of deaths in the United States due to COVID-19, the viral infection caused by the Coronavirus, exceeds 900,000. The total number of deaths globally is now more than 6 million. These astonishing numbers have grown exponentially since early 2020. Just to provide some perspective on how quickly this pandemic has grown: we actually completed most of this manuscript around January 27, 2020. At that time, there were only about 492 cases worldwide, mostly in Wuhan China, with the first case in the United States assumed to be a man who had traveled to Wuhan from Washington state on January 21 (it was later determined that there were cases in California earlier than that, but these cases were not formally reported). The first case of person-to-person transmission in the United States was reported later that week (see Figures 9.1 and 9.2). That same week, the State Department warned U.S. citizens to avoid traveling to China. The first COVID-19 death in the United States occurred on February 28, and the United States issued "do not travel" warnings for areas of Italy and South Korea. The number of deaths due to COVID-19 has taken on an exponential form, and the curve has skyrocketed from zero to one hundred thousand in the United States in less than four months' time. This puts the U.S. COVID-related death rate at almost double all the deaths experienced by U.S. servicemen and women in all the years of the Vietnam war (see Figures 9.3 and 9.4).

COVID-19 was formally labeled a global pandemic by the WHO on March 11. A pandemic is defined as a new disease that affects people with

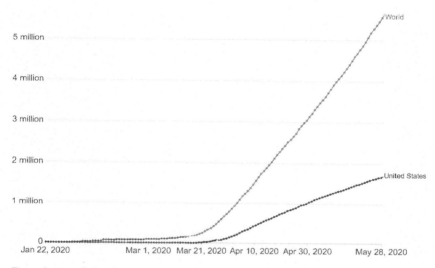

Figure 9.1 Total Confirmed COVID-19 Cases

Source: European CDC − Situation Update Worldwide − Last Updated 28 May, 14:00 (London time) OurWorldInData.org/coronavirus CC BY

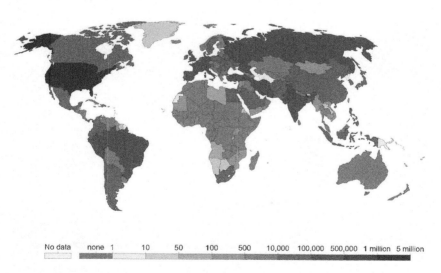

Figure 9.2 Global Distribution of Total Confirmed COVID-19 Cases, May 28, 2020

Source: European CDC − Situation Update Worldwide − Last updated 28 May, 14:00 (London time) OurWorldInData.org/coronavirus CC BY

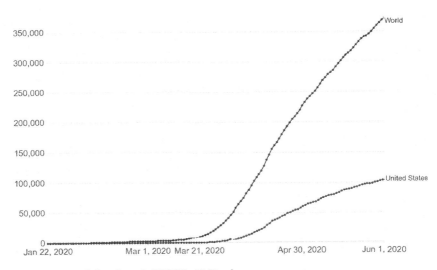

Figure 9.3 Total Confirmed COVID-19 Deaths

Source: European CDC – Situation Update Worldwide – Last updated 1 June, 10:45 (London time) OurWorldInData.org/coronavirus CC BY

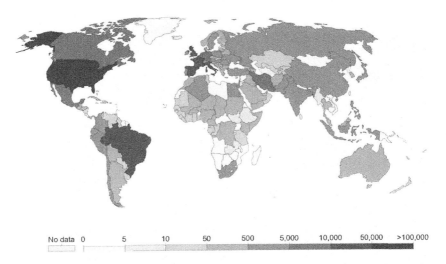

Figure 9.4 Global Distribution of Total Confirmed COVID-19 Deaths, May 28, 2020

Source: European CDC – Situation Update Worldwide – Last updated 28 May, 14:00 (London time) OurWorldInData.org/coronavirus CC BY

intensity, is often fatal, and spreads rapidly infecting large numbers of people in a number of countries (either entire regions or the world). Following the March 11 statement, stock markets in the United States and around the world plummeted. Two days later, President Trump declared a national emergency. Travel came to a standstill, and oil prices also plummeted as demand disappeared. By May 27, 2020, 40 million Americans had lost their jobs and filed for unemployment due to business, school, and college/university closures brought on by the lockdown to limit exposure to the virus. The U.S. unemployment rate went from 3.5% to 14.7% in less than six weeks, the worst reported unemployment since the Great Depression of the 1930s, and this does not even account for those whose who have been unable to file for unemployment insurance due to bottlenecks and heightened reporting requirements (Economic Policy Institute 2020).

Although these job losses were concentrated at first in the travel and energy sectors, white-collar jobs were clearly at risk as well, especially professional white-collar jobs such as lawyers, consultants, accountants, and academics. As with the numbers quoted earlier of disease incidence and deaths due to COVID-19, the loss of 40 million jobs in only six weeks was unprecedented and difficult to fathom. As commented by Zaroli and Schneider in NPR's April 23rd Morning Edition: "That's more than all the jobs added in the past 10 years since the Great Recession."

All of this upheaval was created by a virus that scientists know little to nothing about. Yet a few things became clear as the pandemic has rolled on.

(1) The virus first crossed over to human populations near Wuhan, China, sometime in the fall of 2019.

(2) The virus can spread from person to person, even from carriers that have no symptoms.

(3) There was some debate about transmission via touching surfaces. The major transmission routes were person-to-person via small droplets that are expended when the infected person coughs, sneezes, or exhales. It is possible that transmission happens when someone touches an infected surface and then touches their eyes, nose, or mouth (Doctors without Borders 2020).

(4) Standard protections from the virus include vigorous hand washing, social distancing (the "six foot rule"), proper cough and sneeze etiquette, self-quarantining if one becomes ill or is exposed to someone who is ill, and avoiding crowded public gatherings. Masks are recommended when social distancing is not possible though some worried that this would create a shortage of masks and protective gear for front-line healthcare workers (cf. Doctors without Borders 2020).

(5) Approximately 80% of those infected will develop minor symptoms and recover at home; 15% will develop severe symptoms and require hospitalization, and 5% will become critically ill and need extensive medical intervention to save their life.

(6) COVID-19 seems especially lethal among the elderly and people with respiratory problems. At first, it seemed that children are affected far less, but now doctors are discovering a bizarre form of organ inflammation in children that may be connected to the coronavirus. As of now, vaccination is recommended for everyone over 5 years old.

(7) COVID-19 data collection (especially in the United States) is hampered by the dispersion of health statistics data collection to individual states and wide differences in testing regimens in different parts of the country and around the world.

This information represented something close to a scientific consensus as of mid-May 2020 and little has changed since then.

So we now find ourselves in the midst of an unprecedented global health and fiscal crisis. We focused this book on major changes and trends in the world of professional work, with a special focus on four important themes: (1) the multilevel nature of changes unfolding in professional work and professional careers; (2) the development of a professional precariat; (3) the erosion and devaluation of professional expertise; and (4) the broadening of the "war on science" into a full-scale attack on legitimate expertise and training in all areas of knowledge. COVID-19 did not negate the importance of our four themes, but it does demand we consider their impact both before the emergence of COVID, and now as the pandemic changes, on what is likely to become "the new normal" of our lives post-coronavirus. If anything, the four themes are all pertinent to a fuller understanding of the pandemic and of the dangerously inept response of the US federal government to the pandemic. We will use this brief Epilogue to discuss three issues that derive from the themes we developed in Chapters 2–4. There are many more issues to consider, but in the interest of brevity, we focus here on only three.

1) In Chapter 1, we introduced the important theme that "change in professional work and professional careers is a multilevel phenomenon. . . . Jobs, careers, labor markets, sectors, financial systems, global professional markets, and advances in technologies are all inter-connected across multiple levels of analysis." Following this, there is a multilevel and interconnected set of issues we must consider to understand how changes in professional work and professions have probably influenced the way the COVID pandemic emerged, and how it continues to affect the health and economic lives of millions of people. In Part I, we discussed a number of system-wide macro-level changes that have influenced professions and professional work and have led to declines in stability and status over the past 20 years. The pandemic reminds us once again that all of our macro systems are interrelated: multi-government agencies with global reach, federal systems, state systems, regulatory changes, professional labor markets, the stock market, and the global oil market have taken major hits as a result of this health crisis.

2) Related to (1): globalization demands we study the far-reaching spread of this pandemic and the incredible speed with which that spread occurred. Because of global linkages and the ease of international travel, there are many opportunities for scientists and academics to cross national and regional boundaries. For example, in the early stages of the pandemic, a meeting in Boston of Biogen scientists became what epidemiologists call a "superspreading event," where a small number of meeting attendees lead to a huge number of infections. Stockman and Barker described that after that meeting, the Biogen employees "most feeling healthy, boarded planes full of passengers. They drove home to their families. And they carried the virus to at least six states, the District of Columbia and three countries, outstripping the ability of local public health officials to trace the spread" (April 12, 2020, *New York Times*).

In addition, the most important tool now emerging to help control the further spread of this pandemic at a more micro level, both now (May 2020) and when the virus re-emerges in the fall of 2020, is case tracking: who do people talk to for ten minutes or longer, and how do we follow those contacts when someone emerges as a non-symptomatic disease carrier? Case tracking is an often-used tool in epidemiology to find possible carriers for smaller disease spread problems, but there are few if any examples of the use of this method for global pandemics. The COVID-19 pandemic is perhaps the first case of a global health crisis that requires both a global focus and the ability to think about and trace individual-level networks of interaction. As such, this combination of global and micro-networks is another example of the multilevel set of issues that are linked to the professionals needed to solve this health crisis and the many ways in which the crisis can be bungled when they are ignored.

3) And finally, what happens when needed expertise is lost? When it becomes more difficult to find and engage? When government leaders refuse to listen to the advice of experts and professionals, and (even worse) believe their own pronouncements about science and medicine are as legitimate and valuable as scientific knowledge? What happens when that leadership becomes a major source of misinformation, which is then picked up by social media, and converted into an "infodemic" (WHO 2020)?

We will address each of these issues in the following.

The Widespread, Multilevel Changes in Professional Work Crippled Our Response to the Pandemic and Stifled the Recovery

The changes we discuss in this book have taken place over a long period of time (30 years) and were not due to some small conspiracy hatched in a smoke-filled room (see Chapters 1 and 2). But if you wanted to create an environment where an economic crisis could spread and a pandemic run rampant, the erosion of the professional infrastructure that has occurred in the United States might be the environment you would pick. Consider the following six observations.

First, while we point to the generally stalled state of the diversification of many professional occupations, many of the scientific occupations that are critical to fighting the pandemic (for example, biologists, chemists, MDs, and some kinds of engineers) are increasingly composed of racial/ethnic groups that are viewed with suspicion by former President Trump and his followers (see Chapter 4). Biologists are now 20% Asian, physical scientists and MDs are 30% Asian, and substantial subsets of each group are first-generation immigrants. Our ability to draw in the best talent from other parts of the world, train them at world-class universities, and then gainfully employ them would, under normal circumstances, put us in a strong position to fight the pandemic. But the current cultural mistrust and "cultural war" surrounding diversity are not helping our situation at all nor is the association of science and expertise with "suspicious and disloyal" people.

Second, the costs of training young professionals (especially MDs and lawyers) and the offloading of that training onto would-be entrants mean that much of our professional expertise is misallocated. Most new graduates, almost regardless of their initial preferences, move to high-reward areas of specialization almost all of which are concentrated in large cities. While it is true that the COVID-19 pandemic has been especially damaging to large cities (see McPhillips 2020), the general concentration of expertise around the country has left many regions lacking the basic professional infrastructure to fight the pandemic when it actually comes (Maani and Galea 2020). To put it bluntly, communities without doctors do not build hospitals. Communities with no hospitals cannot take care of ICU patients with COVID-19. The unmet health needs of people in these communities (needs that preceded the pandemic) make them more vulnerable to complications when the virus actually hits, and new infrastructure and professional expertise cannot be summoned with a few phone calls. Unfortunately, this unique structure of incentives breeds still more mistrust of professionals and professional elites.

Third, the healthcare system that we are relying on to take care of pandemic patients was not working well before the pandemic came to the United States. For example, rural areas have long been subject to poorer quality hospital care and nursing home care (cf. Fennell and Campbell 2007; Tyler and Fennell 2015). Healthcare in the United States privatizes profits and socializes losses through a labyrinth of state, local, and private entities, all seeking to reduce expenses and maximize profits. The net result (especially in combination with point two) is that most hospitals lack the basic infrastructure to deal with pandemics and other mass emergencies and there is often very little local or regional coordination (cf. Maani and Galea 2020). Ironically, hospitals laid off nurses and other healthcare staff during the pandemic because they cannot generate the physician billable hours to pay them just to deal with COVID-19 cases (cf. Gonyea 2020). Worse still (from the hospital's standpoint) caseloads contain disproportionate numbers of African American and Hispanic "essential" workers with little or no health insurance (cf. Brooks 2020). In short, there is no national healthcare policy and no national healthcare system to deliver whatever innovations the beleaguered scientific community comes up with.

Fourth, the labor market for most new entrants into the professions has collapsed, in some cases entirely. We have already documented the number of new PhDs in STEM fields with no concrete employment plans at graduation (see Chapter 4). This will almost certainly get worse – Federal funding for laboratories will be harder to secure; the academic job market will collapse entirely as universities lose revenues related to their diminished operations, and private companies and professional practices lay off skilled workers to avoid filing for bankruptcy. Those on the endless "postdoctoral fellow" treadmill will either be stuck there or be laid off as funds dry up or universities reallocate their efforts elsewhere.

Fifth, the "winner-take-all" nature of professional labor markets means that not everyone is going to feel the pain. Instead, those in relatively secure positions (tenured professorships, research directors at biotechnology companies, physicians at major urban hospitals, partners in large, diversified law firms in major cities, etc.) will weather the storm, perhaps (at most) have to take some furlough days, and otherwise remain at the top of the professional pecking order. Those below them and new labor market entrants will see their opportunities shrink or disappear. For example, the number of universities announcing layoffs of non-tenure track faculty has been increasing by the week, and some are closing entire departments and laying off tenure-track faculty (Pettit 2020). Big law firm pay cuts and furloughs are multiplying as well (cf. Weiss 2020).

Finally, it is clear that the pandemic recession is very deep and is affecting the already fragile state of middle-class finances. Many of these problems result from the overall long-term disinvestment in earnings and work that we discuss in Chapter 2. People who live from paycheck to paycheck have little savings to fall back on when they face job loss and mounting bills. Bankruptcy filings are way up (Tucker 2020), but billionaires are still making money and are receiving bailouts from the Federal government (cf. Alexander et al. 2020). Rents and mortgages are not being paid, with some 6.5% of mortgages in "forebearance" (meaning the owner is behind on their payments) which will lead to evictions and foreclosures (cf. Lane 2020). The wholesale disinvestment in work is coming forward to haunt the American economy.

Globalization and the Pandemic

In 2014, Leicht was a program officer at the NSF in Washington DC when the Ebola virus was decimating Africa (28,000 cases and 11,000 deaths in Guiana, Sierra Leone, and Liberia). At one point, the NSF was called by the offices of several members of Congress. The request? "Put together a taskforce of people the NSF has funded to study African diseases. . . ." The problem? Congress in the 1980s mandated that the NSF and NIH could only study "U.S. Diseases," not diseases affecting global populations that might end up here. There were no NSF awardees to name because funding the study of African-origin diseases was prohibited.

Earlier we discussed how the response to the COVID-19 pandemic required global and locally based responses. The NSF example is one where a lack of global understanding led to a short-sighted local response, which then had implications locally and for the global community. U.S.-based scientists were not in a position to help out with a global pandemic because it was not U.S.-based. The global community was then deprived of their insights. The U.S. government and population were left potentially defenseless because the government had prohibited an earlier generation of researchers from studying diseases they assumed were irrelevant.

The inability to see interconnectedness, and the potentially devastating local consequences of that "blindness" can be seen in the widely disparate responses of national and local governments to the COVID-19 crisis. The United States' problems are well known and most have been discussed earlier (we will talk about the political use of misinformation shortly). Differing views on the depth and virulence of the virus in the United States have meant that state and local governments were creating their own responses, everything from almost total and early shutdown (e.g., California) to doing next to nothing (e.g., Texas). Likewise, states are varying in the types of activities they allow after they open up and what is required to do so (compare Georgia with Illinois).

Internationally, the coordination was not much better. Governments controlled by populists (Brazil), repressive theocracies (Iran), or one-party dictators (e.g., Russia) have downplayed the virulence and threat of the virus. The local results have been disastrous (see Figure 9.5). And this does not even account for the problems some countries have had in spite of the best efforts of their creaky and wobbly healthcare systems (e.g., Italy).

All of these varied responses suffer from a major, fundamental flaw – states in the United States, and nation-states on the world stage, do not exist on other planets in the galaxy. The spread and continued virulence of COVID-19 are fueled by a globalized trade and movement of people that no one controls and that means everyone is vulnerable to the policies of the weakest link. People in U.S. states with severe restrictions can simply travel to places where the restrictions do not exist, become infected, and then return to their homes. Internationally, the very same process can happen as the infected from places with few or no restrictions gravitate and/or travel to places that do have restrictions to infect citizens there.

The belief that "we aren't all in this together" has spread to global supply chains for critical goods and the global competition to search for a vaccine. Supply chains for PPE and other essential medical equipment have long since gone global and now appeal to nationalism and the desire to treat "our

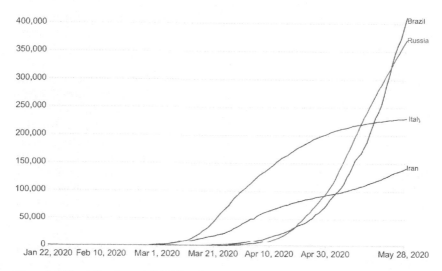

Figure 9.5 Total Confirmed COVID-19 Cases in Brazil, Russia, Italy, and Iran.

Source: European CDC – Situation Update Worldwide – Last updated 28 May, 14:00 (London time) OurWorldInData.org/coronavirus CC BY

nation first" leaves many nations vulnerable to a few suppliers in a small number of places. Fully half of the world's PPE prior to the pandemic came from China (Lopez 2020), and the U.S. government was warned for years that the lack of a reliable supply chain would affect the U.S. ability to deal with any pandemic. There were no stockpiles as these are not profitable. Nobody seemed to understand that no pandemic in our globalized world was going to stay in one place (cf. Foreign Affairs 2020).

The data on the sheer speed of the spread of the virus are startling – the United States went from 50 cases to over 50,000 cases in 30 days, 900,000 in 60 days, and currently, over 80 million Americans have been infected over the past 22 months (April 2020 to February 2022), (Johns Hopkins University 2022). The world total rose from 534 on January 22, 2020, to 78,000 one month later (February 22, 2020), 316,000 on March 22, 2020, 5.1 million on May 22, 2020, and currently stands at 433 million (Roser et al. 2020; Johns Hopkins University 2022).

Then, at a Time When We Need Experts, We Ignore Them or Send Them Packing

A number of writers and reporters have commented on the large numbers of scientists leaving government service since the beginning of the Trump administration (Gowen et al. 2020; Friedman and Plumer 2020). According to the Office of Personnel Management (and analyzed by the *Washington Post*), more than 1,600 federal scientists left government employment in the first two years of Trump's reign. Those exits represent both voluntary exits, firings, and resignations under pressure. The Brookings Institution has regularly tracked turnover in the Trump administration, focusing on the "A Team," made up of members of the executive office of the president. Among these higher-level employees, there has been an 86% turnover rate as of May 15, 2020, and multiple turnovers have occurred in 38% of the A team positions (Dunn Tenpas 2020). This turnover rate is higher than the five most recent presidents (Brookings Institution 2018). Unfortunately, it isn't possible to separate voluntary exits from resignations-under-pressure or from firings in the Brookings data.

Another commonly used strategy to make sure Presidents have access to advise from top scientists has been through advisory councils and committees. One of the most important advisory councils on science issues for the last 20 years was established in 2001 by President George W. Bush and rechartered in 2010 by President Barack Obama: The President's Council of Advisors on Science and Technology (PCAST). Each president is able to charter or re-charter this Council. Council members are appointed by the President and are drawn from research institutions, education, industry, and other NGOs. During the Obama presidency, meetings were frequently held, usually with the President in attendance, and numerous reports were prepared. One of the last projects taken on by the Obama PCAST was specifically on planning and responding to pandemic illness. Before ending their service toward the end of November 2016, the PCAST provided a set of recommendations to the incoming administration on "Confronting the Pandemic Threat" and a proposed infrastructure in a "Playbook for early response to high-consequence emerging infectious disease threats and biological incidents." These two documents provided the incoming president with a roadmap on how to prepare and organize for the next pandemic. However, by January 22, 2017,

> the day after Trump's inauguration, the PCAST website was taken down and all of its reports vanished from the White House website. . . . For two years the directorship of OSTP was vacant. . . . The staff was reduced by two-thirds . . . PCAST lay dormant until November 2019, when Trump appointed

an initial seven members to a rechartered Council (all but one member is from industry, see Table 9.1, Karlawish 2020).

The first meeting of the reconstructed PCAST in February 2020 did not include a discussion of the COVID-19 emerging pandemic. The Pandemic

Table 9.1 PCAST Members in the Past Two Presidential Administrations, United States

PCAST Members – Obama Administration	PCAST Members – Trump Administration
John P. Holdren. Co-Director of PCAST and Director of the Office of Science and Technology Policy. Previously Professor of Environmental Policy and Director of the Program on Science, Technology, and Public Policy at Harvard University's Kennedy School of Government	*K. Birgitta Whaley,* a chemistry professor at the University of California, Berkeley and a scientist at Lawrence Berkeley National Laboratory
Eric Lander co-chair of PCAST and Director of the Broad Institute of MIT and Harvard. He is Professor of Biology at MIT and Professor of Systems Biology at Harvard Medical School and is a member of the Whitehead Institute for Biomedical Research	*Dario Gil,* an electrical engineer and computer scientist, as well as the director of IBM Research
William H. Press, Professor of Computer Sciences at the University of Texas at Austin, Professor of Astronomy and Physics at Harvard University	*A. N. Sreeram,* a senior vice president at the Dow Chemical Company with a doctorate in materials science and engineering from MIT
Maxine Savitz, retired general manager of Technology Partnerships at Honeywell and currently vice-president of the National Academy of Engineering	*Sharon Hrynkow,* chief scientific officer at Cylo Therapeutics, Inc., a biotechnology company that focuses on research around rare diseases
Rosina Bierbaum, Dean of the School of Natural Resources and Environment at the University of Michigan	*Herbert Fisk Johnson III,* the CEO of S. C. Johnson & Son
Christine Cassel, President and CEO of the American Board of Internal Medicine and previously served as Dean of the School of Medicine and Vice President for Medical Affairs at Oregon Health & Science University	*Catherine Bessant,* the chief operations and technology officer at Bank of America
Christopher Chyba is Professor of Astrophysical Sciences and International Affairs at Princeton University	*Shane Wall,* the chief technology officer for Hewlett-Packard and director of HP Labs
Sylvester James Gates, Jr., is John S. Toll Professor of Physics and Director of the Center for String and Particle Theory at the University of Maryland, College Park.	
Mark Gorenberg is Managing Director of Hummer Winblad Venture Partners	

(Continued)

Table 9.1 (Continued)

PCAST Members – Obama Administration	PCAST Members – Trump Administration
Susan L. Graham is Pehong Chen Distinguished Professor of Electrical Engineering and Computer Science Emerita at the University of California, Berkeley	
J. Michael McQuade is Senior Vice President for Science and Technology at United Technologies Corporation	
Chad Mirkin is Founding Director of the International Institute for Nanotechnology, George B. Rathmann Professor of Chemistry, Professor of Chemical and Biological Engineering, Professor of Biomedical Engineering, Professor of Materials Science and Engineering, and Professor of Medicine at Northwestern University	
Mario J. Molina is Professor of Chemistry and Biochemistry at the University of California, San Diego, and the Center for Atmospheric Sciences at the Scripps Institution of Oceanography, as well as Director of the Mario Molina Center for Energy and Environment in Mexico City	
Craig Mundie is Chief Research and Strategy Officer at Microsoft	
Barbara A. Schaal is Professor of Biology at Washington University in St. Louis	
Eric Schmidt is Executive Chairman of Google and a former member of the Board of Directors of Apple Inc.	
Daniel P. Schrag is Sturgis Hooper Professor of Geology in the Department of Earth and Planetary Sciences at Harvard University and Professor of Environmental Science and Engineering in the School of Engineering and Applied Sciences. He is also Director of the Harvard-wide Center for Environment	
Ed Penhoet is Director of Alta Partners	

playbook was "neglected, and its existence has even been denied" (Karlawish 2020). As we write this Epilogue, the nation has borne sad witness to the terrible milestone of over 900,000 COVID-related deaths of U.S. citizens. We entered the pandemic with no plan, no playbook, and an administration that did not listen to scientists, focused on the battered economy, and

Table 9.2 Examples of COVID-19 Misinformation

The virus was created in a Chinese chemical weapons factory and escaped
Bill Gates created the COVID-19 virus to profit from the development of a vaccine
The CDC inadvertently released the COVID-19 virus from one of their labs
The virus is a "Democratic Hoax" to damage Donald Trump
The COVID-19 virus is just like the flu
COVID-19 can be cured with massive doses of vitamin C
COVID-19 can be prevented by consuming hydroxychlorquine
Covid-19 can be cured by blowing a hairdryer up your nose
Covid-19 can be cured by drinking a mixture of water and bleach
COVID-19 is being deliberately mutated in laboratories in Iceland
Most people labeled as COVID-19 fatalities died from other causes

---

did not recognize that the first job is the health crisis. This is what happens when science and expertise are made irrelevant.

Tied to the silencing of experts was the creation of the COVID-19 "infodemic" – the spread of bogus misinformation and conspiracy theories about the virus's origin and potential treatments and cures. To some extent, this dimension of the pandemic simply mirrors more widespread problems in the spread of health misinformation via the web (regarding vaccinations, cancer cures, and so on; see Table 9.2).

The Trump administration and his enablers fueled this misinformation as well.

- Trump dismissed the reports on COVID-19 as "little more than the flu."
- Then he significantly delayed or did not understand the need for widespread testing and left testing activities to the states.
- Then he promoted the use of oxychlorquine as a potential vaccine or prophylactic and began taking it himself, in spite of the total lack of evidence that it works and plenty of evidence that the side effects (including heart palpitations) were dangerous.
- Then his administration claimed the number of cases would "converge toward zero" by May 1.
- When it was clear that social distancing was harming the economy, he declared that the "cure was worse than the disease."
- Then he declared that democratic-led states had mismanaged their responses to the virus and mismanaged their state economies (in spite of evidence that cases were rapidly spreading to areas that were Trump strongholds).
- Trump was in virtually continuous conflict with his own health experts (most notably Anthony Fauci) and attacked any and all sources of information that suggest the U.S. response is too feeble, too decentralized, and too late.

This completely feeble national response left the state and local governments and healthcare providers to their own devices. Individual states

Table 9.3 Examples of U.S. States That Have Suppressed or Not Collected High-Quality Data on the COVID-19 Pandemic

State	Suppression
Georgia	Manipulated trend data to make new case trend appear to be headed downward. Inflated test numbers
Florida	Fired public health employee who refused to manipulate Data to make the state appear healthier
Iowa	Suppressed data tied to meat packing plants. It is "only available on request"
Arizona	Shut down their epidemiological modeling of COVID-19
Washington DC	Excludes data on nursing homes, correctional facilities, and other group residences
New Jersey and Illinois	Only counts nursing home deaths among those with the lab-confirmed presence of the disease

Source: Tahir and Cancryn 2020; Cohen 2020

went after their own medical supplies, and, in some cases, the U.S. Federal Government prevented the delivery of PPE and medical devices the states attempted to purchase for themselves. In practice, this means that we have had 50 individual responses to the pandemic rather than a coordinated national response.

Politicians around the country took their cue from the U.S. administration and either (a) did not enforce social distancing in the belief that the consequences of the pandemic were "greatly exaggerated," (b) systematically ignored information that their populations are vulnerable and their healthcare systems could not cope, or (c) suppressed data on COVID-19 cases, hospitalizations, and deaths leading to protests from local healthcare providers and scientists (see Table 9.3).

The inadvertent or deliberate confusion that has resulted from the systematic sidelining of scientific experts has combined with the very real economic pain of the recession caused by the pandemic shutdown to heighten cultural and economic conflict around the country and (in many cases) the world. The most visible manifestations of this have been demonstrations and protests by citizens seeking to "open up" the economy in spite of widespread evidence that lax social distancing guidelines will increase the number of cases, tax healthcare systems, and lead to more deaths. There is considerable debate among journalists and observers about whether these protests are genuine outcries of economic distress, are fueled by misinformation about the pandemic, or (worse still) are "astroturfed" by specific national organizations looking to sow discord in areas controlled by Democrats (see, Graves 2020).

The future involves living with the COVID-19 virus, widespread vaccination, and testing combined with changes in social distancing practices that have taken some time to take root. However, the overwhelming feeling of many citizens (and even some analysts like us) is that there is nobody in charge and that our government is no longer using experts to craft good policy. In fact, it almost looks as if our populist politicians wait for experts to speak and then do the exact opposite of what is recommended as a form of "cultural rebellion."

Neither the pandemic, the economic recession that has resulted from it, nor our view of the post-pandemic world shows any signs of easing. These latest developments will do little but exacerbate the trends. Widespread changes internal to the world of professional work are now affected by the globalization of the COVID-19 pandemic and the economic recession that resulted, and our response was harmed by widespread misinformation. That misinformation complicated efforts to end the pandemic and prolonged the economic downturn.

Bibliography

Abbott, Andrew. 1988. *The System of Professions*. Chicago: University of Chicago Press.

Abbott, Andrew. 1991. "The Future of Professions: Occupation and Expertise in the Age of Organization." *Research in the Sociology of Organizations*, 8: 17–42.

Abel, Jaison, Richard Dietz, and Yaqin Su. 2014. "Are Recent College Graduates Finding Good Jobs?" *Current Issues in Economics and Finance*. www.researchgate.net/publication/289987055_Are_recent_college_graduates_finding_good_jobs

Adler, P. S., and Kwon, S. W. 2013. "The Mutation of Professionalism as a Contested Diffusion Process: Clinical Guidelines as Carriers of Institutional Change in Medicine." *Journal of Management Studies*, 50(5): 930–62.

Aizcorbe, Ana M., Arthur B. Kennickell, and Kevin B. Moore. 2003. "Recent Changes in U.S. Family Finances: Evidence from the 1998 and 2001 Survey of Consumer Finances." *Federal Reserve Bulletin*. January 27. pgs. 1–36. https://www.federalreserve.gov/pubs/bulletin/2003/0103lead.pdf.

Alberts, Bruce, Marc Kirsshner, Sjirley Tilghman, and Harold Varmus. 2014. "Rescuing US Biomedical Research From Its Systematic Flaws." *PNAS*, April 22. www.pnas.org/content/pnas/111/16/5773.full.pdf

Alexander, Sophie, Tom Maloney, and Tom Metcalf. 2020. "Jeff Bezos Gains $24 Billion While World's Rich Reap Bailout Rewards." *Bloomberg News*, April 14. www.bloomberg.com/news/articles/2020-04-14/bezos-gains-24-billion-while-world-s-rich-reap-bailout-rewards

Alptraum, Lux. 2016. "Millennials, Please Don't Waste Your Money on Graduate School." *Quartz*. https://qz.com/680954/millennials-please-dont-waste-your-money-on-graduate-school/

American Bar Foundation. 2014. *After the JD III: Third Results From a National Study of Legal Careers*. Chicago: American Bar Foundation.

American Bar Association. 2016. *2016 Graduate Employment Data*. Chicago: American Bar Association.

Anderson, K. 2017. "How America Lost Its Mind." *The Atlantic*, September. How America Went Haywire - The Atlantic https://www.theatlantic.com/magazine/archive/2017/09/how-america-lost-its-mind/534231/

Antonio, R. 2000. "After Postmodernism: Reactionary Tribalism." *American Journal of Sociology*. July, 106: 40–87.

Arum, Richard and Josipa Roksa. 2011. *Academically Adrift: Limited Learning on College Campuses*. Chicago: University of Chicago Press.

Arum, Richard and Josipa Roksa. 2014. *Aspiring Adults Adrift: Tentative Transitions of College Graduates*. Chicago: University of Chicago Press.

Avery, Robert et al. 1984. *Survey of Consumer Finances, 1983*. Washington, DC: Federal Reserve Bulletin.

Baker, Phyllis, and Kevin T. Leicht. 2017. "Globalization, Gender, and Development: Toward a Theoretical Understanding of Public Gender-Based Violence against Women and Girls." *Sociology of Development, 3*: 323–45.

Barr, Robin. 2015. "R01 Teams and Grantee Age Trends in Grant Funding." www.nia. nih.gov/research/blog/2015/04/r01-teams-and-grantee-age-trends-grant-funding

Baruch, Y. 2004. "Transforming Careers: From Linear to Multidirectional Career Paths: Organizational and Individual Perspectives." *Career Development International*, January 1.9:58–73.

Batt, Rosemary and Eileen Applebaum. 2013. "The Impact of Finanicalization on Management and Employment Outcomes." Upjohn Institute Working Paper, No. 13–191. Kalamazoo: W.E. Upjohn Institute.

Beck, U. (1992). *The Risk Society: Towards a New Modernity*. Thousand Oaks, CA: Sage.

Beck, U., Giddens, A., and Lash, S. (1994). *Reflexive Modernization: Politics, Tradition and Aesthetics in the Modern Social Order*. Stanford, CA: Stanford University Press.

Becker, Amanda. 2018. "Republican Tax Cuts to Fuel Historic U.S. Deficits: CBO." *Reuters*, April 9. https://www.reuters.com/article/us-usa-fiscal-deficit/republican-tax-cuts-to-fuel-historic-u-s-deficits-cbo-idUSKBN1HG2RW

Belew, S. 2016. "What Is the Difference Between Consulting and Freelancing?" *The Balance: How You Describe Yourself Defines the Services You Offer*. www.thebalance.com/written-consulting-contract-benefits-845899.

Bell, Daniel. 1976. *The Coming of Post-industrial Society*. New York: Basic Books.

Berkopec, N. 2013. "How Can College Students Become Successful Entrepreneurs?" *Quora*. www.slate.com/blogs/quora/2013/09/30/how_can_college_students_become_successful_entrepreneurs.html.

Bidwell, M. 2009. "Do Peripheral Workers Do Peripheral Work? Comparing the Use of Highly Skilled Contractors and Regular Employees." *Industrial & Labor Relations Review, 62*(2): 200–25.

Binder, A. and K. Wood. 2014. *Becoming Right: How Campuses Shape Young Conservatives*. Princeton, NJ: Princeton University Press.

Binder, A., D. Davis, and N. Bloom. 2016. "Career Funneling: How Elite Students Learn to Define and Desire 'Prestigious' Jobs." *Sociology of Education, 89*: 20–39. https://journals.sagepub.com/doi/abs/10.1177/0038040715610883.

Blau, P. M. and O. D. Duncan. 1967. *The American Occupational Structure*. New York: John Wiley and Sons.

Bluetone, Barry and Bennett Harrison. 1981. *The Deindustrialization of America*. New York: Basic Books.

Bluetone, Barry and Bennett Harrison. 1990. *The Great U-Turn: Corporate Restructuring and the Polarizing of America*. New York: Basic Books.

Bonetta, Laura. 2009. "The Evolving Postdoctoral Experience." Pgs. 20–5 in *Career Trends Step By Step: Your Career from Undergrad to Postdoc*. Briana Blaser (Ed.). Washington, DC: American Association for the Advancement of Science.

Bonetta, Laura. 2010. "The Postdoc Experience: Taking a Long-Term View." Pgs. 26–31 in *Career Trends Step By Step: Your Career from Undergrad to Postdoc*. Briana Blaser (Ed.). Washington, DC: American Association for the Advancement of Science.

Braverman, Harry. 1974. *Labor and Monopoly Capital*. New York: Monthly Review Press.

Brewster, Mike. 2003. *Unaccountable: How the Accounting Profession Forfeited a Public Trust*. New York: John Wiley and Sons.

Bricker, Jesse et al. 2017. "Changes in U.S. Family Finances from 2013 to 2016: Evidence from the Survey of Consumer Finances." *Federal Reserve Bulletin, 103.*

Brint, Steven. 1994. *In an Age of Experts: The Changing Role of Professionals in Politics and Public Life.* Princeton: Princeton University Press.

Brint, S. 2013. "The 'Collective Mind' at Work: A Decade in the Life of U.S. Sociology of Education." *Sociology of Education, 86*(4), 273–279. https://doi.org/10.1177/0038040713503304

Brock, David, Hinings, C. R., and Michael Powell. 2012. *Restructuring the Professional Organization: Accounting, Health Care, and Law.* London: Routledge.

Brokaw, Tom. 1998. *The Greatest Generation.* New York: Random House.

Brooks, Rodney A. 2020. "African Americans Struggle With Disproportionate COVID-19 Death Toll." *National Geographic*, April 24. www.nationalgeographic.com/history/2020/04/coronavirus-disproportionately-impacts-african-americans/

Brown, P., H. Lauder, and D. Ashton. 2011. *The Global Auction: The Broken Promises of Education, Jobs, and Incomes.* Oxford: Oxford University Press

Bryan, M. 2015. "Medical Scribe Industry Thrives." *Marketplace.* www.marketplace.org/2015/05/12/health-care/medical-scribe-industry-thrives.

Burawoy, Michael. 1979. *Manufacturing Consent.* Chicago: University of Chicago Press.

Burawoy, Michael. 1985. *The Politics of Production.* Thetford and Norfolk: Thetford Press Ltd.

Burleson, Debra. 2017. "The Hospitalist Model." *Communication Design Quarterly Review, 3*(2015): 50–60.

Burman, Leonard E. 2007. "The Alternative Minimum Tax: Assault on the Middle Class." *The Milken Institute Review*, pgs. 12–23.

Burning Glass Technologies. 2018. *The Permanent Detour: Underemployment's Long-Term Effects on the Careers of College Graduates.* file:///C:/Users/kleicht/Downloads/permanent_detour_underemployment_report.pdf

Burrell, Teal. 2013. "Working With Big Data." *United States Bureau of Labor Statistics.* www.bls.gov/careeroutlook/2013/fall/art01.pdf

Capelli, P. 1999. "Career Jobs Sare Dead." *California Management Review, 42.* 146–167.

Carr-Saunders, A. P., and Wilson, P. A. 1933. *The Professions.* Oxford: Oxford University Press.

Carruthers, Bruce and Terence Halliday. 2009. *Bankrupt: Global Lawmaking and Systemic Financial Crisis.* Stanford: Stanford University Press.

Castells, Manuel. 1998. *End of Millennium, The Information Age: Economy, Society and Culture Vol. III.* Cambridge and Oxford: Blackwell.

Castells, Manuel. 2011. *The Rise of the Network Society, The Information Age: Economy, Society and Culture Vol. I.* Cambridge and Oxford: Blackwell.

Chamorro-Premuzic, Tomas. 2014. "How the Web Distorts Reality and Impairs our Judgement Skills." *Guardian*, May 13. https://www.theguardian.com/media-network/media-network-blog/2014/may/13/internet-confirmation-bias

Chen, David. 2018. "A Surprise Gift: Free Tuition for All NYU Medical Students." *New York Times*, August 16. www.nytimes.com/2018/08/16/nyregion/nyu-free-tuition-medical-school.html

Cherlin, Andrew. 2018. "Marriage Has Become a Trophy." *The Atlantic*, May 20. https://www.theatlantic.com/family/archive/2018/03/incredible-everlasting-institution-marriage/555320/

Chronicle of Higher Education. 2017. "The Post-Truth Issue." www.chronicle.com/specialreport/The-Post-Truth-Issue/84

CAW. 2012. *A Portrait of Part-Time Faculty Members*. The Coalition on the Academic Workforce. CAW Report: A Portrait of Part-Time Faculty Members (academicworkforce.org).

Coccia, Mario. 2012. "Driving Forces of Technological Change in Medicine: Radical Innovations Induced by Side Effects and Their Impact on Society and Healthcare" *Technology in Society*, *34*(4): 271–83

Cohen, Seth. 2020. "Are the Test Numbers Right? Georgia, Florida, and the Deadly Trend of Science Suppression." *Forbes*, May 22. www.forbes.com/sites/sethcohen/2020/05/22/are-the-test-numbers-right-georgia-florida-and-the-deadly-trend-of-science-suppression/#7bfc5be76009

Collins, Randall. 1978. *The Credential Society: An Historical Sociology of Education and Stratification*. New York: Columbia University Press.

Cook, Marty. 2015. "Hospitalist Jobs Growing in Popularity." *Arkansas Business*. www.arkansasbusiness.com/article/107447/hospitalist-jobs-growing-in-popularity

Cortese, Amy. 2016. "A New Wrinkle in the Gig Economy: Workers Get Most of the Money." *The New York Times*, July 20. www.nytimes.com/2016/07/21/business/smallbusiness/a-new-wrinkle-in-the-gig-economy-workers-get-most-of-the-money.htmlCyranoski, David, Natasha Gilbert, Heidi Ledford, Anjali Nayar, and Mohammed Yahia. 2011. "Education: The PhD Factory." *Nature*, *472*(7343): 276–79. www.nature.com/news/2011/110420/full/472276a.html

Daguerre, A. 2014. "New Corporate Elites and the Erosion of the Keynesian Social Compact." *Work, Employment & Society*, *28*(2): 323–34.

Daily Record. 2004. "General Motors Earns Seven Times More from Finance Than Cars." *Maryland Daily*, March 23. https://thedailyrecord.com/2004/03/23/general-motors-earns-seven-times-more-from-finance-than-cars/

Daudigeos, Thibault. 2013. "In Their Profession's Service: How Staff Professionals Exert Influence in Their Organization." *Journal of Management Studies*, *50*(5): 722–49.

Davenport, Coral. 2018. "In the Trump Administration, Science is Unwelcome. So is Advice." *New York Times*, June 9. www.nytimes.com/2018/06/09/climate/trump-administration-science.html

Davenport, Thomas H. 2016. "At The Big Data Crossroads Report." *Amadeus Corporate Blog*, June 23. www.bigdata.amadeus.com/assets/pdf/Amadeus_Big_Data.pdf

Davies, William. 2016. "The Age of Post-Truth Politics." *New York Times*, August 24. https://www.nytimes.com/2016/08/24/opinion/campaign-stops/the-age-of-post-truth-politics.html

Dettling, Lisa J., Joanne W. Hsu, Lindsay Jacobs, and Kevin Moore. 2017. "Recent Trends in Wealth-Holding by Race and Ethnicity: Evidence from the Survey of Consumer Finances." *FEDS Notes*, September 27. https://www.federalreserve.gov/econres/notes/feds-notes/recent-trends-in-wealth-holding-by-race-and-ethnicity-evidence-from-the-survey-of-consumer-finances-20170927.html

Doctors Without Borders. 2020. "Facts and Figures about the Coronavirus Disease Outbreak: COVID-19." www.doctorswithoutborders.org/covid19?source=ADD200U0U01&utm_source=google&utm_medium=cpc&utm_campaign=googlepaid&utm_content=nonbrand&utm_term=covid&gclid=Cj0KCQjwwr32BRD4ARIsAAJNf_2iYIl1dbPzy7ZNi1pPBIB-NJSBd3JVqsK34ZDLVAr1eMKvmlex4I0aAtGOEALw_wcB#How%20is%20coronavirus%20transmitted?

Doeringer, Peter and Michael Piore. 1970. *Dual Labor Markets and Manpower Analysis*. Cambridge: MIT Press.

Dokko, Jane, Megan Mumford, and Diane Schanzenbach. 2015. "Workers and the Online Gig Economy." *The Hamilton Project*. www.hamiltonproject.org/assets/files/workers_and_the_online_gig_economy.pdf

Dunn Tenpas, Kathryn. 2020. "Tracking Turnover in the Trump Administration." *Brookings Institution*, June. www.brookings.edu/research/tracking-turnover-in-the-trump-administration/

Durkheim, Emile. 1933. *The Division of Labor in Society*. New York: Free Press.

Dworskin, Elizabeth. 2016. "Coming to a Doctor's Office Near You: Live-streaming Your Exam With Google Glass." *Washington Post*. www.washingtonpost.com/business/economy/medical-scribes-track-doctors-examinations-from-thousands-of-miles-away/2016/09/27/2c269f54-7c23-11e6-ac8e-cf8e0dd91dc7_story.html

Economic Policy Institute. 2020. "Economic Indicators: Jobs and Unemployment." www.epi.org/indicators/unemployment/

Edwards, Richard. 1979. *Contested Terrain*. New York: Basic Books.

Elance Desk. 2015. Freelancers Union, An Independent Study Commissioned By Freelancers Union and Elance-Odes. "Freelancing in America: A National Survey of the New Workforce." October 1. https://fu-web-storage-prod.s3.amazonaws.com/content/filer_public/7c/45/7c457488-0740-4bc4-ae45-0aa60daac531/freelancinginamerica_report.pdf

Elder, G. 1974. *Children of the Great Depression: Social Change in Life Experience*. Chicago, IL: University of Chicago Press.

Elliott, Daniel J., Robert S. Young, Joanne Brice, Ruth Aguiar, and Paul Kolm. 2014. "Effect of Hospitalist Workload on the Quality and Efficiency of Care." *JAMA Internal Medicine*, 174(5): 786.

Empson, Laura, Daneil Muzio, Josephy P. Bruschak, and Bob Hinings (eds). 2017. *The Oxford Handbook of Professional Service Firms*. Oxford: Oxford University Press.

Evetts, J. 2006. "Trust and Professionalism: Challenges and Occupational Changes." *Current Sociology*, 54: 515–41.

Evetts, J. 2013. "Professionalism: Value and Ideology." *Current Sociology*, 61: 778–96.

Executive Office of the President. 2014. "Big Data: Seizing Opportunities, Preserving Values." May. www.whitehouse.gov/sites/default/files/docs/big_data_privacy_report_may_1_2014.pdf

Fairlie, R. W. 2013. "Entrepreneurship, Economic Conditions, and the Great Recession." *Journal of Economics & Management Strategy*, 22(2): 207–31.

Federal Reserve Bank of New York. 2016. *Quarterly Report on Household Debt and Credit*. New York: Federal Reserve Bank of New York Research and Statistics Group.

Federal Reserve Bank of St. Louis. 2017. Real Median and Mean Family Income in the United States, 2017 CPI-U-RS Adjusted Dollars, Annual, Not Seasonally Adjusted. https://fred.stlouisfed.org

Federal Trade Commission. 2016. "Big Data: A Tool for Inclusion or Exclusion?" January. www.ftc.gov/system/files/documents/reports/big-data-tool-inclusion-or-exclusion-understanding-issues/160106big-data-rpt.pdf

Fennell, Mary L. 2014. "Profound Change in Medical Technologies: Time to Re-examine the Technology Structure Nexus in Health Care?" Pgs. 205–28 in *Advances in Health Care Organizational Theory* (2nd Edition). S. Mick and P. Shay (Eds.). London: Jossey Bass.

Fennell, Mary and Susan Campbell. 2007. "The Regulatory Environment and Rural Hospital Long Term Care Strategies From 1997–2003," *Journal of Rural Health*, 23: 1–9.

Flaherty, Colleen. 2017. "Where the Grass Is Greener." *Inside Higher Ed*, December 18. www.insidehighered.com/news/2017/12/18/study-humanities-and-social-science-phds-working-outside-academe-are-happier-their

Fligstein, Neil and Alex Roehrkasse. 2016 "The Causes of Fraud in Financial Crises: Evidence From the Mortgage-Backed Securities Industry." *American Sociological Review, 81*(4): 617–43.

Florida, Richard L. 2008. *Who's Your City? How the Creative Economy Is Making Where You Live the Most Important Decision of Your Life.* New York: Basic Books.

Foreign Affairs. 2020. *The Next Pandemic: Why the World Was Not Prepared for Covid-19.* Washington, DC: Council on Foreign Relations.

Form, William. 1987. "On the Degradation of Skills," *Annual Review of Sociology, 13*: 29–47.

Foubister, V. 1999. "Doctors Decry Mandatory Hospitalists." *AMNews, 42*: 16–8.

Foucault, Michael. 1977. *Discipline and Punish: The Birth of the Prison.* London: Allen Lane.

Frase, P. 2013. "The Precariat: A Class or a Condition?" *New Labor Forum, 22*(2): 11–4.

Freelancers Union. 2015. *Freelancing in America: A National Survey of the New Workforce.* New York: Freelancers Union.

Freeman, Richard B. 2010. "It's Financialization!" *International Labour Review, 149.* https://onlinelibrary.wiley.com/doi/abs/10.1111/j.1564-913X.2010.00082.x

Frey, Carl and Michael Osborne. 2017. "The Future of Employment: How Susceptible are Jobs to Computerization?" *Technological Forecasting and Social Change, 114*: 254–80.

Friedman, Lisa and Brad Plumer. 2020. "Trump's Response to Virus Reflects a Long Disregard for Science." *New York Times*, April 28. www.nytimes.com/2020/04/28/climate/trump-coronavirus-climate-science.html

Friedson, Elliot. 1986. *Professional Powers: A Study of the Institutionalization of Formal Knowledge.* Chicago: University of Chicago Press.

Froud, Julie, Johal, Sukhdev, Papazian, Viken, and Williams, Karel. 2004. "The Temptation of Houston: A Case Study of Financialisation." *Critical Perspectives on Accounting, 15*: 885–909.

Fuller, Joseph B. and Manjari Raman. 2017. *Dismissed by Degrees: How Degree Inflation Is Undermining U.S. Competitiveness and Hurting America's Middle Class Report.* October 2017. Cambridge, MA: Accenture, Grads of Life, Harvard Business School.

Galanter, Tim and Thomas Palay. 1991. *Tournament of Lawyers: The Transformation of the Big Law Firm.* Chicago: University of Chicago Press.

Gallup, Inc. "How Millennials Want to Work and Live." *Gallup.com.* www.gallup.com/reports/189830/millennials-work-live.aspx

Gellert, G. A., Ramirez, R., and Luke, S. W. 2015. "The Rise of the Medical Scribe Industry: Implications for the Advancement of Electronic Health Records." *The Journal of the American Medical Association, 313*(13): 1315–16.

Georgiou, Aristos. 2019. "Anti-vax Movement Listed by World Health Organization as One of the Top 10 Health Threats for 2019." *Newsweek*, January 15. https://www.newsweek.com/world-health-organization-who-un-global-health-air-pollution-anti-vaxxers-1292493

Giddens, Anthony. 1991. *Modernity and Self-Identity. Self and Society in the Late Modern Age.* Cambridge: Polity.

Giddens, Anthony. 1994. *Beyond Left and Right.* Stanford: Stanford University Press.

Ginther, D. K., Schaffer, W. T., Schnell, J., Masimore, B., Liu, F., Haak, L. L., and Kington, R. 2011. "Race, Ethnicity, and NIH Research Awards." *Science, 333*(6045): 1015–19.

Gitig, Nancy. 2010. "Professional Science Masters Degrees." *Science*, June 18. https://www.science.org/content/article/professional-science-masters-degrees

Gonyea. Don. 2020. "Amid the Pandemic, Hospitals Lay Off 1.4 Million Workers in April." May 10. www.npr.org/2020/05/10/853524764/amid-pandemic-hospitals-lay-off-1-4m-workers-in-april

Goode, William J. 1957. "Community Within a Community: The Professions: Psychology, Sociology, and Medicine." *American Sociological Review, 25*: 902–14.

Goodell, W. 2018. "Scott Pruitt Knows Exactly What He's Doing." *Rolling Stone*, April 4. https://www.rollingstone.com/politics/politics-news/scott-pruitt-knows-exactly-what-hes-doing-629969/ Scott Pruitt Scandal: The EPA Chief Knows What He's Doing – Rolling Stone.

Gordon, David. 1996. *Fat and Mean: The Corporate Squeezing of Americans and the Myth of Managerial Downsizing.* New York: Free Press.

Gordon, David M., Richard Edwards and Michael Reich. 1982. *Segmented Work/Divided Workers.* Cambridge: Cambridge University Press.

Gordon, Tracy. 2012. "State and Local Budgets and the Great Recession," *Brookings.* www.brookings.edu/articles/state-and-local-budgets-and-the-great-recession/

Gowen, Annie, Juliet Eiloerin, Ben Guarino, and Andrew Ba Tran. 2020."Science ranks grow thin in Trump administration." *Washington Post*, January 23. www.washington-post.com/climate-environment/science-ranks-grow-thin-in-trump-administration/2020/01/23/5d22b522-3172-11ea-a053-dc6d944ba776_story.html

Graves, Lisa. 2020. "Who's Behind the 'Reopen' Protests?" *New York Times*, April 22. www.nytimes.com/2020/04/22/opinion/coronavirus-protests-astroturf.html

Ginsberg, Benjamin. 2011. The Fall of the Faculty: The Rise of the Administration-Centered University and Why It Matters. Oxford: Oxford University Press.

Ginsburg, Geoffrey S., and Katheryn A. Phillips. 2018. "Precision Medicine: From Science to Value." *Health Affairs, 37*, www.healthaffairs.org/doi/pdf/10.1377/hlthaff.2017.1624Gould, Julie. "How to Build a Better PhD." *Nature, 528*(7580): 22–5.

Greener, Mark. 2007. "Taking on Creationism. Which Arguments and Evidence Counter Pseudoscience?" *EMBO Reports, 8*: 1107–9.

Greenwood, R., C. R. Hinings, and J. Brown. 1990. "P2-Form Strategic Management: Corporate Practices in Professional Partnerships." *Academy of Management Journal, 33*: 725–55.

Greer, I. 2015. "Welfare Reform, Precarity and the Re-Commodification of Labour." *Work, Employment & Society, 30*(1): 162–73.

Groves, Robert. 2011. "A Possible Data Future for the Observational Social Sciences." *United States Census Bureau.* www.cossa.org/annualmtg/2011/Robert-Groves.pdf

Grusky, David and Kim Weeden. 2008. "Are There Social Classes? An Empirical Test of the Sociologist's Favorite Concept." Pgs. 65–92 in *Social Class: How Does It Work?* Dalton Conley and Annette Laureau. New York: Russell Sage Foundation.

Guardian. 2016. "British Euroskepticism: A Brief History." February 7.www.theguard-ian.com/politics/2016/feb/07/british-euroscepticism-a-brief-history

Hacker, Jacob. 2008. *The Great Risk Shift: The New Economic Insecurity and the Decline of the American Dream.* Oxford: Oxford University Press.

Hacker, Jacob and Paul Pearson. 2006. *Winner-Take-All Politics: How Washington Made the Rich Richer – And Turned Its Back on the Middle Class.* New York: Simon and Scheuster.

Hafferty, F. W., and Light, D. W. 1995. "Professional Dynamics and the Changing Nature of Medical Work." *Journal of Health and Social Behavior, 36*: 132–53.

Halliday, Terrence and Bruce Curruthers. 2009. *Bankrupt: Global Lawmaking and Systemic Financial Crisis.* Palo Alto: Stanford University Press.

Han, Xueying, and Richard P. Applebaum. 2016. "Will They Stay or Will They Go? International Stem Students are Up for Grabs." www.kauffman.org/-/media/kauffman_org/research-reports-and-covers/2016/stem_students_final.pdf

Hanauer, N. 2019. "Better Schools Won't Fix America." *Atlantic Monthly*, July. https://www.theatlantic.com/magazine/archive/2019/07/education-isnt-enough/590611/

Hanlon, G. 1997. "A Profession in Transition? Lawyers, The Market and Significant Others." *The Modern Law Review, 60*: 798–822.

Hanlon, G. 1999. *Professionals, State and the Market: Professionalism Revisited*. London. Palgrave Macmillan

Hembree, Diana. 2018. "CEO Pay Skyrockets to 361 Times That of the Average Worker." *Forbes*, May 22. www.forbes.com/sites/dianahembree/2018/05/22/ceo-pay-skyrockets-to-361-times-that-of-the-average-worker/#297af6f6776d

Hill, Steven. 2015. *Raw Deal: How the Uber Economy and Runaway Capitalism Are Screwing American Workers*. London: St. Martin's.

Hofstadter, Richard. 1963. *Anti-Intellectualism in American Life*. New York, NY: Knopf.

Hopper, Trevor, Phillippe Lassou and Teerooven Soobaroyen. 2017. "Globalization, Accounting, and Developing Countries." *Critical Perspectives on Accounting, 43*: 125–48.

Horta, Hugo. 2009. "Holding a Post-doctoral Position Before Becoming a Faculty Member: Does It Bring Benefits for the Scholarly Enterprise?" *Higher Education, 58*(5): 689–721.

Howard, Daniel J., and Frank N. Laird. 2013. "The New Normal in Funding University Science." *Issues in Science and Technology, 30*. https://issues.org/the-new-normal-in-funding-university-science/

Huang, Edric, Jenny Dorsey, Claire Mosteller, and Emily Chen. 2021. "Understanding Anti-Intellectualism in the U.S." https://www.studioatao.org/post/understanding-anti-intellectualism-in-the-u-s

Hughes, E. C. 1958. *Twenty Thousand Nurses Tell Their Story: A Report on Studies of Nursing Functions Sponsored by the American Nursing Association*. Philadelphia, PA: Lippincott.

Humphreys, Debra and Patrick Kelly. 2014. "How Liberal Arts Majors Fare in Employment: A Report on Earnings and Long-Term Career Paths." *American Associations of Colleges and Universities*, January 22. www.aacu.org/publications-research/publications/how-liberal-arts-and-sciences-majors-fare-employment-report

Hurlburt, S., and McGarrah, M. W. 2016. *Cost Savings or Cost Shifting? The Relationship Between Part-Time Contingent Faculty and Institutional Spending*. New York: TIAA Institute.

Illich, aIvan. 1982. *Medical Nemesis: The Expropriation of Health*. New York: Pantheon Books.

Inglehart, R. 1990. *Cultural Shift in Advanced Industrial Society*. Princeton: Princeton University Press.

Issa, Erin El. 2018. "American Credit Card Debt Statistics: 2017." Nerdwallet. www.nerdwallet.com/blog/credit-card-data/household-credit-card-debt-study-2017/

Jaeger, C. B. 2016. "Law 2.0." http://stories.vanderbilt.edu/law-2-point-0

Japec, Lilli et al. 2015. "AAPOR Report on Big Data." *American Association for Public Opinion Research: AAPOR Big Data Task Force*. www.aapor.org/AAPOR_Main/media/MainSiteFiles/images/BigDataTaskForceReport_FINAL_2_12_15_b.pdf

Johns Hopkins University 2022. "Coronavirus Resource Center" https://coronavirus.jhu.edu/

Jones, Lamont. 2018. "Study: Student Loan Debt for Millennials Becoming More Manageable." *Diverse Issues in Higher Education*, August 8th. https://www.diverseeducation.

com/students/article/15102987/study-student-loan-debt-for-millennials-becoming-more-manageable

Kahn, Lisa. 2010. "The Long-Term Labor Market Consequences of Graduating From College in a Bad Economy." *Labour Economics*, 17: 303–16.

Kaiser, Jocelyn. 2017. "NIH Plan to Reduce Overhead Payments Draws Fire." *Science*. www.sciencemag.org/news/2017/06/nih-plan-reduce-overhead-payments-draws-fire

Kalleberg, A. L. 2009. "Precarious Work, Insecure Workers: Employment Relations in Transition." *American Sociological Review*, 74(1): 1–22.

Kalleberg, A. L. 2011. *Good Jobs, Bad Jobs: The Rise of Polarized and Precarious Employment Systems in the United States, 1970s-2000s.* New York: Russell Sage Foundation.

Kalleberg, A. L., and Leicht, K. T. 1991. "Gender and Organizational Performance: Determinants of Small Business Survival and Success." *The Academy of Management Journal*, 34(1): 136–61.

Karlawish, Jason. 2020. "A Pandemic Plan was in Place. Trump Abandoned It – and Science – in the Face of COVID19." *Statnews*, May 17. www.statnews.com/2020/05/17/the-art-of-the-pandemic-how-donald-trump-walked-the-u-s-into-the-covid-19-era/

Kauffman Foundation. 2016. "What the Changing Nature of Work Means for Entrepreneurship." *Entrepreneurship Policy Digest*, August 9. Ewing Marion Kauffman Foundation | Kauffman.org

Kennickell, Arthur and Janice Shack-Marquez. 1992. *Changes in Family Finances from 1983 to 1989: Evidence From the Survey of Consumer Finances.* Washington, DC: Federal Reserve Bulletin.

Khoury, Muin J. et al. 2012. "Multilevel Research and the Challenges of Implementing Genomic Medicine." *Journal of the National Cancer Institute Monographs*, 44: 112–20.

Khurana, R. 2007. *From Higher Aims to Hired Hands: The Social Transformation of American Business Schools.* Princeton, NJ: Princeton University Press.

Kinsella, M., G. Fowler, J. Boland and D. Weiner. 2020. "Trump Administration Abuses Thwart Pandemic Response." https://www.brennancenter.org/our-work/research-reports/trump-administration-abuses-thwart-us-pandemic-response

Kipping, M., and Kirkpatrick, I. 2013. "Alternative Pathways of Change in Professional Service Firms: The Case of Managerial Consulting." *Journal of Management Studies*, 50: 777–807.

Kolata, Gina. 2016. "So Many Research Scientists, So Few Openings as Professors." *The New York Times*, October 4. www.nytimes.com/2016/07/14/upshot/so-many-research-scientists-so-few-openings-as-professors.html

Koller, V., S. Kopt, and M. Miglbauer. 2019. *Discourses of Brexit.* New York: Routledge.

Krippner, Greta. 2012. *Capitalizing on Crisis: The Political Origins of the Rise of Finance.* Cambridge: Harvard University Press.

Kuhlmann, E. 2006. "Traces of Doubt and Sources of Trust: Health Professions in an Uncertain Society." *Current Sociology*, 54: 607–20.

Kuratko, D. 2005. "The Emergence of Entrepreneurship Education: Development, Trends, and Challenges." *Entrepreneurship Theory and Practice*, 29: 577–97. The Emergence of Entrepreneurship Education: Development, Trends, and Challenges (sagepub.com).

Lane, Sylvan. 2020. "More than 6 Percent of U.S. Mortgages in Forbearance: Analysis." *The Hill*, April 24. https://thehill.com/policy/finance/494504-more-than-6-percent-of-us-mortgages-in-forbearance-analysis

Larsen, M.S. 1977. *The Rise of Professionalism: A Sociological Analysis.* Berkeley, CA: University of California Press.

Lazonick, William. 2013. "From Innovation to Financialization: How Shareholder Value Ideology Is Destroying the U.S. Economy." in *The Political Economy of Financial Crises.* Gerald Epstein and Martin H. Wolfson (Eds.). Oxford: Oxford University Press.

Lederman, Doug. 2014. "Credential Creep Confirmed." *Inside Higher Ed,* September 9. www.insidehighered.com/news/2014/09/09/demand-degrees-grows-many-fields-havent-required-them

Lee, V. and A. Looney. 2018. *Headwinds for Graduate Student Borrowers: Rising Balances and Slowing Payment Rates.* Washington, D.C.: Brookings Institution

Leicht, K. 2013. "Institutions and Professions." In the *Wiley Encyclopedia of Health, Wellness, Behavior, and Society.* New York: Wiley.

Leicht, K. T. 2015. "Market Fundamentalism, Cultural Fragmentation, Post-Modern Skepticism, and the Future of Professional Work." *Journal of Professions and Organization, 3*(1): 103–17.

Leicht, K. T. and Mary Fennell. 2001. *Professional Work: A Sociological Approach.* Oxford, UK: Blackwell.

Leicht, K.T. and Mary L. Fennell. 2008a. "Institutionalism and the Professions." In *Handbook of Organizational Institutionalism.* Roy Suddaby (Ed.). Thousand Oaks, CA: Sage Publications.

Leicht, K. T. and Mary L. Fennell. 2008b. "Who Staffs the U.S. Leaning Tower? Organizational Change and Diversity." *Equal Opportunities International, 27*: 88–106.

Leicht, K. T., Fennell, M., and Witkowski, K. 1995. The Effects of Hospital Characteristics and Radical Organizational Change on the Relative Standing of Health Care Professions. *Journal of Health and Social Behavior, 36*(2): 151–67. www.jstor.org/stable/2137222

Leicht, K. T., and Scott T. Fitzgerald. 2008. *Post-Industrial Peasants: The Illusion of Middle Class Prosperity.* New York: Worth Publishers.

Leicht, K. T., and Scott T. Fitzgerald. 2022. *Middle-Class Meltdown in America* (2nd edition). New York: Routledge.

Leicht, K. T., and Charles L. Harper. 2018. *Social Change: America and the World.* London: Routledge.

Leicht, K. T., and Elizabeth C. W. Lyman. 2006. "Markets, Institutions, and the Crisis of Professional Practice." *Research in the Sociology of Organizations, 24*: 19–47. Leonhardt, David. 2019. "The Rich Really Do Pay Lower Taxes Than You." *New York Times,* October 6. www.nytimes.com/interactive/2019/10/06/opinion/income-tax-rate-wealthy.html

Levin Institute and State University of New York. n.d. "What Is Globalization?" www.globalization101.org/what-is-globalization/

Lieberson, Stanley. 1980. *A Piece of the Pie: Blacks and White Immigrants Since 1880.* Berkeley: University of California Press.

Lin, Ken-Hou and Donald Tomaskovic-Devey. 2013. "Financialization and U.S. Income Inequality, 1970–2008." *American Journal of Sociology, 118*: 1284–329.

Littler, Craig. 1982. *The Development of the Labor Process in Capitalist Societies.* Exeter: Heinemann Educational.

Lohr, Steve. 2017. "A.I. Is Doing Legal Work. But It Won't Replace Lawyers, Yet." *The New York Times,* 9 March 19. A.I. Is Doing Legal Work. But It Won't Replace Lawyers, Yet. - The New York Times (nytimes.com).

Long, Heather and Jeff Stein. 2019. "U.S. Deficit Hits $984 Billion, Soaring during the Trump Era." www.washingtonpost.com/business/2019/10/25/us-deficit-hit-billion-marking-nearly-percent-increase-during-trump-era/

Lopez, German. 2020. "Why Americans Ran Out of Protective Masks: And What Can Be Done About it." *VOX*, March 27. www.vox.com/policy-and-politics/2020/3/27/21194402/coronavirus-masks-n95-respirators-personal-protective-equipment-ppe

Lopez, Lenny, Leroi S. Hicks, Amy P. Cohen, Sylvia Mckean, and Joel S. Weissman. 2009. "Hospitalists and the Quality of Care in Hospitals." *Archives of Internal Medicine, 169*.

Lunt, Neil, Richard Smith, Mark Exworthy, Stephen T. Green, Daniel Horsfall and Russell Mannion, 2011 "Medical Tourism: Treatments, Markets and Health System Implications: A scoping review." OECD Directorate for Employment, Labour and Social Affairs. https://www.oecd.org/els/health-systems/48723982.pdf

Lyons, S., L. Schweitzer, E. Ng, and L. Kuron. 2012. "Comparing Apples to Apples: A Qualitative Investigation of Career Mobility Patterns Across Four Generations." *Career Development International*, August 10. 33:333–357

Maani, Nason and Sandro Galea. 2020. "COVID-19 and Underinvestment in Public Health Infrastructure in the United States." *Milbank Quarterly*, May 14. www.milbank.org/quarterly/articles/covid-19-and-underinvestment-in-the-public-health-infrastructure-of-the-united-states/

Maguire, Phyllis. 2014. "The High Price of Heavy Workloads." *Today's Hospitalist.* www.todayshospitalist.com/the-high-price-of-heavy-workloads/

Manyika, James et al. 2013. "Big Data: The Next Frontier in Competition, Innovation and Productivity." *McKinsey & Co*, October 9. www.mckinsey.com/business-functions/digital-mckinsey/our-insights/big-data-the-next-frontier-for-innovation

Manza, Jeff and Clem Brooks. 1999. *Social Cleavage and Political Change: Voter Alignment and U.S. Party Coalitions.* New York: Oxford University Press.

Mars, M. M., Slaughter, S., and Rhoades, G. 2008. "The State-Sponsored Student Entrepreneur." *The Journal of Higher Education, 79*(6): 638–70.

Massey, Douglas. 1996. "The Age of Extremes: Concentrated Affluence and Poverty in the 21st Century." *Demography, 33*: 395–412.

McAllister, D. C. (January 24, 2017). Sorry journalists: Trump isn't the first president to threaten the press. The Federalist. Retrieved February 20, 2017 from thefederalist.com/2017/01/24/sorryjournalists-trump-isnt-first-president-threaten-press/

McKinsey & Company. 2016. "Indepenendent Work: Choice, Necessity and the Gig Economy." *McKinsey Global Institute.* www.mckinsey.com/~/media/McKinsey/Featured%20Insights/Employment%20and%20Growth/Independent%20work%20Choice%20necessity%20and%20the%20gig%20economy/Independent-Work-Choice-necessity-and-the-gig-economy-Executive-Summary.ashx

McMurtrie, B. 2015. "Now Everyone's an Entrepreneur." *Chronicle of Higher Education*, April 20. http://innovation.umd.edu/wp-content/uploads/2016/11/Now-Everyone%E2%80%99s-an-Entrepreneur-The-Chronicle-of-Higher-Education-Excerpt.pdf

McPhillips, Deirdre. 2020. "This Map Shows How Vulnerable Cities Are to COVID-19." US News, April 17. www.usnews.com/news/cities/articles/2020-04-17/map-these-us-cities-are-most-vulnerable-to-coronavirus

Meiboom, Ariadne A., Henk de Vries, Cees Hertogh, and Fedde Scheele. 2015. "Why Medical Students Do Not Choose a Career in Geriatrics: A Systematic Review." *BMC Medical Education, 15*. www.ncbi.nlm.nih.gov/pmc/articles/PMC4470031/

Menon, A. 2017. "Why the British Chose Brexit." *Foreign Affairs*, November/December. https://www.foreignaffairs.com/reviews/review-essay/2017-10-16/why-british-chose-brexit

Michtalik, Henry J., Hsin-Chieh Yeh, Peter J. Pronovost, and Daniel J. Brotman. "Impact of Attending Physician Workload on Patient Care: A Survey of Hospitalists." *JAMA Internal Medicine*, *173*(5): 375.

Miller, Mark. 2018. "Ten Years After Onset of Great Recession, How Are U.S. Retirees Doing?", *Reuters*, September 27. https://www.reuters.com/article/us-column-miller-retirement/ten-years-after-onset-of-great-recession-how-are-u-s-retirees-doing-idUSKCN1M7165

Mishel, Lawerence, and Jesica Schnieder. 2017. *CEO Pay Remains High Relative to the Pay of Typical Workers and High-Wage Earners*. Washington, DC: Economic Policy Institute.

Mooney, Chris. 2005. *The Republican War on Science*. New York: Basic Books.

Mooney, Chris. 2012. *The Republican Brain: The Science of Why They Deny Science and Reality*. Hoboken: John Wiley and Sons Inc.

Moses, B. 1997. *Career Intelligence: Mastering the New Work and Personal Realities*. Toronto: Stoddard.

Murse, T. 2017. "What Is Sequestration?" *About.com*. http://uspolitics.about.com/od/thefederalbudget/a/ What-Is-Sequestration.htm

Muzio, D., and Ackroyd, S. 1999. "On the Consequences of Defensive Professionalism: Recent Changes in the Legal Labor Process." *Journal of Law and Society*, *32*: 615–42.

Muzio, D., D. Hodgson, J. Faulconbridge, J. Beaverstock, and S. Hall. 2011. "Towards Corporate Professionalization: The Case of Project Management, Management Consultancy and Executive Search." *Current Sociology*, *59*(4): 443–64. https://doi.org/10.1177/0011392111402587

Muzio, D. and I. Kirkpatrick. 2011. "Introduction: Professions and Organizations—A Conceptual Framework." *Current Sociology*, *59*: 389–405.

Muzio, D., Brock, D., and Suddaby, R. 2013. "Professions and Institutional Change: Towards an Institutionalist Sociology of the Professions." *Journal of Management Studies*, *50*(5): 699–721

National Institutes of Health. 2022. "NIH Research Grants: Total Funding, Current and Constant Dollars, 1950–2017." https://report.nih.gov/funding/nih-budget-and-spending-data-past-fiscal-years/budget-and-spending.

Nelson, J. R., Wellikson, L., and Wachter, R. M. 2012. "Specialty Hospitalists: Analyzing an Emerging Phenomenon." *The Journal of the American Medical Association*, *307*(16): 1699–700.

New York Times Editorial Board. 2017. "President Trump's War on Science." *New York Times*, September 9. www.nytimes.com/2017/09/09/opinion/sunday/trump-epa-pruitt-science.html

Nichols, Tom. 2017a. "How America Lost Faith in Expertise." *Foreign Affairs*, February 22. https://www.foreignaffairs.com/articles/united-states/2017-02-13/how-america-lost-faith-expertise

Nichols, Tom. 2017b. *The Death of Expertise: The Campaign Against Established Knowledge and Why it Matters*. Oxford: Oxford University Press.

Olgiati, V. 2006. "Shifting Heuristics in the Sociological Approach to Professional Trustiworthiness: The Sociology of Science." *Current Sociology*, *54*: 533–47.

Olson, Elizabeth. 2016a. "Goodbye to 'Honeys' in Court, by Vote of American Bar Association." *The New York Times*. www.nytimes.com/2016/08/10/business/dealbook/aba-prohibits-sexual-harassment-joining-many-state-bars.html

Olson, Elizabeth. 2016b. "Leading New York Law Firms Lag in Including Women and Minorities." *The New York Times*. www.nytimes.com/2016/10/17/business/dealbook/leading-new-york-law-firms-lag-women-and-minorities-diversity.html?_r=0

Olson, Elizabeth. 2016c. "More Law Degrees for Women, but Fewer Good Jobs." *The New York Times*, November 30. www.nytimes.com/2016/11/30/business/dealbook/more-law-degrees-for-women-but-fewer-good-jobs.html?_r=0;.

O'Shea, R., H. Chugh, and T. Allen. 2008. "Determinants and Consequences of University Spinoff Activity: A Conceptual Framework." *The Journal of Technology Transfer*, *33*: 653–66.

Osnowitz, Debra, and Kevin D. Henson. 2016. "Leveraging Limits for Contract Professionals." *Work and Occupations*, August 1. https://journals.sagepub.com/doi/abs/10.1177/0730888416642599

Paradis, Tim. 2009. "The Statistics of the Great Recession." *Huffington Post*, October 10. www.huffintonpost.com/2009/10/10/the-statistics-of-the-great-recessin316548.html

Parsons, Talcott. 1937. *The Structure of Social Action*. New York: MacGraw-Hill.

Patten, Eileen and Kim Parker. 2012. "A Gender Reveal on Career Aspirations: Young Women now Top Young Men in Valuing a High-Paying Career." *Pew Research Center*. www.pewsocialtrends.org/2012/04/19/a-gender-reversal-on-career-aspirations/

Pedulla, David S. 2011. "The Hidden Costs of Contingency: Employers' Use of Contingent Workers and Standard Employees' Outcomes." Working Paper Series. Center for the Study of Social Organization, July. www.princeton.edu/csso/working-papers/WP6.pdf

Pettit, Emma. 2020. "Faculty Cuts Begin, with Warnings of More to Come." *Chronicle of Higher Education*, May 15. www.chronicle.com/article/Faculty-Cuts-Begin-With/248795

Phillips, Kevin. 1993. *Boiling Point: Democrats, Republicans, and the Decline of Middle Class Prosperity*. New York: Knopf.

Pippenger, Nathan. 2017. "Know Nothing Nation." *Chronicle of Higher Education*, January 25. www.chronicle.com/article/Know-Nothing-Nation/238873?cid=cp84

Porter, Katherine (ed). 2012. *Broke: How Debt Bankrupts the Middle Class*. Stanford, CA: Stanford University Press.

Powell, Kendall. 2015."The Future of the Postdoc." *Nature*, 7 April. www.nature.com/news/the-future-of-the-postdoc-1.17253

Randazzo, S. 2018. "The New Hot Law Job: Litigation Finance." *Wall Street Journal*, July 5. https://www.wsj.com/articles/the-new-hot-law-job-litigation-finance-1530783000

Reed, M. I. 1996. "Expert Power and Control in Late Modernity: An Empirical Review and Synthesis." *Organization Studies*, *17*: 573–97.

Reed, M. 2007. "Engineers of Human Souls, Faceless Technocrats, or Merchants of Morality?: Changing Professional Forms and Identities in the face of Neo-Liberal Challenge." In *Human Resource Management: Ethics and Employment*. R. M. Ashly, T. Pinnington, and Campbell (Eds.). Oxford, UK: Oxford University Press.

Reich, Robert. 2013. *Aftershock: The Next Economy and America's Future*. New York: Vintage Books.

Reskin, Barbara. 1993. "Sex Segregation in the Workplace." *Annual Review of Sociology*, *19*: 241–70.

Reskin, Barbara and Patricia Roos. 1990. *Job Queues/Gender Queues: Explaining Women's Inroads into Male Occupations*. Philadelphia, PA: Temple University Press.

Rhoades, G. 2014. "We are All Contingent: Reorganizing Higher Education and Society." *On Campus: The National Publication of AFT Higher Education*, *33*(4): 4–6.

Richmond, Douglas. 2010. "The Partnership Paradigm and Law Firm Non-Equity Partners." *Kansas Law Review*, *58*: 507–51.

Rideout, E. and D. Gray. 2013. "Does Entrepreneurship Education Really Work? A Review and Methodological Critique of the Empirical Literature on the Effects of University-Based Entrepreneurship Education." *Journal of Small Business Management*, June. 51:329–351.

Rifkin, Jeremy. 1995. *The End of Work*. New York: Putnam.

Robbins, Liz and Christina Goldbaum. "A Suicidal Nanny, an Underground Industry, and 3 Babies Stabbed. *New York Times*, October 11. www.nytimes.com/2018/10/10/nyregion/queens-daycare-stabbing-nanny.html

Robeznieks, Andis. 2019. "7 Big Reasons Why EHRs Consume Physicians' Days and Nights." *American Medical Association*, May 15. www.ama-assn.org/practice-management/digital/7-big-reasons-why-ehrs-consume-physicians-days-and-nights

Rockey, Sally. 2015. "Straight Talk: More Data on Age and the Workforce," https://nexus.od.nih.gov/all/2015/03/25/age-of-investigator/

Rodgers, Daniel. 2017. "When Truth Becomes A Commodity." *Chronicle of Higher Education*, January 15. www.chronicle.com/article/When-Truth-Becomes-a-Commodity/238866?cid=cp84

Rosenthal, Elisabeth. 2013. "In Need of a New Hip, but Priced Out of the U.S." *New York Times*, August 3. www.nytimes.com/2013/08/04/health/for-medical-tourists-simple-math.html

Roser, Max, Hannah Ritchie, Esteban Ortiz-Ospina, and Joe Hasell. 2020. "Coronavirus (COVID-19) Cases and Deaths." https://ourworldindata.org/covid-cases

Roth, J. 1974. "Care of the Sick: Professionalism vs. Love." *Scientific Medical Management*, 1: 173–80.

Rubin, Beth. 1996. *Shifts in the Social Contract: Understanding Change in American Society*. California: Pine Forge Press.

Rubin, Jennifer. 2017. "Trump's Best People Aren't Even Average." *Washington Post*, July 25. https://www.washingtonpost.com/blogs/right-turn/wp/2017/07/25/trumps-best-people-arent-even-average/

Rubenstein, W. 1997. "The Role of 'Hospitalists' in the Healthcare System." *New England Journal of Medicine*. February 6.

Ruggeri, Kai, Ladislav Zalis, Christopher R. Meurice, Ian Hilton, Terry Lisa Ly, Zorana Zupan, and Saba Hinrichs. 2015. "Evidence on Global Medical Travel." *Bulletin of the World Health Organization*, 93(11): 785–89. www.who.int/bulletin/volumes/93/11/14-146027.pdf.

Rutenberg, Jim. 2017. "Alternative Facts and the Costs of Trump-Branded Reality." *New York Times*, January 22. www.nytimes.com/2017/01/22/business/media/alternative-facts-trump-brand.html

Saks, Mike. 2016. "A Review of Theories of Professions, Organizations, and Society: The Case for Neo-Weberianism, Neo-Institutionalism, and Eclecticism." *Journal of Professions and Organization*, 3: 170–87.

Saks, Mike and Daniel Muzio (eds.). 2018. *Professions and Professional Service Firms: Private and Public Sector Enterprises in the Global Economy*. London: Routledge.

Sanbonmatsu, J. 2003. *The Postmodern Prince: Critical Theory, Left Strategy, and The Making of a New Political Subject*. New York: NYU Press.

Sandefur, Rebecca. 2016. "What We Know and Need to Know About the Legal Needs of the Public." *University of South Carolina Law Review*, 67: 443–60.

Santos, J. M., and Hugo Horta. 2015. "The Generational Gap of Science: A Dynamic Cluster Analysis of Doctorates in an Evolving Scientific System." *Scientometrics*, 104(1): 381–406.

Sassen, Saskia. 2001. *The Global City: New York, London, Tokyo* (2nd edition). Princeton: Princeton University Press.

Sassen, Saskia. 2014. *Expulsions: Brutality and Complexity in the Global Economy*. Cambridge: Harvard University Press.

Scheiber, Noam. 2017. "The Pop-Up Employer: Build a Team, Do a Job, Say Goodbye." *New York Times*, July 12. https://www.nytimes.com/2017/07/12/business/economy/flash-organizations-labor.html

Schmitt, John, and Kris Warner. 2009. "The Changing Face of Labor, 1983–2008." *Center for Economic and Policy Research*." http://cepr.net/documents/publications/changing-face-of-labor-2009-11.pdf

Scott, W. R. 2008. "Lords of the Dance: Professionals as Institutional Agents." *Organization Studies*, *29*(2): 219–38.

Selingo, Jeffrey J. 2017. "Perspective. Why Getting a Good Job Is so Much Harder for Today's College Graduates." *The Washington Post*. https://www.washingtonpost.com/news/grade-point/wp/2017/03/10/why-getting-a-good-job-is-so-much-harder-for-todays-college-graduates/

Semuels, Alana. 2008. "Understanding the Two Loan Giants." *Los Angeles Times*, September 8. https://www.latimes.com/archives/la-xpm-2008-sep-08-fi-qanda8-story.html

Shane, S. 2009. "Why Encouraging More People to Become Entrepreneurs is Bad Public Policy." *Small Business Economics*, *33*: 141–9.

Shorter, Gary. 2008. *CRS Report for Congress: Bear Stearns, Crisis, and 'Rescue' for a Major Provider of Mortgage-Related Products*. Washington, DC: Congressional Research Service.

Singh, Upinder, et al. 2018. "Policy Recommendations for Optimizing the Infectious Diseases Physician-Scientist Workforce." *Journal of Infectious Diseases*, September. 218:S49–S54.

Sites, Carolyn. 2017. "Hospitalist Compensation Models Evolve Toward Production, Performance-Based Variables." *The Hospitalist*, January 26. https://www.the-hospitalist.org/hospitalist/article/125608/hospitalist-compensation-models-evolve-toward-production-performance

Skaggs, Bruce C. and Kevin T. Leicht. 2006. "Management Paradigm Change in the United States: A Professional Autonomy Perspective." *Research in the Sociology of Work*, *15*: 125–52.

Standing, G. 2011. "Labor Market Policies, Poverty and Insecurity." *International Journal of Social Welfare*, *20*: 260–69.

Standing, G. 2014. *The Precariat: The New Dangerous Class* (2nd edition). London: Bloomsbury Academic.

Stevens, M., E. Armstrong, and R. Arum. 2008. "Sieve, Incubator, Temple, Hub: Empirical and Theoretical Advances in the Sociology of Higher Education." *Annual Review of Sociology*, *34*: 127–51. https://sites.lsa.umich.edu/elizabetharmstrong/wp-content/uploads/sites/218/2015/01/Stevens-Armstrong-Arum-annurev.soc_.34.040507.134737-1.pdf

Stiglitz, Joseph. 2012. *The Price of Inequality: How Today's Divided Society Endangers Our Future*. New York: W.W. Norton.

Stockman, Farah and Kim Barker. 2020. How a Premier U.S. Drug Company Became a Virus 'Super Spreader'." *New York Times*, April 12. www.nytimes.com/2020/04/12/us/coronavirus-biogen-boston-superspreader.html

Streek, Wolfgang. 2014. *Buying Time: The Delayed Crisis of Democratic Capitalism*. London: Verso.

Suddaby, R. and T. Viale. 2011. "Professionals and Field-Level Change: Institutional Work and the Professional Project." *Current Sociology, 59*: 423–42.

Suddaby, Roy and Daniel Muzio. 2015. "Theoretical Perspectives on the Professions." Pgs. 25–47. *The Oxford Handbook of Professional Service Firms.* Oxford, UK: Oxford University Press.

Suddaby, Roy, David Cooper and Royston Greenwood. 2007. "Trans-national Regulation of Professional Services: Governance Dynamics of Field Level Organizational Change." *Accounting Organizations & Society, 32*: 333–62.

Sukel, Kayt. 2019. "Official CVS/AETNA merger: Greater Convenience, Less- Cost Reform." *Drug Topics*, October 17. www.drugtopics.com/article/official-cvsaetna-merger-greater-convenience-less-cost-reform

Susskind, Richard and Daniel Susskind 2017. *The Future of the Professions: How Technology Will Transform the Work of Human Experts.* Oxford: Oxford University Press.

Suskind, Ron. 2006. "Faith, Certainty, and the Presidency of George W. Bush." October 17. www.nytimes.com/2004/10/17/magazine/faith-certainty-and-the-presidency-of-george-w-bush.html

Sutton, J., F. Dobbin, J. Meyer, and W. R. Scott. 1994. "The Legalization of the Workplace." *American Journal of Sociology.* 99:944–971. https://doi.org/10.1086/230368.

Swagel, Phillip. 2010. "The Costs of the Financial Crisis: The Impact of the September 2008 Economic Collapse." Briefing Paper #18. New York: Pew Charitable Trust Economic Policy Group.

Sweet, S., Besen, E., Pitt-Catsouphes, M., and McNamara, T. K. 2014. "Do Options for Job Flexibility Diminish in Times of Economic Uncertainty?" *Work, Employment & Society, 28*(6): 882–903.

Tahir, Darius and Adam Cancryn. 2020. "Bad State Data Hides Coronavirus Threat as Trump Pushes Reopening." *Politico*, May 27. www.politico.com/news/2020/05/27/bad-state-coronavirus-data-trump-reopening-286143

Tankersley, Jim. 2018. "Trump's Tax Cut One Year Later – What Happened?" *New York Times*, December 27. www.nytimes.com/2018/12/27/us/politics/trump-tax-cuts-jobs-act.html

The Coalition on the Academic Workforce. 2012. "A Portrait of Part-Time Faculty Members: A Summary of Findings on Part-Time Faculty Respondents to the Coalition on the Academic Workforce Survey of Contingent Faculty Members and Instructors." June 2012, Pgs. 1–52. www.academicworkforce.org/CAW_portrait_2012.pdf

Thompson, Paul. 2013. "Financialization and the Workplace: Extending and Applying the Disconnected Capitalism Thesis." *Work, Employment and Society, 27*: 472–88.

Thurow, Lester. 1969. *Poverty and Discrimination.* Washington, DC: Brookings.

Toppo, Greg. 2017. "Why you might want to think twice before going to law school." *USA Today*, June 28. https://www.usatoday.com/story/news/2017/06/28/law-schools-hunkering-down-enrollment-slips/430213001/

Trainor, B. 2000. "The Challenge of Postmodernism to the Human Service Professions." *Journal of Applied Philosophy, 17*: 81–92.

Treasurydirect.gov. 2020. "Total Federal Debt Outstanding." www.treasurydirect.gov/govt/reports/pd/histdebt/histdebt_histo5.htm

Tucker, Hank 2020. "Coronavirus Bankruptcy Tracker: These Major Companies are Failing Amid the Shutdown." *Forbes*, May 3. www.forbes.com/sites/hank-tucker/2020/05/03/coronavirus-bankruptcy-tracker-these-major-companies-are-failing-amid-the-shutdown/#17db09193425

Tyler, Denise and Mary L Fennell. 2015. "Rebalance Without the Balance: A Research Note on the Availability of Community-based Services in Areas Where Nursing Homes Have Closed." *Research on Aging*, 1–15.

Ulrich, K. 2018. "The Future of Entrepreneurship is Students." *Forbes*, May 24. https://www.forbes.com/sites/karlulrich/2018/05/24/the-future-of-entrepreneurship-is-students/?sh=49d460307255

U.S. Census Bureau. 2019. *Current Population Survey*. Washington, DC: U.S. Department of Commerce.

U.S. Census Bureau. 2018. *Table H-3. Mean Household Income Received by Each Fifth and Top 5 Percent, All Races: 1967 to 2017*. New York: Current Population Survey, Annual Social and Economic Supplements.

U.S. Department of Labor. 2019. "*The Occupational Outlook Handbook*." https://www.bls.gov/ooh/

U.S. National Institutes of Health. 2022. "NIH Budget Mechanism Detail." *NIH Databook Report ID 226*.

U.S. Senate Select Committee on Intelligence. 2019. *Russian Active Measures Campaigns and Interference in the 2016 U.S. Election Volume 1: Russian Efforts Against Election Infrastructure with Additional Views*. S. Rept. 116-290 - russian active measures campaigns and interference in the 2016 u.s. Election, volumes i-v | congress.gov | library of congress

Van der Zwan, Natascha. 2014. "Making Sense of Financialization." *Socio-Economic Review*, *12*: 99–129.

Vedder, Richard. 2016. "The Value of a College Degree Is Diminishing Over Time." *Center for College Affordability and Productivity*. file:///C:/Users/kleicht/Downloads/Value%20of%20College%20Diminishing(1).pdf

Vintzileos, Anthony M. 2015. "Obstetrics and Gynecology Hospitalist Fellowships." *Obstetrics and Gynecology Clinics of North America*, *42*(3): 541–48.

Wachter, R. M., and Lee Goldman. 1996. "The Emerging Role of "Hospitalists" in the American Health Care System." *The New England Journal of Medicine*, *335*: 514–17.

Walcott, John. 2019. "Trump's Go-It-Alone Strategy on North Korea Led to a White House Fight." *Time*, April 25. https://time.com/5576489/kim-jong-un-vladimir-putin-donald-trump/

Warren, Elizabeth and Amelia Warren Tyagi. 2003. *The Two-Income Trap: Why Middle-Class Parents are Going Broke*. New York: Basic Books.

Webb, J. 1999. "Work and the New Public Service Class?" *Sociology*, *33*: 747–66.

Weber, Max. 1947. *The Theory of Social and Economic Organization*. Translated by A.M. Henderson and Talcott Parsons. New York: Free Press.

Weiss, Debra. 2020. "BigLaw Pay Cits and Layoffs Are Likely to Multiply, Experts Say: Which Firms Are Doing It?" *ABA Journal*, April 2. www.abajournal.com/news/article/biglaw-pay-cuts-and-layoffs-are-likely-to-multiply-experts-say-which-firms-are-doing-it

Wellikson, Laurence, John Nelson, and Robert Wachter. 2012. "Specialty Hospitalists: Analyzing an Emerging Phenomenon." *Journal of the American Medical Association*, *307*(16): 1699.

Wile, Rob. 2017. "The Richest 10% of Americans Now Own 84% of the Stocks." *Money*, December 19. http://money.com/money/5054009/stock-ownership-10-percent-richest/

Wilensky, H. L. 1964. "The Professionalization of Everyone?" *American Journal of Sociology*, *70*: 137–58.

Wilkins, David B., and Maria J. Esteban Ferrer. 2018. "The Integration of Law Into Global Business Solutions: The Rise, Transformation, and Potential Future for the Big Four Accountancy networks in the Global Legal Services Market." *Law and Social Inquiry, 43*: 981–1026.

Williams, Mark V. 2008. "Hospitalists and the Hospital Medicine System of Care Are Good for Patient Care." *Archives of Internal Medicine, 168*(12): 1254.

Wilson, William Julius. 1997. *When Work Disappears: The World of the Urban Poor.* New York: Alfred Knopf.

Woolander, Steffie and David Himmelstein 1991. "The Deteriorating Administrative Efficiency of the U.S. Healthcare System." *New England Journal of Medicine, 324*: 1253–58.

Wriight, E. O. 2005. "Foundations of a Neo-Marxist Class Analysis." Pg. 4039 in *Approaches to Class Analysis.* E.O. Wright (Ed.). Cambridge, UK: Cambridge University Press.

Zappavigna, M. 2019. "Ambient Affiliation and #Brexit: Negotiating Values About Experts Through Censure and Ridicule." Pgs. 48–68 in *Discourses of Brexit.* V. Koller, S. Kopf, and M. Miglbauer (Eds.). London: Routledge. http://dx.doi.org/10.4324/9781351041867

Index

Note: Page numbers in *italics* indicate a figure and page numbers in **bold** indicate a table on the corresponding page.

206   *Index*

Made in the USA
Monee, IL
21 August 2023